ORGANIZED
VIOLENCE

ORGANIZED VIOLENCE

CAPITALIST WARFARE IN LATIN AMERICA

EDITED BY

**DAWN PALEY AND
SIMON GRANOVSKY-LARSEN**

 University of Regina Press

Printed and bound in Canada at Friesens. The text of this book is printed on 100% post-consumer recycled paper with earth-friendly vegetable-based inks.

Cover design: Duncan Campbell, University of Regina Press
Text design: John van der Woude, JVDW Designs
Copy editor: Kirsten Craven
Proofreader: Rhonda Kronyk
Indexer: Jenn Harris

Library and Archives Canada Cataloguing in Publication

Title: Organized violence : capitalist warfare in Latin America / edited by Dawn Paley and Simon Granovsky-Larsen.
Names: Paley, Dawn, 1981- editor. | Granovsky-Larsen, Simon, editor.
Description: Includes bibliographical references and index.
Identifiers: Canadiana (print) 20190055898 | Canadiana (ebook) 20190056010 | ISBN 9780889776289 (hardcover) | ISBN 9780889776104 (softcover) | ISBN 9780889776111 (PDF) | ISBN 9780889776128 (HTML)
Subjects: LCSH: Violence—Economic aspects—Latin America.
Classification: LCC HN110.5.Z9 V5 2019 | DDC 303.6098—dc23

10 9 8 7 6 5 4 3 2 1

University of Regina Press, University of Regina
Regina, Saskatchewan, Canada, s4s 0a2
tel: (306) 585-4758 fax: (306) 585-4699
web: www.uofrpress.ca

We acknowledge the support of the Canada Council for the Arts for our publishing program. We acknowledge the financial support of the Government of Canada. / Nous reconnaissons l'appui financier du gouvernement du Canada. This publication was made possible with support from Creative Saskatchewan's Book Publishing Production Grant Program.

CONTENTS

LIST OF TABLES, FIGURES, AND ILLUSTRATIONS

Map 1: Featured Conflict Sites in Mexico and Central America

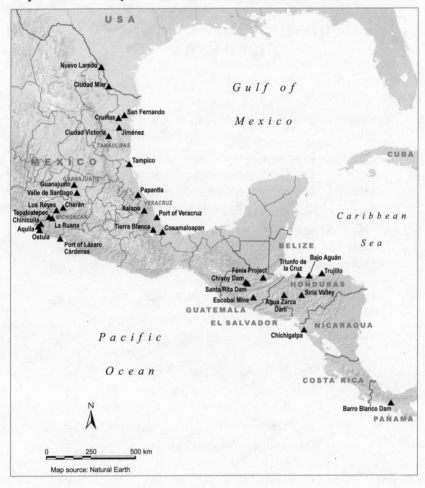

Map source: Natural Earth

Map 2: Featured Conflict Sites in South America

ORGANIZED VIOLENCE AND THE EXPANSION OF CAPITAL

Simon Granovsky-Larsen and Dawn Paley

n early 2007, a public prosecutor in a suit with short, spiky hair, backed by hundreds of police and dozens of individuals with their faces covered to prevent identification, entered the lakeside lands occupied by Indigenous Q'eqchi' people near the town of El Estor, Guatemala. Conflict had been ongoing for generations (Grandin 2004), and it came to a head again after local people grew tired of subsisting on tiny lots, and began to build houses on farmlands claimed at the time by Vancouver-based mining company Skye Resources. The lands had lain fallow for decades before Syke Resources attempted to reactivate the project, which was sold to Hudbay in 2008 and again to the Solway Group in 2011.

Filmmakers and journalists—including one of the editors of this volume—documented the evictions, which escalated from forced removal of community members by hired labourers, to the participation of soldiers and the burning of houses the next day, to the gang rape of eleven women in a more remote community days later. Following the dramatic and painful incidents in 2007, Adolfo Ich Chamán was shot and hacked to death by company security guards in 2009, and Germán Chub was shot and paralyzed in the same incident (see chocversushudbay.com).

The spectacular and organized violence set off against Q'eqchi' people near Lake Izabal ten years ago was intended to clear the way for a nickel mine: Skye Resources planned to restart the Fénix Project, first floated by the Canadian mining company Inco in the 1960s. An array of state and non-state armed actors has participated in repressive violence in the region since the first arrival of Inco. During the evictions in early 2007, Guatemalan soldiers ran between houses in formation, taking up position around the community members as their houses burned. Mynor Padilla, a former army colonel and head of security for the mine, was tried and eventually acquitted of the 2009 shootings in 2017.

In 2011, Hudbay sold the project to the Solway Group, a private Russian company based in Cyprus. Disgraced President Otto Pérez Molina, a former general and an architect of Guatemala's genocidal internal armed conflict who is now in jail on corruption charges, inaugurated the mine in El Estor in 2014. The project is still mired in controversy. A twelve-day peaceful blockade of the open-pit mine in 2017 was met with repression, as local fishers demanded an end to the contamination of nearby Izabal Lake. One demonstrator was killed and four police injured. City hall was set ablaze (Cuffe 2017).

After more than ten years of observing the case of El Estor and the struggles of local communities against the nickel mine, it is clear that the underlying dynamics in the conflict are about what Mina Lorena Navarro Trujillo (2012) calls *despojo multiple* (dispossession in multiple dimensions): physical dispossession from lands and goods, but also political and social dispossession. Families forced off of lands that could support them not only lose access to those lands, they also lose important community ties and are stripped of the potential to organize their own governance systems, or to push for access to services like water, electricity, or education. Mainstream press coverage, however, largely follows the state line, which is to criminalize Q'eqchi' people who resist toxic mining and assert sovereignty over lands their families have occupied since time immemorial.

Through the case of the Fénix mine in El Estor, Guatemala, we can begin to see how criminalization and repression work to undermine resistance. This violence is portrayed as necessary for the security of all, when, in fact, it is mainly necessary to ensure the security of transnational capital—in this case, a Canadian/Russian mining company. A handful of ongoing court cases in Canada—one involving eleven rape survivors and another involving the wounded Chub and Ángelica Choc, wife of murdered Ich Chamán—has revealed intersections between power brokers, armed groups, and mineral extraction in Guatemala.

All across Mexico, Central America, and South America, there are conflicts similar to the one in El Estor, with one key difference: there is little international media attention. Instead, members of local communities are forced from coveted housing blocks, valuable coastal lands, or communal territories to make way for new industrial projects. In many cases, whole communities are criminalized; state troops using lethal force are portrayed as having arrived to clean up or pacify an area. And, to varying degrees, the mass media repeats official discourse from offices in Mexico City or New York: that violence in the Americas today is an unintended consequence of drug trafficking and illegal activity, a side effect of criminal efforts to control drug distribution in cities, or to dominate trafficking routes in remote areas. Together with the authors of this volume, we point to how discourses centred on the so-called wars on drugs and crime serve corporate and state interests, depoliticizing violence that often appears to have more to do with extraction, production, finance, or social control than it does with cocaine or gangs. All too often, little mind is paid to a key driver of violent conflict the world over: securing profit and the expansion of capital through the control of land, labour, and natural resources.

HEMISPHERIC WAR FOR CAPITAL

In this book we contextualize patterns of violence in countries generally considered to be allies of the United States: Mexico, Guatemala, Honduras, Colombia, and Paraguay. This is not to diminish violence, and state violence in particular, in countries such as Bolivia, Ecuador, and Venezuela, where domestic and foreign policy has been less aligned with US foreign policy goals, but where, to differing extents, economic participation by transnational corporations is encouraged and where extractivism is a key economic driver (North and Grinspun 2016; Postero 2017; Webber and Carr 2012). The countries the authors focus on in this volume are solid US allies, their domestic policies structured around responding to the dictates and desires of the United States and, increasingly,

Canada. The authors examine subordinate countries within the current phase of imperialism in the hemisphere, one in which military intervention, transnationalized capitalist expansion, and a return to coup d'états follow the economic and political interests of northern governments and investors, as well as their elite local allies, interests that pay particular attention to the whims of the dominant power of the continent, the United States (Gordon and Webber 2016; Harvey 2004; Klassen 2014; Robinson 2014; Shipley 2017).

Our choice to focus on US-allied states can be understood in part through a return to the notion of worthy and unworthy victims developed by Herman and Chomsky in their book *Manufacturing Consent*. "A propaganda system will consistently portray people abused in enemy states as *worthy* victims, whereas those treated with equal or greater severity by its own government or clients will be *unworthy*" (Chomsky and Herman 1988, 37). Thirty years after the fall of the Berlin Wall, the once (mostly) black and white geopolitical world map that contrasted the "free world" and "state socialism" has been replaced by the drab greyscale of neoliberalism: no matter the gradient, each nation is stained by its participation in global capitalism.

In the Americas, there are governments that have held public positions against the United States, most often shrouded in traditional discourses of anti-imperialism (Venezuela, Ecuador, Bolivia, Cuba). In countries with tense relations with Washington, the expansion of capital carries on under different names, and often in wretched conditions absent dramatic violence. Hugo Chávez encouraged "21st century socialism," while Bolivia's Vice-President Álvaro García Linera speaks of a transition towards socialism via "Andean-Amazonian capitalism" by increasing state participation in the economy, building the proletariat, and strengthening communitarianism (García Linera 2006). By and large, these strategies are akin to alternative formulas for managing capitalism in extremely unequal societies, even as transnational capital continues to exercise economic dominance (Webber 2014).

Ongoing popular and Indigenous protest and organization—to the extent they have not been captured through Left governance and the expansion of the state to increasingly remote areas—continue to mobilize for autonomy and dignity, and in defence of urban spaces and rural territories that allow for some degree of economic, political, and cultural autonomy (Zibechi 2012). In countries like Argentina and Chile, the expansion of capital today is, with some important exceptions, taking place in a manner that appears peaceful, especially in comparison with the countries studied in this book. It is important to recall that this appearance of peace rests on the wars of the 1970s and 1980s, in which thousands of dissidents, activists, unionists, campesinos, and others were disappeared or murdered (Menjívar and Rodríguez 2005).

To the chagrin of progressive commentators who prefer to focus on the "Pink Tide," there remain a host of states in Latin America where elite politics continue to be subsumed to the dictates of transnational capital, as well as to the political beck and call of Washington and Ottawa (North and Clark 2017). Devising a list of client states is as problematic as it is necessary, as these nations correspond to a crucial subset, a key shade of grey, in a geopolitical map of global neoliberalism. One way to establish clientelism could be to count the number of confirmed us military bases: ten in Colombia; a strategic major base at Soto Cano in Honduras, and twelve others accessed by the us Army and the us Drug Enforcement Administration in the same country; and the presence of us military troops in Guatemala, Honduras, Panama, Peru, and elsewhere. This metric, however, is weakened when we take into consideration the us military base and illegal prison at Guantanamo Bay, Cuba, the country with the most oppositional position vis-à-vis the United States in the hemisphere.

Another metric of clientelism could be to take the us government at its word. Mexico, which, because of its unique location and history has no us military bases, "is one of the United States' closest and most valued partners" (White House 2016). Chile, possibly the country with the most transnationalized economy in South America, is "one of the United States' strongest partners in Latin America" (us Department of State 2016). Trading blocks like the Pacific Alliance, which includes Colombia, Peru, Chile, and Mexico, also delineate clear and strong ties with Washington.

Alternatively, we could discern pro-us or imperialist relations through a series of coup d'états that have pushed governance rightward, from the military coup in Honduras in 2009 (as well as the fraudulent elections of 2013 and 2017) to the legislative coups in Paraguay (2012) and Brazil (2016) (Castillo 2016). Then again, we could use us foreign aid as a barometer: Colombia topped the list at nearly $400 million projected for 2017, followed by Haiti ($218 million), Guatemala ($145 million), Mexico ($135 million), Honduras ($105 million), and Peru ($81 million). By comparison,

Bolivia was not projected to receive any foreign assistance from the United States in 2017, and other Central and South American countries received much smaller amounts (ForeignAssistance.gov 2016). Or perhaps we could use the "openness" of national economies as a barometer, but here again there are shades of grey: Mexico had a fully nationalized energy sector that was far more restrictive to foreign investment than that of Venezuela or Bolivia until constitutional changes opened the door to foreign investment in late 2013.

We are encouraged to perceive countries less aligned to the United States as undemocratic nations that use repression to undermine basic rights, while client states are held up as democracies where violence—including extreme violence and acts of state terror like aerial bombings or mass disappearances—are divorced from politics and positioned as a necessary response to criminal activity. The peace process in Colombia, through which the Fuerzas Armadas Revolucionarias de Colombia (Revolutionary Armed Forces of Colombia—FARC) guerrillas were demobilized (see Chapter 6), completes this illusion, removing armed struggle for left-wing ideals, however flawed, from the equation. But neoliberal peace is not meaningful peace.

It is urgent that we update the propaganda model described by Herman and Chomsky. We have established that systems of US clientelism in the hemisphere remain vibrant, and that victims of state and parastate violence in these countries are rendered particularly *unworthy* of attention. In the countries we examine in this book, there is a routine depoliticization of ongoing acts of terror (including massacres and disappearances) and other forms of economic, social, and political violence that forces outward migration and internal displacement. Rather, as mentioned, violence in US-allied countries tends to be linked, by governments and the mainstream media, to criminal activity or the drug trade. What is not often told is that this violence can take on a reactionary character, and its victims were, often in nontraditional ways, participating in local autonomies or acts of resistance, or building towards alternative futures (Dinerstein 2015).

In this book, our overarching goal has been to bring conversations about contemporary violence and capitalism in Mexico, Central America, and South America into dialogue. We look at economic transformation under neoliberalism alongside violence not as separate phenomena, but as generative and mutually reinforcing elements that buttress capitalism in its current stage.

ORGANIZED VIOLENCE AND THE EXPANSION OF CAPITAL

A nuanced look at current affairs requires us to go beyond easy notions of Pink Tide progressivisms in South America and of dehumanized drug cartel monsters in Mexico, Colombia, and Central America. We take an approach that instead allows us to understand events in their specific regional and global context without falling into determinism, examining economic processes at the same time as we address ongoing acts of coercive violence. It is clear that the grinding, daily violence of capitalism proliferates worldwide, and we are living in times of unprecedented inequality: by 2017, five men owned over $410 billion of wealth, compared to $400 billion shared among the poorest half of the world's population (Buchheit 2017). As we wrapped up the final draft of this volume in early 2018, austerity programs and privatization, advanced under the banner of reform, efficiency, and competition, remained the macroeconomic policies du jour in Mexico, Guatemala, Honduras, Colombia, and Paraguay, the countries examined within. These economic policies fit within a broader frame of global capitalism, a system that has made unwavering use of violence in order to ensure power, allowing for the continuous expansion of capital. In the words of Geoff Mann, "Capitalism is premised upon two kinds of power: (1) private economic power that comes from the control of property and profit-making; and (2) coercive power exercised by states in (and often beyond) bounded national territories" (2013, 48).

Following Mann's definition of power within capitalism, in this volume we introduce the notion of organized violence as connected to the structural political-economic conditions of capitalism, a definition that allows us to consider systematically the violence perpetrated by drug cartels, guerrillas and soldiers, or paramilitaries and police.

Existing academic literature tends to define the concept of organized violence in relation to the nature of the organized group. Perhaps the most common use of the term comes from the research and dataset of the Uppsala Conflict Data Program (UCDP), which understands organized violence as being comprised of three subsets: state-based armed conflict, non-state conflicts, and one-sided violence by either state-based or non-state groups (Allansson, Melander, and Themnér 2017). Other major works on contemporary organized violence adopt the UCDP definition implicitly in looking to a determinant factor in the organization of people into armed groups (see Koonings and Kruijt 2004; Daly 2016).

While not disagreeing with this categorization, we believe a key factor is missing in this understanding of organized violence: recognizing the relationship between violence and its surrounding political-economic context. This is the way the concept of *organized violence* is mobilized across the chapters of this volume: violence as organized not only due to the formal structure of armed groups but also organized in its relationship to capitalism. We do not consider more localized instances of violence, such as armed robbery, or its violent retribution by community members to fall within this definition. These acts may be organized as such, and they are, of course, not untouched by the socio-economic system within which they occur, but they are not necessarily connected directly to economic projects, to the state, or to the interests of local, national, or transnational elites.

As examples, then, drug cartels discussed in chapters on Mexico in this volume are instances of organized violence due to their relationship to a war driven by neoliberalism and economic expansion; the violence of Paraguayan police and *sicario* hit men alike (see Chapter 4) present instances of organized violence because they are connected to the expansion of transnational soya projects, to the interests of local landowning elites, and to the US-led militarization of the country; and, as Paula Balduino de Melo demonstrates using testimony from Afro-Colombian women in Chapter 5, the left-wing FARC guerrillas in Colombia also exercise organized violence that responds to US-led militarization and disputes the control of resource-rich territory.

In the early twenty-first century, a plethora of group categories carry out organized violence according to our definition. Along with the more formal armed actors that dominated violence in the twentieth century—military (local and foreign, including significant involvement by the United States), police, death squads, and guerrilla armies—today, headlines (and body counts) in Latin America are dominated by armed groups with opaque entanglements with overtly political affairs. Paramilitary armies continue to operate alongside official armed forces, especially in Colombia and southern Mexico. Drug cartels have increased their firepower and enmeshed their activities into networks of cooperation and coercion with police forces and armies, sharing many traits with paramilitary organizations. As documented in Part II of this volume, these groups, which control territory and commerce through tactics ranging from spectacular displays of violence to house-to-house extortion, dominate much of the terrain between Mexico and Colombia. Separate from cartels, but with a great deal of overlap, youth gangs—and especially the *maras* of northern Central America—exercise horrific violence in their efforts to bring neighbourhoods and populations under their influence, always in concert with certain elements of the state structure (see, for example, Domínguez 2018). Finally, groups that are smaller in size and area of operation also exercise significant influence: local death squads and *sicario* hit men who provide anonymity for those who hire them, and private security companies, lending legitimacy to the violence of economic interests.

Koonings (2012; see also Koonings and Kruijt 2004) separates these armed actors into categories of "new" and "old" violence. Old violence, for Koonings, was essentially political, with a purpose to protect or challenge state power. While militaries and guerrillas fit this category, their engagement in violence was reduced significantly as dictatorships gave way to formal democracies, and large-scale armed conflicts drew to a close over the 1980s and 1990s. The remainder of armed groups outlined above, which together comprise the main drivers of new violence in Koonings's binary, instead exercise violence in pursuit of economic or social goals.

The categories of new and old violence suggested by Koonings demonstrate a central concern with the state—the state as armed actor, or state power as an ultimate goal—that is shared by many analyses of contemporary armed groups. With violence now increasingly privatized and dispersed, recent theoretical work on violence in Latin America has contributed in important ways to our understanding of the relationship between state institutions and non-state armed groups. Méndez, O'Donnell, and Pinheiro grapple with the problem of "lawless violence" in *The (Un)Rule of Law and the Underprivileged in Latin America* (1999), which highlights the ways in which incomplete democratic transitions encourage, often intentionally, a weakening of the state's supposed monopoly of violence. Arias and Goldstein (2010) explore the ways in which non-state violence helped in the creation and maintenance of democratic states, and offer the term "violent pluralism" to discuss the operations of non-state violent actors within state institutions. Pearce (2010) argues that the importance of non-state violence for Latin American states has a much longer history than recent democratic transitions. A "perverse" form of state formation was historically common,

Pearce argues: local elites intentionally undermine the state's monopoly of violence in order to hang onto the use of violence in support of their own power. This argument is supported by Holden's work on Central America (2004), which discusses the importance of private armies in the formation of newly independent states.

Acts of violence can be difficult to accurately document and track. Court cases regarding paramilitary activity around mining sites in Colombia, for example, demonstrate how plausible deniability by the corporate sector is deployed in the face of the testimonies of affected community members (see Chapter 6). As the cases presented in many chapters of this volume attest, when states award symbolic and material impunity to armed actors, these groups often carry out coercive violence that reinforces state power and corporate profits.

If the state and armed groups of all kinds are deeply involved in many scenarios, there are equally enmeshed relationships between states and private economic interests. In the neoliberal era, when many commentators conclude that the state is retreating from the management of domestic economies and global finance, these cases show that states, in fact, continue to set local conditions for capital accumulation and hold on tightly to their role as economic arbiters. We find no contradiction between the provision of legal and material guarantees for investors to ensure the viability of megaprojects in states that erode the rights of local people through austerity and violence. Rather, the dual processes of security and rule of law for capital on the one hand, and insecurity and injustice for people and communities on the other, are, in fact, attractive to investors (see Chapter 6). Regulation and deregulation, legislation, and even the blind eye turned to illegal acts all allow states to have unmatched influence over shaping the context for capital accumulation.

Similarly, states continue to set the stage for organized violence in the neoliberal period. Non-state armed actors throughout the region operate within a context of state-driven militarization and state-sanctioned impunity for repressive violence. When instigating or hiring out organized violence, private economic actors do so within favourable conditions largely set out through the actions of both local states and the intervention of their foreign counterparts.

Whether in the current period of post-authoritarian transition or in earlier stages, non-state armed groups have without a doubt worked across Latin America in ways that support the functioning of the state and the interests of those whose power is represented by governments and institutions. However, the state is not the only location of power that deserves our attention when exploring the function and deployment of organized violence. The question is not only to what extent violence upholds and serves the state but what other interests are advanced by the use of organized violence? Shifting the analysis away from a focus on the actions of states alone allows us to recognize the importance of economic interests in driving organized violence—as well as the role of that violence as a linchpin of the economic system. We approach the diverse perpetrators of organized violence today, from state forces to drug cartels and local *sicarios*, as emerging neoliberal formations that differ from their Cold War antecedent. Instead of military juntas and associated death squads, unclear conglomerations of armed groups are active in complex systems that appear to mimic a subcontracting of coercive violence in the interest of guaranteeing the established power of the state and economic actors (Paley 2018; see also Correa-Cabrera 2017).

A focus on the economic drivers of violence is not meant to be deterministic or exclusive. Organized violence does not operate exclusively to generate profit. States and the interests they represent continue to shape the national contexts within which organized violence operates, and they participate in violence either openly or from behind the plausible deniability facilitated through the formal and informal subcontracting of violence to non-state armed actors. Organized violence can be applied in protection of the political or social power of individuals and groups, and is not necessarily connected to profit (Pansters 2012). But to set our focus on the relationship between organized violence and capitalism brings into perspective the reliance of the current economic model on brute force.

Indeed, capitalism has always relied on force in order to operate and expand, from the acquisition of resources through primitive accumulation and imperialism, through to the continued violence of exploitative labour (Marx 1976; Polanyi 2001). It is widely recognized—especially in critical research on extractive industries and most clearly in David Harvey's work on "accumulation by dispossession"—that the current period of the expansion of capitalism in the form of economic globalization relies on renewed vigour in the application of violence in order to secure profit (Butler 2015; Deonandan and Dougherty 2016; Harvey 2004; Robinson 2014). As local elites become increasingly transnationalized, and transnational capital pushes into new areas, the tasks of securing territory, resources, and labour have relied heavily on the well-established terrain of organized violence (Gordon and Webber 2016; Hristov 2014; Solano 2015).

Today, a multitude of state- and non-state armed groups across the region operate to secure the expansion of capital in the midst of a historical moment that tries to tell us that political conflict in Latin America—along with "history" itself (Fukuyama 1992)—is a thing of the past. Taken together, the chapters of this volume demonstrate that capitalism in contemporary Latin America, as a socio-political-economic system, relies on the continued use of organized violence in order to function and expand. In some senses, *who* applies violence is of less importance in the current stage of capital expansion than *to what end* it is applied. Be it a member of the military, police, paramilitaries, private security, or a death squad that pulls the trigger, capitalist expansion across many countries carries with it a necessity to eliminate opposition in order to operate and secure resources. A brief look at some of the cases examined in this volume shows that this claim holds.

The case of Tahoe Resources' Escobal silver mine in Guatemala, recounted by Luis Solano in Chapter 3, demonstrates an apparent coordination of violence across distinct armed groups. As communities surrounding the mine site organized in opposition to the project by hosting community plebiscites and demanding that the results be respected by the government, a range of violent attacks were used to silence them. First, private security guards shot into a crowd of unarmed protesters, wounding seven. The military later became involved, with the declaration of localized martial law (the *estado de sitio*, or "state of siege," category of military intervention) that quelled open opposition and led to the arrest of many community leaders. When that did not end organized resistance to the mine, *sicarios* targeted key organizers, killing two leaders and wounding a number of others. We cannot say definitively that this set of events was coordinated, but evidence presented in court cases against Tahoe in Canada and Guatemala has documented counter-insurgency-style intelligence gathering and strategic planning aimed at ending community opposition, with the involvement of Tahoe managers, a variety of Guatemalan state institutions, and private security operators.

Tyler Shipley's discussion of Honduras in Chapter 2 presents a scenario similar to that explored in Guatemala, with a gamut of armed actors working towards similar ends in a range of situations. In order to construct tourist villages on Garifuna land, company thugs and the Honduran military intimidated and attacked people, assassinated leaders, and evicted entire communities. Company security and the army have both been involved in repressing community opposition to the Agua Zarca dam project on the Gualcarque River. When four people were arrested for the murder of activist and organizer Berta Cáceres, we learned that the group was made up of individuals connected either to the company or the military. And, as Shipley writes, in communities near Goldcorp's San Martín mine, police and paramilitaries routinely round up and intimidate community leaders, while private security guards have killed one person and injured two more.

While it may appear that Honduran state forces are in the hire of transnational corporations, Shipley asserts that there is, in fact, a "complex interplay between foreign capital, the local oligarchy, the Honduran military, [and] organized criminal networks." The violence visited on Hondurans opposed to these economic projects is carried out with the goal of advancing the projects themselves, and the "development" of Honduras in general, rather than for the isolated interests of a particular armed group. Violence in Honduras, echoing with the other cases explored in this volume, is organized to secure the expansion of capital.

Perhaps the most well documented cases of organized violence and the extractive industries in Latin America have taken place in Colombia. In Chapter 6, Rosalvina Otálora Cortés explores how the expansion of transnational coal mining has been accompanied by military and paramilitary activity targeting local residents and union organizers. Otálora questions whether transnational corporations will continue to invest at the same levels in Colombia following the adoption of peace accords in late 2016, given that a framework of formal peace may not be as beneficial to corporate interests.

In Mexico, particularly in the oil- and gas-rich state of Tamaulipas, as documented in Chapter 7 by Guadalupe Correa-Cabrera and Carlos Daniel Gutiérrez-Mannix, but also in the case of mineral exploitation in the state of Michoacán as explored by Ana Del Conde and Heriberto Paredes Coronel in Chapter 8, the extractive industries have become a node of ongoing conflict that manifests as the exercise of control over local residents by organized criminal groups. In Chapter 9, Antonio Fuentes Díaz examines how Mexican Federal Police, soldiers, and marines participate in complex subterfuge with criminal groups who have made strategic alliances with local police forces and small town self-defence groups, and vice versa. In these cases, it is agribusiness and the extractive industries that have employed violence in a multitude of ways. In their chapter on Veracruz, Michelle Arroyo Fonseca and Jorge Rebolledo Flores discuss how the involvement of government elites criss-crosses with the activities of criminal groups as the extraction of resources becomes a formula through which to ensure political survival. In each of the chapters on Mexico, official narratives about drug trafficking and criminality obscure the potential for corporate gain or personal enrichment of state agents through violence.

It should be noted that while the cases above involve agribusiness and the extractive industries, we can trace the use of organized violence across other economic sectors as well, including logistics and transportation infrastructure. In the words of Deborah Cowen, "logistics space is produced through the intensification of both capital circulation and organized violence—although in ways that might be difficult to recognize" (2014, 11). The difficulty in deciphering the actors involved in and the broader ramifications of intensifying violence is certainly true in major Mexican port cities, including the Pacific port of Lázaro Cárdenas, Michoacán (see Chapter 10), and the Atlantic port of Veracruz in Veracruz state (see Chapter 11).

OVERVIEW OF THE BOOK

The chapters of this book are grouped into two parts: one covering the countries of Central and South America, and another dedicated to Mexico. Part I opens with a regional overview by Mary Finley-Brook, examining oil, natural gas, hydropower, and biofuel projects to identify patterns in energy sector violence. Through the discussion of dozens of cases across ten countries, Finley-Brook outlines the many roles of capital inputs in driving, legitimating, and promoting energy projects linked to murder, violence, and toxic contamination. This picture is expanded by Tyler Shipley in Chapter 2, which locates violence in contemporary Honduras within the interplay between foreign capital, the local oligarchy, the Honduran military, organized criminal networks, and social movements. Shipley describes the intricate networks of often-violent coercion that promote large-scale economic projects, going into rich detail from fieldwork with communities resisting dams, tourist property development, and mining.

The scale of examination zooms in once again in Chapter 3, as Luis Solano recounts the militarized campaign against communities opposed to the construction of Tahoe Resources' Escobal silver mine in Guatemala. Within a context of violence by private security and paramilitaries, criminalization and arrest of community leaders, and a broad-based campaign of militarization by the Guatemalan state, Solano describes the extent to which both the conditions enabling violence, as well as those in search of justice, are tied to transnational processes.

In Chapter 4, Arturo Ezquerro-Cañete approaches the Paraguayan soya industry, centring his analysis on the disastrous eviction of a plantation occupation in 2012, which took the lives of eleven campesinos and six police officers. Ezquerro-Cañete links soya crop expansion to the violence of resource extraction, and shows how the Paraguayan state is willing to criminalize, militarize, and murder in order to assist in the growth of the soy sector. In Chapter 5, Paula Balduino de Melo looks at the forms of social and economic organization employed by the Afro-descendant population along Colombia's southern Pacific region, and how these interact with the various armed groups in the country. The chapter focuses on women's roles within resistance to armed actors, arguing that the *matronaje* system of female leadership allows Afro-Pacific collectives to resist violent displacement and exile through the continued operation of traditional territorial practices. Chapter 6, by Rosalvina Otálora Cortés, examines the role of transnational corporations within the Colombian war. The chapter focuses on the coal industry, demonstrating the direct relationship between foreign companies and paramilitary groups. Otálora Cortés concludes her analysis with a reflection on the Colombian peace process and the role of transnational corporations in possible scenarios of diminishment or continuation of organized violence.

Part II moves the regional focus to Mexico, which has been a key recipient of US foreign aid for anti-narcotics-related security programs since the beginning of the Merida Initiative in 2008 (Meyer 2017). The carnage and terror of the war on drugs in Mexico has shaken the nation since former President Felipe Calderón sent troops into the state of Michoacán in December of 2006. Over the last twelve years, tragic events in Mexico have stirred up concern and social mobilization around the world, especially following the forced disappearance of forty-three students from the Ayotzinapa Normal School in Guerrero in 2014. And the war carries on: December 2017 was the most violent month in Mexico since 1997, and 2017 the most violent year (Angel 2017; SEGOB and SESNSP 2018, 4).

In Chapter 7, Guadalupe Correa-Cabrera and Carlos Daniel Gutiérrez-Mannix explore a complex web of criminal, state, and corporate relations in strategic border zones and oil- and gas-rich territories of Tamaulipas. Their perspective allows a close reading of one of Mexico's most dangerous states, from which little institutional or journalistic information is available. This chapter looks at the confusion of narratives and the problems with using official sources and dominant language to describe a series of armed actors with interests and networks that go far beyond drug trafficking.

The next three chapters of the book all deal with different aspects of resources, infrastructure, and violence in the western state of Michoacán, the world's largest producer of avocados, as well as a key region for transportation and mining. Chapters 8 and 9 both deal with organized community resistance to illegal mining, military occupation, and campaigns of terror and extortion against local residents. In Chapter 8, Ana Del Conde and Heriberto Paredes Coronel make use of extensive fieldwork and journalistic investigations to sketch out the on-the-ground realities of state cooperation with drug runners. We hear directly from community members from two towns, one in the mountains and another on the coast, about local struggles against militarization and resource theft. Antonio Fuentes Díaz rounds out the focus on Michoacán in Chapter 9 with an exploration of the various community defence formations, particularly in the Tierra Caliente region. We see the variance in these structures and the potentials and pitfalls of autonomous security patrols and their eventual incorporation or criminalization by state forces. In Chapter 10, Patricia Alvarado Portillo looks at the illegal export of iron ore and the clandestine import of precursor chemicals (for manufacturing synthetic drugs) and narcotics through the port of Lázaro Cárdenas. This in-depth study of a much ignored port city traces the presence of criminal groups and state security forces in a transnationalized *hinge area* of global commerce.

Chapter 11 draws our attention to the embattled state of Veracruz, which stretches along the oil-rich Gulf of Mexico, and where corruption at the state and municipal levels is rampant (as this volume went to print, former Governor Javier Duarte remained in the Reclusorio Norte prison in Mexico, after cutting short his term by fleeing to Guatemala). Michelle Arroyo Fonseca and Jorge Rebolledo Flores discuss the relation of elite groups in Veracruz to different styles of corruption and look at how these elites interface with trafficking organizations, often in resource-rich areas, for the mutual benefit of both groups, and at a high cost to the majority of the state's population.

In Chapter 12, Elva F. Orozco Mendoza challenges readers to consider organized violence as also linked to the expansion of the prison system in the central Mexican state of Guanajuato. Narrated through a lens of grassroots resistance to incarceration, this chapter encourages us to consider *dispossession by incarceration*, and examines the ways in which jailing people impacts families and encourages forms of accumulation that subsidize the prison system, while at the same time enforcing hierarchies of corruption inside the country's jails. This chapter, while farthest from an analysis of extractive capitalism in the traditional sense, urges us to centre the prison system in our understanding of capitalism and the state under neoliberalism.

Organized Violence: Capitalist Warfare in Latin America is rounded out by a short conclusion discussing some of the book's key insights, pointing to areas for future study, and briefly highlighting evolving forms of resistance to violence. It is our hope that this book provides concrete examples and areas from which we can think through many instances of organized violence that are often presented as random and chaotic. By analyzing patterns of militarization and violence within a clear frame of capitalism and, especially—but not only—of the extractive industries, this volume proposes that we may be able to arrive at new understandings that help us better work to transform systems of injustice throughout the hemisphere.

REFERENCES

Allansson, Marie, Erik Melander, and Lotta Themnér. 2017. "Organized Violence, 1989–2016." *Journal of Peace Research* 54 (4): 574–87.
Angel, Arturo. 2017. "Récord violento con gobierno de EPN: Mayo tiene la cifra más alta de homicidios desde 1997." *Animal Político*, June 21. http://www.animalpolitico.com/2017/06/homicidios-violencia-record-epn/.

Arias, Enrique Desmond, and Daniel M. Goldstein, eds. 2010. *Violent Democracies in Latin America*. Durham, NC: Duke University Press.

Buchheit, Paul. 2017. "Now Just Five Men Own Almost as Much Wealth as Half the World's Population." *Common Dreams*, June 12. https://www.commondreams.org/views/2017/06/12/now-just-five-men-own-almost-much-wealth-half-worlds-population.

Butler, Paula. 2015. *Colonial Extractions: Race and Canadian Mining in Contemporary Africa*. Toronto: University of Toronto Press.

Castillo, Antonio. 2016. "Brazil Ousting Demonstrates the New Coup Rocking Latin America." *The Conversation*, September 4. https://theconversation.com/brazil-ousting-demonstrates-the-new-coup-rocking-latin-america-64871.

Chomsky, Noam, and Edward S. Herman. 1988. *Manufacturing Consent: The Political Economy of the Mass Media*. New York: Pantheon Books.

Correa-Cabrera, Guadalupe. 2017. *Los Zetas Inc.: Criminal Corporations, Energy, and Civil War in Mexico*. Austin: University of Texas Press.

Cowen, Deborah. 2014. *The Deadly Life of Logistics: Mapping Violence in Global Trade*. Minneapolis: University of Minnesota.

Cuffe, Sandra. 2017. "Un comunitario asesinado fue la respuesta del gobierno a las demandas de los pescadores." *Prensa Comunitaria*, May 27. http://www.prensacomunitaria.org/el-estor-un-comunitario-asesinado-fue-la-respuesta-del-gobierno-a-las-demandas-de-los-pescadores.

Daly, Sarah Zukerman. 2016. *Organized Violence after Civil War: The Geography of Recruitment in Latin America*. Cambridge: Cambridge University Press.

Deonandan, Kalowatie, and Michael L. Dougherty. 2016. *Mining in Latin America: Critical Approaches to the New Extraction*. New York: Routledge.

Dinerstein, Ana Cecilia. 2015. *The Politics of Autonomy in Latin America: The Art of Organizing Hope*. New York: Palgrave Macmillan.

Domínguez, Andrea. 2018. "Capturan a líder de la Mara Salvatrucha: Un coronel del Estado Mayor del Ejército." *Guatevisión*, April 18. https://www.guatevision.com/noticia/capturan-a-lider-de-la-mara-salvatrucha-un-coronel-del-ejercito/.

ForeignAssistance.gov. 2016. "Map of Foreign Assistance Worldwide." http://beta.foreignassistance.gov/explore.

Fukuyama, Francis. 1992. *The End of History and the Last Man*. New York: Free Press.

García Linera, Álvaro. 2006. "El 'capitalismo andino-amazónico.'" *Le Monde Diplomatique*, January. https://www.lemondediplomatique.cl/El-capitalismo-andino-amazonico.html.

Gordon, Todd, and Jeffery R. Webber. 2016. *Blood of Extraction: Canadian Imperialism in Latin America*. Halifax: Fernwood.

Grandin, Greg. 2004. *The Last Colonial Massacre: Latin America in the Cold War*. Chicago: University of Chicago Press.

Harvey, David. 2004. "The 'New' Imperialism: Accumulation by Dispossession." *Socialist Register* 40: 63–87.

Holden, Robert W. 2004. *Armies without Nations*. Oxford: Oxford University Press.

Hristov, Jasmin. 2014. *Paramilitarism and Neoliberalism: Violent Systems of Capital Accumulation in Colombia and Beyond*. London: Pluto Press.

Klassen, Jerome. 2014. *Joining Empire: The Political Economy of the New Canadian Foreign Policy*. Toronto: University of Toronto Press.

Koonings, Kees. 2012. "New Violence, Insecurity, and the State: Comparative Reflections on Latin America and Mexico." In *Violence, Coercion, and State-Making in Twentieth-Century Mexico: The Other Half of the Centaur*, edited by Wil G. Pansters, 255–78. Stanford: Stanford University Press.

Koonings, Kees, and Dirk Kruijt, eds. 2004. *Armed Actors: Organised Violence and State Failure in Latin America*. London: Zed Books.

Mann, Geoff. 2013. *Disassembly Required*. Oakland, CA: AK Press. http://www.akpress.org/disassemblyrequired.html.

Marx, Karl. 1976. *Capital: A Critique of Political Ecomomy*, vol. I. London: Penguin Books.

Méndez, Juan E., Guillermo O'Donnell, and Paulo Sérgio Pinheiro, eds. 1999. *The (Un)Rule of Law and the Underprivileged in Latin America*. Notre Dame, IN: Notre Dame University Press.

Menjívar, Cecilia, and Néstor Rodríguez, eds. 2005. *When States Kill: Latin America, the U.S., and Technologies of Terror*. Austin: University of Texas Press.

Meyer, Peter. 2017. "U.S. Foreign Assistance to Latin America and the Caribbean: Trends and FY2017 Appropriations." 7–5700. Washington, DC: Congressional Research Service. https://fas.org/sgp/crs/row/R44647.pdf.

Navarro Trujillo, Mina Lorena. 2012. "Las luchas socioambientales en México como una expresión del antagonismo entre lo común y el despojo múltiple." *Observatorio Social de América Latina* 32 (November): 135–53.

North, Liisa L., and Ricardo Grinspun. 2016. "Neo-Extractivism and the New Latin American Developmentalism: The Missing Piece of Rural Transformation." *Third World Quarterly* 37 (8): 1483–1504.

North, Liisa L., and Timothy D. Clark, eds. 2017. *Dominant Elites in Latin America: From Neo-Liberalism to the "Pink Tide."* London: Palgrave Macmillan.

Paley, Dawn. "Guerra Neoliberal y contrainsurgencia ampliada: Vida en el holocausto de Torreón, Coahuila." PhD dissertation, Bénemerita Universidad Autónoma de Puebla, October 2018.

Pansters, Wil G. 2012. "Zones of State-Making: Violence, Coercion, and Hegemony in Twentieth-Century Mexico." In *Violence, Coercion, and State-Making in Twentieth-Century Mexico: The Other Half of the Centaur*, edited by Wil G. Pansters, 3–40. Stanford: Stanford University Press.

Pearce, Jenny. 2010. "Perverse state formation and securitized democracy in Latin America." *Democratization* 17 (2): 286–306.

Polanyi, Karl. 2001. *The Great Transformation: The Political and Economic Origins of Our Time*. Boston: Beacon Press.

Postero, Nancy. 2017. *The Indigenous State: Race, Politics, and Performance in Plurinational Bolivia*. Oakland: University of California Press.

Robinson, William I. 2014. *Global Capitalism and the Crisis of Humanity*. Cambridge: Cambridge University Press.

SEGOB (Secretaría de Gobernación) and SESNSP (Secretariado Ejecutivo del Sistema Nacional de Seguridad Pública). 2018. *Informe de víctimas de homicidio, secuestro y extorsión 2017*. http://secretariadoejecutivo.gob.mx/docs/pdfs/victimas/Victimas2017_122017.pdf.

Shipley, Tyler. 2017. *Ottawa and Empire: Canada and the Military Coup in Honduras*. Toronto: Between the Lines.

Solano, Luis. 2015. *Under Siege: Peaceful Resistance to Tahoe Resources and Militarization in Guatemala*. International Platform against Impunity in Guatemala, MiningWatch Canada, and Network in Solidarity with the People of Guatemala. http://miningwatch.ca/sites/default/files/solano-underseigereport2015-11-10.pdf.

US Department of State. 2016. "U.S. Relations with Chile." Washington, DC, September 7. http://www.state.gov/r/pa/ei/bgn/1981.htm.

Webber, Jeffrey. 2014. "Managing Bolivian Capitalism." *Jacobin*, January. https://www.jacobinmag.com/2014/01/managing-bolivian-capitalism/.

Webber, Jeffrey, and Barry Carr. 2012. *The New Latin American Left: Cracks in the Empire*. Lanham, MD: Rowman and Littlefield.

The White House. 2016. "Fact Sheet: United States-Mexico Relations." Washington, DC, July 22. https://www.whitehouse.gov/the-press-office/2016/07/22/fact-sheet-united-states-mexico-relations.

Zibechi, Raul. 2012. *Territories in Resistance: A Cartography of Latin American Social Movements*. Translated by Ramor Ryan. Oakland, CA: AK Press.

PART I
CENTRAL AND
SOUTH AMERICA

CHAPTER 1

EXTREME ENERGY INJUSTICE AND THE EXPANSION OF CAPITAL

Mary Finley-Brook

T he World Bank predicts that Latin American electricity consumption will double by 2030, following more than $430 billion of investment in the energy sector (Yépez-García, Johnson, and Andrés 2011). Energy expansion has been an essential cornerstone of neoliberal economic reform; as such energy projects have received considerable financial and technical support from development banks and aid agencies. Although justified for regional development and national economic growth, energy development has been carried out in ways that complement broader governance transitions through which regional elites consolidate power and resources, creating what Harvey (2005) identifies as accumulation by dispossession. Energy projects in rural areas disrupt subsistence economies and in some instances force resettlement (as is the case with Colombia's Afro-Pacific population, discussed in Chapter 5). Impacted populations that defend land rights may face violent attacks. Military and paramilitary responses to resource-related protests often exhibit excessive force, leading to intimidation, injury, and death.

Energy expansion, like much resource and infrastructure development in Latin America, relies on the transnational capitalist class to direct resources to projects with uneven social impacts such that vulnerable groups are displaced and their livelihoods threatened while economic and political elites profit (Finley-Brook and Thomas 2011; Robinson 2014). This often takes the form of "disaster capitalism," which Klein (2007, 4) defines as "orchestrated raids on the public sphere in the wake of catastrophic events, combined with the treatment of disasters as exciting market opportunities." In Honduras and elsewhere, wealthy and powerful families and their foreign partners take advantage of chaos and weak institutional capacity to profit from the exploitation of marginalized peoples and places (see Chapter 2). These patterns are particularly nefarious because access to electricity and the reduction of energy poverty can create vital improvements in standards of living for low-income populations, and yet large-scale electrification efforts often ignore the needs of the poor and focus on the consolidation of energy for profitable markets and wealthy consumers. Commercial-scale projects frequently export electricity or channel power towards modern urban centres and industrial hubs.

Extreme energy injustice (EEI) involves murder or preventable death and structural violence from systemic oppression. To understand how processes are unjust, it can be helpful to examine the tenets of energy justice (see Table 1.1): *procedural justice* with access to decision-making power; *distributive justice* with equitable allocation of risks and opportunities; and *recognition justice* involving respect for all peoples regardless of race, ethnicity, gender, faith, or income (McCauley et al. 2013). Protest movements often emerge from violations in political, economic, cultural, and territorial rights. Conflict triggers stem from frustration with maldistribution and disrespect (Vásquez 2014).

Table 1.1: Tenets of Energy Justice

Procedural Justice	Distributive Justice	Recognition Justice
self-governance; inclusion; interactive participation	equitable allocation of costs and benefits	respect; diversity

Source: Modified from Finley-Brook and Holloman (2016).

Countries with violent habits tend to develop industries resilient to violence. Sectors that are resource-bounded, meaning they involve location-specific inputs, are often more resilient to crime and bloodshed; this contrasts with industries with low obstacles to relocate, in which case firms can leave a conflict area and produce elsewhere (Ríos 2016). Remaining in situ regardless of tensions and fatalities, energy and electricity companies internalize violence as a cost of production. In some instances, violence may even facilitate inward flows of foreign direct investment (Maher 2015). For example, when military forces target protesters and quell opposition to extraction, investors may perceive this as a positive signal.

We recognize that capitalist practices range across time, space, and sector. In Latin America, the role of the state in the energy sector was weakened by neoliberalism, or the vigorous turn to free market capitalism pushed by the components of the so-called Washington Consensus, including privatization, trade liberalization, and deregulation (Williamson 1990). Nevertheless, current processes reinsert the state as a powerful motivator of energy sector expansion in collaboration with private sector partners (Springer 2010; Lu, Valdivia, and Silva 2017). Although not a wholesale shift from neoliberalism, in Latin American neo-extractivism—which North and Grinspun (2016, 1484), following Gudynas, define as the contemporary "phenomenon of a more active state and social policies funded by extraction"—the state facilitates private sector control of energy production and transportation to address infrastructural weaknesses and fill supply gaps. Although disparities are present within and between countries of the region, trends do exist. In conflict-ridden countries, capital investments drive and legitimate intimidation and oppression. Millions of dollars of aid flow to locations where private sector and state personnel instigate, assist, and condone violence to advance energy development.

To explore these trends, this chapter addresses organized violence in hydropower installations and with fossil fuel and biofuel production. In exploring cases, research demonstrates not only assassination and physical brutality but also the types of slow, everyday violence found in highly toxic energy extraction or production sites. The last sections of the chapter explore energy systems as an objective, cause, and means of conflict while exploring methods to increase ethics and transparency among donors and multilateral and bilateral financial institutions as a means to reduce violence in the sector.

Energy is a foundation of production and capital accumulation, tying this research to other chapters in this volume. As noted in the Introduction to this collection, "[organized] violence is portrayed as necessary for the security of all, when, in fact, it is mainly necessary to ensure the security of transnational capital." This is clear in the energy sector, as some of the most negatively impacted populations do not even receive electricity from the projects that displace or harm them. Another clear pattern in the energy sector, and one highlighted in several chapters of this book, is the danger of organizing for social transformation. These stories also speak to the determination of grassroots agents of change who organize in spite of the risk to personal safety.

ILLUSTRATIVE CASES AND PATTERNS

In 1992, the Indigenous U'wa people in Colombia threatened to commit mass suicide if Occidental Petroleum extracted oil from their territory (Miranda 2006). The U'wa used what has become a common defence strategy: to publicly demand that shareholders and funders retract project support. Many of the illustrative cases in this chapter have received funding from the same international institutions (i.e., the International Finance Corporation, the Central American Bank of Economic Integration, or the Netherlands Development Corporation), which shows that some institutions are willing to work regularly in risky environments with increased likelihood of conflict (see Table 1.3; see also Chapter 2 on Honduras). Although pressure campaigns are sometimes successful with large development banks and aid agencies in the United States and Europe, pressure becomes complicated when energy projects involve complex webs of subcontractors, subsidiaries, consortiums, and temporary holding companies. Pressure campaigns seem least successful when firms tied to violence are strongly connected to national political and economic elites, such as the Facussé and Atala families in Honduras, who function outside legal structures and norms (Salazar Pérez 2009; Gillison 2014; Lakhani 2014).

Energy firms usually deny responsibility for the murder of project opponents, even when witnesses identify former or active police or military as those carrying out the homicides (Bill et al. 2012; Carson et al. 2015; International Rivers 2016). While identifying who gave the orders for assassinations is challenging, the central objective of this chapter is to point out the extent of the problem. Overall patterns in our illustrative cases suggest complacency, particularly when repeated attacks occur at the same site or in the same country. In these instances, where violent oppression is widespread and common, we suggest that governments, firms, and donors should each be held accountable, whether they are responsible for instigating, perpetuating, or merely tolerating the use of violence or the violation of basic human rights like access to clean water.

Analysis of illustrative cases is broken down into three energy sectors, with discussions of hydropower, oil and gas, and green fuels. Hydropower is the most common energy source in Latin America, so it receives the greatest attention. We extend notions of violence to three cases involving toxic energy where there have been harmful releases of pollutants leading to public health emergencies with wide-ranging sickness and death. Spills and accidents have been left without remediation. As profitable energy resources are extracted, some low-income areas have become pollution hotspots, essentially serving as sacrifice zones.

BLOODY HYDRO

Latin American hydropower has been tied to repression for decades. In Guatemala, four hundred Indigenous villagers were massacred and thousands were displaced for the Chixoy Dam in the 1980s (Stewart 2004). Direct involvement of the World Bank throughout the project cycle meant the bank either knew or should have known about this violence. Bank involvement reinforced transnational support for local demands. First, local populations fought for a shrine to those massacred and later for reparations. Even with clear evidence of culpability, a settlement was not reached until 2014 (Prensa Libre 2014). Violent hydro development has not been contained to the past. Figure 1.1, depicting murders of anti-dam activists, shows an alarming upward trend after 2012.[1] The

---

1   International Rivers, founded in 1985, keeps a running tab of anti-dam activists murdered around the world. While it is possible this tally is incomplete, most of these activists were social movement leaders, and many had previously received death threats or warnings, so human rights groups were apprised of the potential for conflict. International Rivers is the most reliable source of this information because it works in close collaboration with regional, national, and local organizations with on-the-ground connections and knowledge.

persistence of anti-dam activists is striking, as they see their livelihoods and cultural traditions under threat. Many continue to mobilize against projects even after receiving death threats or after comrades are killed.

Figure 1.1: Anti-Dam Activists Murdered in Latin America, 2008–2015

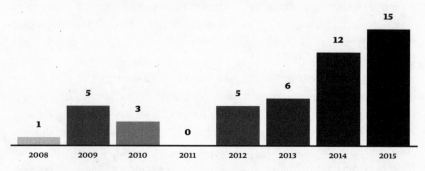

Source: *International Rivers (2016).*

As shown in Table 1.2, Guatemala had the highest dam-related homicide rates, with twenty-one assassinations in just six years (2009–2015), and peak violence at the Santa Rita project with nine murders.

Table 1.2: Assassinated Anti-Dam Activists by Country, 2000–2016

Country	Dams Linked to Homicide	Murders (#)
Guatemala	Unión Fenosa (various), Canbalam, Santa Rita, Tres Marías, Santa Cruz, Palo Viejo, Vega I, Vega II, Caparja	21
Honduras	Babilonia, Intibucá, Agua Zarca, Tigre, Las Minitas, Los Encinos	12
Mexico	El Cajón, La Parota, Cerro de Oro, Cuamono, Picachos	7
Brazil	Belo Monte, Tucuruí, Jirau	5
Colombia	Urra 1, Hidrosogamoso, Hidroituango	5
Panama	Barro Blanco	4
Ecuador	Baba	1
Peru	Chadin II	1

Source: *Updated from International Rivers (2016).*

Since we are unable to detail all of the above cases due to the high number, Table 1.3 presents three internationally prominent projects.

Table 1.3: Comparative Analysis of Three Dams

	Agua Zarca, Honduras	**Barro Blanco, Panama**	**Santa Rita, Guatemala**
Force	Murder of seven Indigenous anti-dam activists since 2011.	Murder of an anti-dam activist and three Ngäbe community members, including a minor.	Murder of four protesters; three killed during evictions; two local youth shot; scorched earth-style evictions.
Project Owner (Country Headquarters)	Desarrollos Energéticos (Honduras)	Generadora del Istmo (Panama)	Latin American Renewables Infrastructure Fund (US)
Project Funders	FMO, FinnFund, CABEI, IFC	DEG, FMO, CABEI	DEG, FMO, AECID, SIFEM, IFC
Did Funders Pull Funds?	Yes (except CABEI)	No	Under compliance investigation since 2015.
Organized Divestment Campaign	Yes	Yes	No
Carbon Offsets	No	CDM (cancelled in 2016)	ETS, CDM

Sources: CIEL (2016); International Rivers (2016); Neslen (2015); FMO (n.d.); Bill et al. (2012).
AECID = Spanish Agency for International Cooperation
CABEI = Central American Bank for Economic Integration
CDM = Clean Development Mechanism (UN)
DEG = German Investment and Development Corporation
ETS = European Trading System
FMO = Netherlands Development Finance Corporation
IFC = International Finance Corporation (World Bank)
SIFEM = Swiss Investment Fund for Emerging Markets

Western Panama has undergone rapid dam building, leading to violence and displacement in Indigenous territories (Finley-Brook and Thomas 2011). There was strong opposition when the Tasbará I dam was originally suggested in the early 1980s, and protest resurfaced with Generadora del Istmo's (GENISA) Barro Blanco proposal on the same Tasbará River. Barro Blanco protesters blocked the Pan-American Highway in 2012. Police used artillery to clear the road, and more than one hundred protesters were injured and four later died, including a minor shot by a police officer at close range. A total of 171 people were incarcerated: those detained were beaten and deprived of sleep, water, and food (Bill et al. 2012). Civilians were shot at from low-flying helicopters and disruption in cell phone service created isolation. Resistance and state repression continued over the next four years.

An international campaign from ActionAid, BankTrack, Both ENDS, and others pressuring donors to divest from Barro Blanco fell on deaf ears, and funds were distributed. Construction halted temporarily with a court injunction, following evidence that the concession lacked proper consultation (CIEL 2016). The government subsequently fined GENISA $775,200 but did not cancel the project; once construction of a dam has started, it is hard to stop. Barro Blanco construction has reached final stages and reservoir flooding was initiated in 2016. After nearly a decade of pressure for the United Nations Clean Development Mechanism (CDM) to reject carbon offsets from this dam, in 2016 the Panamanian government finally withdrew approval from the project. This is a landmark decision, as it is the only time a state has withdrawn support after prior CDM approval (Carbon Market Watch 2016). While CDM carbon credits cannot be exchanged as a result, the flooding of the reservoir still threatens Indigenous communities who continue to oppose the project.

Other prominent Latin American dam projects marked by violence are found in Guatemala. As in Panama, Guatemala's hydro development expanded quickly and plans to construct dozens of additional dams continue. Guatemalan dam-building firms sometimes use private security forces as hit men, creating an atmosphere of impunity where extra-judicial killings seem legitimated. The bloodiest case, Santa Rita, replicated scorched-earth tactics from the civil war (1960–1996). Hundreds of soldiers burned houses and forcefully resettled thousands of Maya Q'eqchi' to make room for the Santa Rita dam (Telesur 2014).

The Santa Rita hydro project reflects global support for lower carbon energy and has been advertised as a green project with carbon offsets to be traded internationally. The developer, the Latin American Renewables Infrastructure Fund, aims to develop wind and hydropower using global finance, including a loan from the World Bank's International Finance Corporation. One could expect funding agencies to learn from prior experiences with Guatemala's Chixoy, Xacbal, and Cambalam dams, all of which involved conflict and negative media attention. Geary (2015) criticizes the World Bank's International Finance Corporation (IFC) for hands-off loan administration through intermediaries in a high-risk country like Guatemala, with its history of violence-ridden dam projects.

In Honduras, the Agua Zarca hydroelectric dam is the most contentious of four dams in the Gualcarque River basin, a sacred place for the Lenca people (see Chapter 2 of this volume). Local opponents formed a human blockade, deterring entrance of equipment for a year. Since 2013, six leaders from the Consejo Cívico de Organizaciones Populares e Indígenas de Honduras (Civic Council of Popular and Indigenous Organizations of Honduras—COPINH) have been murdered due to their advocacy against the dam. Intense global outcry followed the assassination of COPINH member Berta Cáceres (Blitzer 2016), recipient of a 2015 Goldman Environmental Award, who had applied for and received precautionary measures from the Inter-American Commission on Human Rights. The Honduran government was obligated to provide Cáceres with police protection, although this was absent on the night of her death. After the assassination of another COPINH member two weeks after Cáceres's murder, European donors froze Agua Zarca support. In May of 2016, Honduran soldiers and an employee of Desarrollos Energéticos (DESA), the local company building the dam, were charged with killing Cáceres (Blitzer 2016). The Netherlands Development Finance Corporation (FMO) announced it would exit the project after the charges were laid, but more than a year passed before FMO finally cut ties with DESA and the project ground to a halt. FMO has since reinstated support for other Honduran projects. More than thirty international civil society organizations are pressuring FMO to adopt specific measures in its sustainability policy to prevent and address reprisals against human rights defenders, speaking out on FMO-financed activities (Asmann 2016).

Some US state officials have sought to pressure the Honduran government to protect civil liberties. In the 2016 legislative session, forty-two representatives co-sponsored an unsuccessful "Berta Cáceres Human Rights in Honduras Act" in Congress to cut funds to Honduran military and security forces since they have been tied to atrocities. Honduras is a security partner in the US wars on drugs and gang violence. In 2014 alone, the United States sold more than one million dollars worth of arms to Honduras. In 2016, the United States gave Honduras $67.1 million in support—while some of this was categorized under democratization programs, significant support is allocated for military finance and training. Critics argue US government funds for Honduran military and security forces should be suspended until impunity is reversed (Weisbrot 2016). Nonetheless, annual budgetary allocations and military support remain high.

FOSSIL FUEL DISPLACEMENT AND ASSASSINATIONS

Repression and human rights violations are often higher in oil-producing states than in those without petroleum resources (DeMeritt and Young 2013). In Colombia's oil-producing regions, state and paramilitary forces protect oil interests and infrastructure through arrests, torture, murder, and disappearances (Carson et al. 2015; Maher 2015; see also Chapter 6 for a similar pattern in coal-producing regions). Anti-communist rhetoric is used to justify displacing farmers and Indigenous peoples to acquire land for exploration. The degree of foreign responsibility is still being determined in a legal case against British Petroleum (BP), which owns a portion of Ocensa Oil Company. Amnesty International claims to have informed BP of the abduction and murder of union members and that the company did nothing to stop the attacks (Silva Numa 2014).

In recent years, Mexico has taken steps to open oil and gas lands to foreign investment, and drug cartels have moved in to take advantage of profits (see Chapter 7). Fearing for their safety, residents of Guadalupe, Chihuahua, fled in large numbers. If people did not leave, houses were targeted with arson and inhabitants were burned out or murdered. The municipal government in Guadalupe passed a policy to legally seize land and homes if property taxes are unpaid, allowing it to then resell properties to oil and gas speculators (Matalon 2015).

In 2012, the Mexican government approved the Agua Prieta pipeline through ninety kilometres of Yaqui territory in northern Mexico without the free, prior, and informed consent of the Yaqui people. The pipeline, which will transport gas from Arizona in the United States to Sonora, Mexico, garnered international attention in 2016 when a protester against the project was killed and the lawyer representing the Yaqui was kidnapped (Telesur 2016a, 2016b). Due to the voracity with which the state is supporting the project despite opposition, the case is being called Mexico's "Standing Rock," referencing a dispute with thousands of Native Americans protesting against pipeline construction in North Dakota. The Agua Prieta pipeline highlights the need to analyze energy transnationally, between regions, and within global trends, rather than viewing Latin American energy transitions in isolation.

Like those to the north, South American pipelines have also been surrounded by tension and, in some cases, violence. In Brazil, a leader in a fishers' union fighting a Petrobras oil pipeline was murdered in 2009 following death threats and the aggressive confiscation of union members' nets and boats (Frayssinet 2009). Fishers were protesting against the pipeline because catches in the bay had declined since construction, and they observed damage to flora and fauna, as well as violations of environmental permits.

Research on Latin American natural gas exploration is preliminary and deserves additional attention. Indigenous peoples' protests against oil and gas extraction often stem from lack of trust in public-private resource management and concern about inequitable development. A 2009 massacre in Bagua, Peru, arose from protest over legislative degrees that would open Indigenous peoples' territories to oil and gas extraction as part of free trade with the United States. Amazonian protesters blockaded a highway in 2009 for two months until six hundred police used lethal force to remove them, leaving dozens dead and nearly one hundred with bullet wounds (Hughes 2010). In Bolivia in 2003, protests known as the "Gas Wars" left dozens dead at the hands of police. The motive of the protest was to put the brakes on gas privatization, extraction, and export, as well as to increase public participation in resource decision making (Perrault 2006).

Bebbington and Bury (2013) point out that the development of liquid natural gas technology has made it possible to transport gas over long distances and has reshaped the geographies of global markets. Gas is a competitive commodity sought around the world. Based on a Bolivian case study with the Spanish firm Repsol, Peralta et al. (2015) suggest that the involvement of foreign actors with knowledge of the dangers of

gas production can lead to companies developing environmental standards above those required in Latin American host states. They argue
this is most likely to be done when weak standards threaten the viability
of the firm's operations. Whether this is true in other contexts would
need to be explored: the Peruvian Camisea concession, one of the largest
gas projects in the region, is discussed in a subsequent section on toxic
energy due to excessive contamination. Moreover, Peralta et al. (2015) are
not optimistic about foreign gas firms being willing to promote or accept
changes in state rules regarding access to and use of natural resources
because their operations benefit from the exclusion of local populations.
Both environmental impacts from gas extraction and transport and the
implications of the gas industry on land and resource access deserve
additional attention from researchers.

GREEN GRABBING

Human rights abuses and examples of violent displacement exist with
biofuel plantations around the world (Scheidel and Sorman 2012).
Expansion of palm biofuels has contributed to land concentration and
conflict in Colombia, where hundreds were killed by paramilitaries in
the late 1990s (Ballvé 2009; Zimerman 2014; Maher 2015). Land grabbing
displaced thousands of Afro-Colombians when Urapalma and a dozen
other palm companies seized at least fifty-two thousand acres of land
(Ballvé 2009; Zimerman 2014). Fraud investigations revealed companies set up fake community associations to receive phony land titles
and access public funds meant to incentivize palm production (Ballvé
2009). In addition to state subsidies, the US Agency for International
Development (USAID) funded more than $20 million of palm expansion
in Colombia in an effort to promote a crop thought capable of competing
with coca profits (see Chapter 6 for a further discussion of USAID and
the displacement of Afro-Colombians).

In a second country, Honduras, there were more than forty executions
in Bajo Aguán linked to land conflicts driven by palm biofuel expansion
(Bird 2012; Lakhani 2014). Wealthy land grabbers have been accused of
paying for the murder of peasants asserting land rights (*La Prensa* 2010;
Knight 2016; Lakhani 2016). Between 2009 and 2011, state troops relocated dozens of families by force and set up security checkpoints to control movement. Murder, kidnapping, torture, sexual violence, and other

repressive acts were widely documented from police and military, as well as paramilitary troops and private security forces. Miguel Facussé, owner of the Honduran firm Dinant, acknowledged the responsibility of his security guards for violence against local inhabitants (*La Prensa* 2010). Oppression of opposition leaders continues to the present, with the murder of two leaders from the Movimiento Unificado Campesino (Unified Campesino Movement) in October of 2016.

The complacency of international finance institutions in a high-violence location like Honduras is concerning. After complaints were taken to the Office of the Compliance Advisor/Ombudsman (CAO) (2016), IFC was found guilty of noncompliance with various institutional policies (see Table 1.4).

Table 1.4: Review of IFC Oversight of Dinant Corporation, Honduras

IFC accepted an overly narrow definition of risk without adequate consideration of project context or available sources of information.
In a sector and country where conflict and violence around land were or should have been known, IFC's review was not "commensurate to risk."
IFC failed to ensure the communities living most proximate to Dinant's properties were consulted during its environmental and social assessment.
IFC disbursed US$15 million to a client that was in apparent noncompliance with its environmental and social undertakings in a risk environment that had deteriorated significantly.
IFC investment team did not keep staff working on the environmental and social assessment appraised of developments in relation to land disputes and occupations around the client's plantations of which they were aware.
There is no indication that IFC supervised its client's obligations to investigate credible allegations of abusive acts by security personnel.

Source: Condensed from CAO (2016).

A commonality between Dinant palm production and the hydro cases discussed above is the sale of carbon offsets through the UN's CDM (Finley-Brook 2016). Before verification of Dinant's CDM application, the CDM executive board was aware of more than two dozen alleged murders of local farmers but approved the project anyway, stating that it met existing CDM requirements (Neslen 2011). CDM verification requires state approval to assure positive social impacts, but state agencies have supported offsets from energy firms even when they violate human rights (Finley-Brook 2016).

EXTREME ENERGY INJUSTICE

The following EEI cases involve, or have the potential to involve, hundreds of deaths (see Table 1.4). Many Latin American states do not adequately regulate the use and disposal of toxic chemicals and waste, and, in cases of harmful exposure, private sector actors are often unwilling to rectify the situation or even take responsibility. The Chevron-Texaco case is the only one to have gone to international litigation, although national cases have been attempted unsuccessfully in Peru. Ecuador's oil pollution has created a high-stake legal battle of "protracted lawfare" (Joseph 2012, 70). The case has the potential to change precedence for litigation from harm due to resource extraction. In the meantime, oil extraction in the Amazon is causing a public health emergency (San Sebastián and Hurtig 2004), much like sugar cane biofuel has done in parts of Central America (Wegman et al. 2015).

As cases in Table 1.5 demonstrate, assigning responsibility for toxic exposure is complicated. For example, Petroecuador continued oil production and improper waste disposal after Texaco left. In Nicaragua, agrochemicals used for decades in the area surrounding Nicaragua Sugar Estates are now banned due to proven health impacts, although toxic residues will persist in the environment for a long period. In the Peruvian Amazon, illegal gold mining using mercury may also have contributed to the poisoning of Nahua people. These factors complicate responsibility for cleanup and compensation, as does the fact that Camisea and Chevron-Texaco ownership changed over time (Kimerling 2013; Yañez Quiroz 2015). Assigning responsibility for remediation is beyond the scope of this chapter, which seeks to highlight the concerning pattern of creating unresolved public health emergencies as a result of socially and ecologically irresponsible energy development.

The Ecuadorian Amazon is crossed with oil pipelines due to Texaco's twenty-six years of operations that left hundreds of unlined waste pits (Joseph 2012; Kimerling 2013). According to expert testimony in legal cases, the low estimate for fatalities is 1,400, but the death count could reach as much as ten times higher or more, depending on the speed and effectiveness of remediation (Joseph 2012). The parent oil company Chevron, which acquired Texaco in a 2001 merger, refuses to remediate or pay an $18 billion court settlement designated for impacted communities.

Table 1.5: Comparative Analysis of Toxic Hotspots

	Lago Agrio, Ecuador	Chichigalpa, Nicaragua	Block 88, Peru
Energy Type	petroleum	sugar cane bagasse and ethanol	natural gas
Contamination and Risk	Oil spills and waste implicated in a range of diseases and symptoms, including leukemia and reduced fertility; estimated minimum death toll is 1,400.	Deaths of seven hundred inhabitants (2002–present) from chronic kidney disease believed to be tied to surrounding agrichemical systems.	Extreme poverty, malnutrition, and water contamination; suspected mercury poisoning of Nahua tribe.
Firm Owner	Texaco (later Chevron-Texaco) (us); Petroecuador (Ecuador)	Nicaragua Sugar Estates of Pellas Group (Nicaragua)	Camisea consortium: Pluspetrol, Hunt Oil, and others (multinational)
Project Funders	internal	IFC	EXIM, Citibank; IDB

Sources: Hill (2014, 2016); Kimerling (2013, 2016); Lakhani (2015).
EXIM = Export-Import Bank of the United States
IFC = International Finance Corporation (World Bank)
IDB = Inter-American Development Bank

In the Peruvian Amazon, devastation followed oil and gas expansion (Feather 2014). When oil companies entered what is now Block 88 in the 1980s, as many as 50 percent of the Nahua tribe died due to their lack of immunity to outside diseases. Block 88 includes a reserve for Indigenous peoples in voluntary isolation or those undergoing "initial contact" (Munilla 2010; Feather 2014). After years of negotiation and development, and $3.7 billion of investment, production began on Camisea, a massive project of gas fields, pipelines, and processing facilities. The Camisea consortium continued to expand, although Indigenous federations tried to halt plans for additional extraction in national courts (Hill 2014). There have been strong economic returns for Camisea shareholders, but poverty and malnutrition remain widespread in the surrounding areas (Hill 2016). Environmental and health impacts from a series of spills and pipeline ruptures have not been studied adequately. In 2015, it was discovered that 80 percent of the Nahua tribe suffers from mercury poisoning, and one child died with mercury poisoning symptoms (Hill 2016).

Some biofuels cause ecological harm in terms of biodiversity impact, water overuse and contamination, or pesticide burden. In Central America, sugar cane workers are experiencing an epidemic of chronic kidney disease from nontraditional causes (CKDNT), estimated to have killed twenty thousand, with deaths occurring predominantly among sugar cane workers. In Chichigalpa, Nicaragua, home of Nicaragua Sugar Estates, there have been seven hundred deaths since 2002 (Schmidt 2014). Nicaragua Sugar Estates historically produced sugar and rum but diversified to ethanol and bagasse biofuel following IFC funding in 2006 (Finley-Brook 2012).

Causes of CKDNT appear multifactorial; experts have not demonstrated a direct link between chemical exposures, although research is ongoing. Poor hydration and heat exposure in the fields appear to contribute to disease onset (Wegman et al. 2015). Impacted families say the company and the state have not done enough to address work conditions likely to contribute to CKDNT (Lakhani 2015). Nicaragua Sugar Estates insisted for years that there was no occupational link (Wegman et al. 2015). Impacted families assert it is difficult to receive adequate medical attention from the state or the company since workers are forced to prove they became ill on the job. Workers are let go or are not hired back in subsequent seasons when company-mandated blood tests reveal the onset of CKDNT (Finley-Brook 2012; Wegman et al. 2015). CKDNT is a public health emergency, and the state and the private sector need to act immediately to improve research and treatment and regulate work conditions to prevent more loss of life. In contrast, in 2014, police shot and killed a protester demanding better medical treatment and compensation for family members of the diseased (Schmidt 2014). In 2015, impacted families marched 130 kilometres to the capital to protest but were not received by government representatives (Lakhani 2015). Critics contend President Daniel Ortega has not responded to the CKDNT crisis due to his beneficial political relationship with the owner of Nicaragua Sugar Estates, Carlos Pellas, the wealthiest businessman in the country and an influential leader in the Chamber of Industries. The government provided tax breaks and other financial incentives to Nicaragua Sugar Estates to develop energy products from sugar cane.

Potentially demonstrating a lack of concern for human life, IFC approved a new grant in 2013 to another Nicaraguan sugar company, Consorcio Naviero Nicaraguense (Navinic). Navinic workers have since fallen ill and some have died (Wegman et al. 2015). Due to IFC involvement, Office of the Compliance Advisor/Ombudsman cases were opened on Nicaragua Sugar Estates and Navinic loans and the Navinic case is being monitored. After monitoring dispute resolution processes between impacted community members and Nicaragua Sugar Estates, from 2012 to 2015, the earlier CAO case was closed without significant changes that would deter similar lending in the future. Funerals for former sugar workers continue on a weekly basis in Chichigalpa (see also Chapter 4 for cases of poisoning from soya production in Paraguay).

DISCUSSION: EXPANSION OF CAPITAL AND ENERGY CONFLICTS

Månsson (2014) defines three ways in which energy systems are linked to violence (see Table 1.6). We focus on the two more common categories of energy systems as *objectives* and *causes* of conflict. Although less common, energy did became a *means* for conflict, with pipeline sabotage during Colombian and Peruvian civil conflicts. Identifying patterns in conflict occurrence can inform work to proactively avoid violence. If violence already occurred, assessing how a system contributed can help delink energy from conflict.

Energy as an Objective of Conflict

For private and state developers, energy provides the objective for conflict. Energy development is an essential component of infrastructure corridors and industrial operations. The Central America Electrical

Interconnection System links one country to the next, expanding opportunities for export-oriented manufacturing and services. Exports provide the base of the Central American Free Trade Agreement with the United States, a cornerstone of the regional economy. In South America, the Initiative for the Integration of Infrastructure in South America drives regional expansion. The scale of extraction and industrial output continues to intensify. If growth in energy infrastructure cannot keep up, unreliable electricity could become a limiting factor to growth, as it often was in the past under national systems. From this perspective, social movement actors are identified as villains for their role in preventing so-called development and progress.

Table 1.6: Local Energy System-Conflict Interactions

Reason for Conflict	The energy system is the *objective* of conflict.	The energy system is a *means* for conflict.	The energy system is a *cause* of conflict.
Justification	There is competition for resources and power.	A third party induces disturbance.	A resource threat or scarcity occurs.
Example	A member of a state military assassinates a project opponent fighting for their land rights.	A guerrilla group commits an act of pipeline terrorism.	Villagers protest displacement or environmental degradation.

Source: Modified from Månsson (2014, 107).

Energy as a Cause of Conflict

Energy projects are the cause of conflicts for impacted populations. Recognizing the extent and depth of violations, as shown in Table 1.7, helps explain the growth of civil society opposition surrounding energy projects mentioned in this chapter. Latin American energy justice is tied to broad social and economic demands linked to distributive and procedural injustices and structural violence.

Table 1.7: *Energy Injustice, Structural Violence, and Conflict Triggers*

Causes of Conflict	Common Examples
Excessive Use of Force	• Extra-judicial killings, torture, kidnappings, disappearances, death threats, coercion, and repression occurred.
Procedural Injustice	• The right to free, prior, and informed consent is violated in most cases. • Weak, if any, public consultation carried out before project initiation.
Distributive Injustice	• Populations displaced for energy infrastructure live in poverty, often without electrification. • Resource and land access is diminished for local populations without adequate compensation.
Recognition Injustice	• Political and economic systems are exclusionary.
Structural Violence	• Racism and classism are evident in daily interactions. • Local harm from energy projects is grave (i.e., loss of land rights or resource access, contamination of drinking water).
Triggers	• Civil society is frustrated with and distrustful of the government. • Pan-Indigenous and transnational advocacy movements are strengthening and expanding.

Source: *Compiled by the author; inspired by Holmes (2013).*

Conflict triggers are common because public fatigue and anger towards social injustices encourage solidarity among networks of civil society organizations addressing legal rights, human rights, Indigenous rights, environmental justice, or other related campaigns. Important actors who work to shape and strengthen policies of state, private, and finance institutions include watchdog groups (e.g., Banktrack, BankWatch, CorpWatch, Carbon Market Watch, Carbon Trade Watch) and legal support groups, and those documenting and witnessing atrocities (e.g., Amnesty International, the Center for International Environmental Law, International Rivers, Oxfam). Transnational partnerships are increasingly common between grassroots groups and international allies, who publicly shame those violating rights and draw attention to financial and institutional connections among powerful national and global actors. While transnational activist alliances are stronger than ever, international advocates can do little to stop the murder of in-country allies. Unfortunately, local advocates are left to denounce human rights violations, even though they would prefer a more proactive role to stop them altogether. To stop bloodshed will require strict violence-free policies, stronger advocacy, and better oversight from development banks, project financiers, and energy market consumers.

ENERGY AND CARBON ACCOUNTABILITY

Shipping lanes, transmission lines, and pipelines weave the Americas together, and Latin American oil and biofuels move across the globe. With lengthening energy supply chains, consumer agency becomes an important outlet to pressure for state reform and corporate social responsibility. Given international concerns about climate change and the impetus towards low-carbon energy, there are opportunities to cultivate connections between conflict-free energy and clean energy. This is going to require a major shift in how things are done. A focus on governance is essential to eliminate repression, as there is broad disconnect between rhetoric and reality. For example, Latin American business elites from projects mentioned previously, such as Carlos Pellas with Nicaragua Sugar Estates, earn international private-sector accolades for growth, innovation, and environmentally and socially responsible production (Schmidt 2014, 2015). Project owners mentioned in this chapter are integrated into powerful political and economic networks domestically and internationally, and they act with relative impunity. International companies and financial institutions are eager to support energy development, especially if it is categorized as clean, and human rights protections in carbon offset markets remain incomplete and inadequate (Finley-Brook and Thomas 2011; Neslen 2015; Finley-Brook 2016; Finley-Brook and Holloman 2016).

Immediate steps to reduce deadly energy include commitments to conflict-resolution mechanisms, monitoring, and improved funding screens to identify and reject projects with human rights violations during lending and finance decisions. There needs to be zero tolerance when violence occurs after contracts are signed or after financial transfers begin. Today, in contrast, when funding agencies are faced with allegations of repression within projects, some defend repressive actions, preferring to condone violence rather than accept culpability.

Ultimately, solutions to systemic violence are necessary to address extreme energy injustice. Faced with funding cuts due to ethical concerns, project developers may turn to other sources requiring less accountability. This highlights the fact that the Latin American energy sector requires broad reforms—for example, dismantling racism and reforming corruption or misuse of power—to assure terror-free and nontoxic sources of energy.

REFERENCES

Asmann, Parker. 2016. "Environmentalists Face Renewed Repression in Honduras." http://nacla.org/news/2016/10/27/environmental-activists-face-renewed-repression-honduras.

Ballvé, Teo. 2009. "The Dark Side of Plan Colombia." *The Nation*, June 15. https://www.thenation.com/article/dark-side-plan-colombia/.

Bebbington, Anthony, and Jeffrey Bury. 2013. *Subterranean Struggles: New Dynamics of Mining, Oil and Gas in Latin America*. Austin: University of Texas Press.

Bill, Doris, Mariela Arce, Félix W. Solis, Washington L. Sandoya, and David de Leon. 2012. *Informe de gira de observación de derechos humanos luego de las protestas contra la minería e hidroeléctricas en la Comarca Ngäbe-Buglé*. Panama: Comisión de Paz y Justicia.

Bird, Anne. 2012. "Drugs and Business: Central America Faces Another Round of Violence." *NACLA Report on the Americas* 45 (1): 35–36.

Blitzer, Jonathan. 2016. "Should the U.S. Still Be Sending Military Aid to Honduras?" *The New Yorker*, August 17. https://www.newyorker.com/news/news-desk/should-the-u-s-still-be-sending-military-aid-to-honduras.

CAO (Office of the Compliance Advisor/Ombudsman). 2016. "Honduras Dinant-01/CAO Vice President Request." http://www.cao-ombudsman.org/cases/case_detail.aspx?id=188.

Carbon Market Watch. 2016. "In Landmark Decision, Panama Withdraws UN Registration for Barro Blanco Hydrodam." https://carbonmarketwatch.org/2016/11/10/press-statement-in-landmark-decision-panama-withdraws-un-registration-for-barro-blanco-hydrodam-project/.

Carson, Mary, Adrian Gatton, Rodrigo Vásquez, and Maggie O'Kane. 2015. "Gilberto Torres Survived Colombia's Death Squads. Now He Wants Justice." *The Guardian*, May 22. https://www.theguardian.com/world/2015/may/22/gilberto-torres-survived-colombias-death-squads-now-he-wants-justice.

CIEL (Center for International Environmental Law). 2016. "Flooding Begins on UN- Approved Hydro Dam as Indigenous Defenders Are Forcibly Removed." https://intercontinentalcry.org/barro-blanco-flooding-begins-un-approved-hydro-dam-Indigenous-defenders-forcefully-removed/.

DeMeritt, Jacqueline H. R., and Joseph K. Young. 2013. "A Political Economy of Human Rights: Oil, Natural Gas, State Incentives to Repress." *Conflict Management and Peace Studies* 30 (2): 99–120.

Feather, Conrad. 2014. *Violating Rights and Threatening Lives: The Camisea Gas Project and Indigenous Peoples in Voluntary Isolation*. Moreton-in-Marsh, UK: Forest People's Program.

Finley-Brook, Mary. 2012. "El Tratado de Libre Comercio entre Centroamérica, República Dominicana y Estados Unidos (CAFTA-DR) y el desarrollo desigual." *Mesoamérica* 54: 54–93.

———. 2016. "Justice and Equity in Carbon Offset Governance: Debates and Dilemmas." In *The Carbon Fix: Forest Carbon, Social Justice and Environmental Governance*, edited by Stephanie Paladino and Shirley Fiske, 74–88. London: Routledge.

Finley-Brook, Mary, and Erica L. Holloman. 2016. "Empowering Energy Justice." *International Journal of Environmental Research and Public Health* 13 (9): 926.

Finley-Brook, Mary, and Curtis Thomas. 2011. "Renewable Energy and Human Rights Violations: Illustrative Cases from Indigenous Territories in Panama." *Annals of the Association of American Geographers* 101: 863–72.

FMO (Netherlands Development Finance Corporation). n.d. "Agua Zarca." https://www.fmo.nl/agua-zarca.

Frayssinet, Fabiana. 2009. "Brazil: Murder, Death Threats amid Environmental Protests." *Interpress Service*, May 26. http://www.ipsnews.net/2009/05/brazil-murder-death-threats-amid-environmental-protests/.

Geary, Kate. 2015. *The Suffering of Others*. Oxford: Oxfam International.

Gillison, Douglas. 2014. "Blind to Problems, World Bank Invested in Honduran Bank, Audit Says." https://100r.org/2014/08/blind-to-problems-world-bank-invested-in-honduran-bank-audit-says/.

Harvey, David. 2005. *A Brief History of Neoliberalism*. Oxford: Oxford University Press.

Hill, David. 2014. "Two Lawsuits to Stop Peru's Biggest Gas Project in Indigenous Reserve." *The Guardian*, February 25. https://www.theguardian.com/environment/andes-to-the-amazon/2014/feb/25/peru-biggest-gas-project-indigenous-reserve-two-lawsuits.

———. 2016. "Pioneer Gas Project in Latin America Fails Indigenous Peoples." *The Guardian*, June 3. https://www.theguardian.com/environment/andes-to-the-amazon/2016/jun/02/pioneer-gas-latin-america-indigenous-peoples.

Holmes, S. 2013. *Fresh Fruit, Broken Bodies: Migrant Farmworkers in the United States*. Oakland: University of California Press.

Hughes, Neil. 2010. "Indigenous Protest in Peru: The 'Orchard Dog' Bites Back." *Social Movement Studies.* 9 (1): 85–90.

International Rivers. 2016. "Murdered for Their Rivers: A Roster of Fallen Dam Fighters." https://www.internationalrivers.org/resources/murdered-for-their-rivers-a-roster-of-fallen-dam-fighters-11499.

Joseph, Sarah. 2012. "Protracted Lawfare: The Tale of Chevron Texaco in the Amazon." *Journal of Human Rights and the Environment* 3 (1): 70–91.

Kimerling, Judith. 2013. "Oil, Contact, and Conservation in the Amazon: Indigenous Huaorani, Chevron, and Yasuni." *Colorado Journal of International Law and Policy* 24 (1): 43–115.

———. 2016. "Habitat at Human Rights: Indigenous Huaorani in the Amazon Rainforest, Oil, and Ome Yasuni." *Vermont Law Review* 44: 445–524.

Klein, Naomi. 2007. *The Shock Doctrine: The Rise of Disaster Capitalism.* New York: Metropolitan Books.

Knight, Nika. 2016. "Leader of Honduran Campesino Movement Assassinated." *Common Dreams*, October 19. https://www.commondreams.org/news/2016/10/19/leader-honduran-campesino-movement-assassinated.

La Prensa. 2010. "Honduras: Facussé acusa a Ham por los asesinatos." *La Prensa* (Honduras), November 16. https://www.laprensa.hn/sucesos/481387-97/honduras-facussé-acusa-a-ham-por-los-asesinatos.

Lakhani, Nina. 2014. "Honduras and the Dirty War Fuelled by the West's Drive for Clean Energy." *The Guardian*, January 7. https://www.theguardian.com/global/2014/jan/07/honduras-dirty-war-clean-energy-palm-oil-biofuels.

———. 2015. "Nicaraguans Demand Action over Illness Killing Thousands of Sugar Cane Workers." *The Guardian*, February 16. https://www.theguardian.com/world/2015/feb/16/-sp-nicaragua-kidney-disease-killing-sugar-cane-workers.

———. 2016. "Two More Honduran Land Rights Activists Killed in Ongoing Violence." *The Guardian*, October 19. https://www.theguardian.com/world/2016/oct/19/honduras-land-rights-activists-killed-unified-peasant-movement.

Lu, Flora, Gabriela Valdivia, and Nestor L. Silva. 2017. *Oil, Revolution, and Indigenous Citizenship in Ecuador.* London: Palgrave Macmillan.

Maher, David. 2015. "The Fatal Attraction of Civil War Economies: Foreign Direct Investment and Political Violence, A Case Study of Colombia." *International Studies Review* 17: 217–48.

Månsson, André. 2014. "Energy, Conflict and War: Towards a Conceptual Framework." *Energy Research and Social Science* 4: 106–16.

Matalon, Lorne. 2015. *Borderland, Exodus: Towns on Path of Proposed Mexican Pipeline Suffer Rash of Violence.* Marfa, TX: Marfa Public Radio.

McCauley, Darren, Raphael J. Heffron, Hannes Stephan, and Kirsten Jenkins. 2013. "Advancing Energy Justice: The Triumvirate of Tenets." *International Energy Law Review* 3: 107–10.

Miranda, Lillian Aponte. 2006. "The U'wa and Occidental Petroleum: Searching

for Corporate Accountability in Violations of Indigenous Land Rights."
American Indian Law Review 31 (2): 651–73.

Munilla, Isabel. 2010. *People, Power, and Pipelines: Lessons from Peru in the Governance of Gas Production Revenues*. Washington, DC: Oxfam.

Neslen, Arthur. 2011. "EU Carbon Credits Scheme Tarnished by Alleged Murders in Honduras." *The Guardian*, October 3. https://www.theguardian.com/environment/2011/oct/03/eu-carbon-credits-murders-honduras.

———. 2015. "'Green' Dam Linked to Killings of Six Indigenous People in Guatemala." *The Guardian*, March 26. https://www.theguardian.com/environment/2015/mar/26/santa-rita-green-dam-killings-indigenous-people-guatemala.

North, Liisa, and Ricardo Grinspun. 2016. "Neo-Extractivism and the New Latin American Developmentalism: The Missing Piece of Rural Transformation." *Third World Quarterly* 37 (8): 1483–1504.

Peralta, Pablo Ospina, Anthony Bebbington, Patric Hollenstein, Ilana Nussbaum, and Eduardo Ramírez. 2015. "Extraterrestrial Investments, Environmental Crisis and Collective Action in Latin America." *World Development* 73: 32–43.

Perrault, Thomas. 2006. "From the Guerra del Agua to the Guerra del Gas: Resource Governance, Neoliberalism, and Popular Protest in Bolivia." *Antipode* 38 (1): 150–72.

Prensa Libre. 2014. "Gobierno promulga política de reparacíon de daños por Chixoy," November 6. http://www.prensalibre.com/departamental/chixoy-afectados-hidroelectrica-rio-negro-energia-politica-publica-reparacion-comunidades_0_1243675718.html.

Ríos, Viridiana. 2016. *The Impact of Crime and Violence on Economic Sector Diversity*. Cambridge, MA: Harvard University, Wilson Center.

Robinson, William I. 2014. *Global Capitalism and the Crisis of Humanity*. New York: Cambridge University Press.

Salazar Pérez, Robinson. 2009. "Honduras: Golpe de estado y altercación de los escaques del ajedrez político en América Latina." *Periferias* 18: 47–63.

San Sebastián, Miguel, and Anna Karin Hurtig. 2004. "Oil Exploitation in the Amazon Basin of Ecuador: A Public Health Emergency." *Revista Panamerican de Salud Pública* 15 (3): 205–11.

Scheidel, Arnim, and Alevgul H. Sorman. 2012. "Energy Transitions and the Global Land Rush: Ultimate Drivers and Persistent Consequences." *Global Environmental Change* 22: 588–95.

Schmidt, Blake. 2014. "Meet Carlos Pellas, Nicaragua's First Billionaire." *Bloomberg News*, November 4. https://www.bloomberg.com/news/articles/2014-11-05/meet-carlos-pellas-nicaragua-s-first-billionaire.

———. 2015. "Central American Billionaires Discovered amid Citi Asset Sales." *Bloomberg News*, April 21. https://www.bloomberg.com/news/articles/2015-04-21/central-american-billionaires-discovered-amid-citi-asset-sales.

Silva Numa, Sergio. 2014. "BP, demandada por 73 campesinos." *El Espectador*,

October 23. https://www.elespectador.com/noticias/nacional/
bp-demandada-73-campesinos-articulo-523884.

Springer, Simon. 2010. "Neoliberalism and Geography: Expansions,
Variegations, Formations." *Geography Compass* 4 (8): 1025–38.

Stewart, Julie. 2004. "When Local Troubles Become Transnational: The
Transformation of a Guatemalan Indigenous Rights Movement."
Mobilization: An International Journal 9 (3): 259–78.

Telesur. 2014. "Desalojo violento en comunidad campesina de Guatemala."
https://www.telesurtv.net/news/Desalojo-violento-en-comunidad-
campesina-de-Guatemala-20140815-0051.html.

———. 2016a. "Lawyer for Yaqui Tribe Fighting Mexico's DAPL Kidnapped."
http://www.telesurtv.net/english/news/Lawyer-for-Yaqui-Tribe-Fighting-
Mexicos-DAPL-Kidnapped-20161215-0002.html.

———. 2016b. "Mexico Clash Over Pipeline Leaves 1 dead in Yaqui Community."
http://www.telesurtv.net/english/news/Mexico-Clash-Over-Pipeline-
Leaves-1-Dead-in-Yaqui-Community-20161022-0015.html.

Vásquez, Patricia, I. 2014. *Oil Sparks in the Amazon: Local Conflicts, Indigenous
Populations, and Natural Resources*. Athens: University of Georgia Press.

Wegman, David, Jason Glaser, Richard J. Johnson, Christer Hogstedt, and
Catharina Wesseling. 2015. "Mesoamerican Nephropathy—New Evidence
and the Need to Act Now." *International Journal of Occupational and
Environmental Health* 21 (4): 333–36.

Weisbrot, Mark. 2016. "Honduran Opposition Leaders Are Murdered While
US Supports Government." http://thehill.com/blogs/pundits-blog/
international/302635-in-honduras-opposition-leaders-are-murdered-
while-us.

Williamson, John. 1990. "What Washington Means by Policy Reform." In *Latin
American Adjustment: How Much Has Happened?* edited by John Williamson,
7–20. Washington, DC: Institute for International Economics.

Yañez Quiroz, Luis. 2015. *Opportunities and Missteps: Lessons from the International
Finance Corporation (IFC) Investment Policy in Peru*. Lima, Peru: Oxfam.

Yépez-García, Rigoberto Ariel, Todd M. Johnson, and Luis Alberto Andrés. 2011.
*Meeting the Balance of Electricity Supply and Demand in Latin America and the
Caribbean*. Washington, DC: The World Bank.

Zimerman, Artur. 2014. "Violence against Peasants in Latin America: Land
Deals and the Food/Fuel Crop." *International Journal of Contemporary
Sociology* 51 (2): 117–42.

CHAPTER 2

"THE MOST DANGEROUS COUNTRY IN THE WORLD"
VIOLENCE AND CAPITAL IN POST-COUP HONDURAS

Tyler Shipley

I n the sensationalized news stories of the north, Honduras is quite often presented as "the most dangerous country in the world." This statement is not without some truth: in the two years following the military coup of 2009, the homicide rate in Honduras shot up to 86.5 per one hundred thousand people, making it the highest in the world. It remained in the top spot until 2014, when the Honduran state rearranged its definition of homicide to make the numbers appear smaller (Gagne 2014). When the media picked up and repeated the claim that Honduras was the most dangerous country in the world, then, it was not a lie; but it was not exactly the whole truth, either. The mainstream media presentation of Honduras's exceptionally high homicide rate often implies a kind of random violence, as though any person walking down the street at any time might well be shot and killed. This violence is presented as though it was an unavoidable consequence of Honduran politics and culture, or something inherent in the very nature of the country.

To be sure, random acts of violence, from robbery and assault to sexual violence and murder, have become a routinized part of life in many places in Honduras. However, they are not disconnected from the broader dynamics of conflict in the country, which are far less random or chaotic than media descriptions often imply. Much of the violence in Honduras is linked—sometimes quite directly, sometimes by a few degrees of separation—to processes of neoliberal capital accumulation and the resistance they engender. Daily forms of violence, from petty crime to gang conflicts, are rooted in the poverty, dislocation, and despair of contemporary Honduras, and these reflect much more organized forms of violence that take shape around a deep-rooted social conflict between the small minority of wealthy oligarchs and foreign business owners and the majority of poor and working people who are increasingly challenging their authority.

This chapter will explore the complicated dynamics of contemporary violence in Honduras, drawing links between the resurgence of the political Right in Honduras and the expansion of foreign investment in the country following the 2009 coup d'état. I will offer a modest corrective to mainstream discussion about Honduras, which tends to assume the violence is a product of internal dynamics. I locate violence in Honduras within a complex interplay between foreign capital, the local oligarchy, the Honduran military, organized criminal networks, and the Honduran social movement that has, since the early 2000s, been organized in opposition to the overwhelming power marshalled by the above-mentioned elite networks. What emerges from a careful analysis of contemporary Honduras is a complex terrain of violence, wherein, at its heart, conflict follows capital. Whether in mining, manufacturing, energy, or entertainment, the extraction of wealth from Honduras—and Hondurans—is a violent process, and one that generates resistance and repression.

As the editors note in their Introduction to this volume, what is analytically paramount in understanding the current cycle of capital expansion in this region is not necessarily tracing *which* actors carry out violence as much as *why* they do so. As Granovsky-Larsen and Paley put it in the Introduction to this volume, "Be it a member of the military, police, paramilitaries, private security, or a death squad that pulls the trigger, capitalist expansion across many countries carries with it a necessity to eliminate opposition in order to operate and secure resources." Indeed, Honduras may be an emblematic case, insofar as the array of armed actors is vast, their specific interests are varied, and their direct relationship to state power is not always clear. At the same time, it remains the case that—as per Granovsky-Larsen and Paley—the needs of private economic actors are a critically important connection point between much of the seemingly disconnected outbursts of violence (see Introduction). This chapter will sketch some of the fault lines of this conflict, offering a brief summary of the networks and patterns of violence that have taken root in Honduras since the 2009 coup, demonstrating that Honduras is, indeed, the most dangerous country in the world for those who interfere with the interests of capital.

NEOLIBERALISM AND THE 2009 COUP

Colonialism has cast its shadow over Honduras—in several very different forms—for over five hundred years (Booth, Wade, and Walker 2010; MacLeod 2008; Torres-Rivas 1993). But the particular characteristics of the current crisis in Honduras have their roots in two events: the initial establishment of neoliberalism in the 1990s, and the reassertion of oligarchic control in the 2009 coup d'état. Honduran workers and campesinos (small farmers or peasants) had built well-organized networks to protect their interests between the 1950s and 1970s, following a major national strike in 1954 (North and CAPA 1990). But much of this social infrastructure was destroyed during the virtual occupation of the country by the US in the 1980s, during which time hundreds of activists were assassinated and their organizations liquidated. The US military used Honduras as a base for its wars against Nicaragua, El Salvador, and Guatemala, and spent $1.6 billion between 1980 and 1992, beefing up the Honduran military for regional counter-revolutionary activity, which included violent crackdowns on peasant organizations, trade unions, and the growing anti-war movement. The United States built bases, airstrips, and training centres in Honduras, stationed tens of thousands of US troops there, and trained at least twenty thousand Contra fighters for operations in Nicaragua (Lapper 1985). Meanwhile, the Honduran military doubled in size, and civilian branches of governance—like immigration, customs, and telecommunications—were increasingly militarized, while new installations and facilities were built across the country and counter-insurgency units, like the notorious death squad Battalion 3-16, were established (de Ochoa 1987).

As such, when neoliberalism was imposed in the 1990s, the capacity to push back was diminished (Robinson 2003). The Honduran state capitulated to the dictates of the Washington Consensus, and foreign capital was enticed into the country by the dismantling of social, environmental, and labour laws that would have constrained corporate profits (Barahona 2005). Neoliberalism hit average Hondurans hard, plunging many into intense poverty, exacerbated by the devastating effects of Hurricane Mitch in 1998 (Pine 2008). Regional networks of resistance, however, began to rebuild in the late 1990s and, by the mid-2000s, had formed a national social movement capable of applying serious pressure on the state. This was reflected during the presidency of Manuel Zelaya, a traditional politician from the Honduran oligarchy who recognized the growing strength of the well-organized social movement and found it necessary to draw closer to that movement in the hopes that it would bolster his own political position (Tomás Andino, interview, May 9, 2012). As such, Zelaya's presidency was increasingly marked by a willingness to work with social movements on projects of progressive social reform, ranging from raising the minimum wage to halting mining concessions to lowering energy costs by joining the Alianza Bolivariana para los Pueblos de Nuestra América (Bolivarian Alliance of the Peoples of Our America). This culminated in an effort to reopen the Honduran Constitution to a popular assembly, with the goal of refounding the country along more just and equitable lines. The growing momentum—and concrete victories—of the social movement threatened to disrupt the process of the accumulation of wealth for the Honduran oligarchy and its transnational partners and isolated Zelaya from the most powerful sections of Honduran society (Mejía, Fernández, and Menjívar 2009).

Zelaya was overthrown in a military coup in June 2009, ushering in an era of far-right military domination of the country, intensive repression of social movements, and a vigorous new effort to facilitate the plunder of Honduran wealth and resources by foreign capital. The coup was denounced across the western hemisphere but given tacit support from Ottawa and Washington; US Secretary of State Hillary Clinton bragged in her memoirs about the skilful way she "rendered the question of Zelaya moot" (Lakhani 2016b), and the Canadian government worked harder than any to legitimate the coup government and blame Zelaya for the crisis (Shipley 2013; Gordon and Webber 2013). The coup was consolidated through fraudulent elections in 2009, 2013, and 2017 (Mackey 2017;

Weisbrot 2013), and the present government of Juan Orlando Hernández has further dismantled the vestiges of the Honduran welfare state while establishing a new military-police unit and changing the Constitution to allow himself to run for re-election, an ambition falsely attributed to Manuel Zelaya to justify his overthrow in 2009 (Wilkinson 2015).

The coup and subsequent reassertion of oligarchic power threw Honduras into social catastrophe as poverty and violence intensified, especially around sites of capital accumulation. Violence was brought to bear against outspoken members of the social movement, critical journalists, student activists, human rights advocates, and other opponents of the coup; at least forty people (but probably many more) were killed in the six months that followed Zelaya's removal, and untold hundreds were beaten, detained, kidnapped, "disappeared," or tortured (Berta Oliva, interview, November 26, 2009). As time passed, it became clear the people who formed the resistance—and were subsequently targeted for violence—were most often those already located within spaces of social conflict in Honduras. Campesinos struggling to protect their land from encroaching agribusiness development; Indigenous and Garífuna communities battling against foreign-owned megaprojects like mines and hydroelectric dams; workers in sweatshop-style *maquiladoras*; teachers demanding better funding for schools from a government giving tax breaks to foreign companies; taxi drivers forced to pay off criminal gangs running protection rackets with tacit state support; neighbourhoods banding together to resist attempts to privatize social provisions like pools and parks—these and other groups of Hondurans, like queer and trans people, who were already on the front lines of the struggle against neoliberalism, were the most likely targets of the new wave of violence (Frank 2012; Shipley 2016).

Since 2009, the country has been ruled by a faction of the oligarchy that is deeply intertwined with the interests of transnational capital, in both its legal and illegal forms. The Honduran state, courts, and armed forces have been described as "completely infiltrated" by organized crime, a fact that is widely known if only carefully spoken (Meza 2014, 132). This collusion is manifest in the paradoxical combination of, on the one hand, sporadic high-profile arrests of politicians connected to organized crime—like Arnaldo Urbina Soto, a politician arrested after he presumably ran afoul of the criminal gangs with which he was associated—and, on the other hand, the systematic removal of police who try to combat this corruption more broadly—the most notable case being that of the former director of the National Police, Ramón Antonio Sabillón Pineda, dismissed in 2014 (Maria Luisa Borjas, interview, February 19, 2015). Though the coalition of these forces is by no means stable or permanent, they are united by their interest in creating a Honduras that is amenable to the generation of profits, whether in the mining of gold, the production of T-shirts, or the transportation of narcotics. Here it must be added that the United States, under the auspices of the so-called war on drugs, has further contributed to the militarization of Honduras, having expanded its presence in those parts of the country associated with drug trafficking. The United States now has access to at least thirteen bases, from which US troops and Drug Enforcement Administration (DEA) agents carry out strategic assaults on suspected narcotics traffickers, a practice that has often brought violence to poor communities engaged in social struggle (Alvarado 2015).

This ruling coalition has at its disposal a complete arsenal of armed forces with which to bring violence to its opponents, from the official organs of the police and military to the shadowy networks of paramilitaries and private security companies. The rest of this chapter will take up specific case studies in organized violence in Honduras, highlighting the ways that individual incidents of violence are embedded within the broader coercive and conflictual relationships between capital and communities. Nevertheless, the emphasis on particular cases should be understood as examples to illustrate a much broader dynamic. Important cases not addressed in detail here include the deadly conflict between palm oil plantation owners and campesinos in the Aguán Valley (Edelman and León 2013); recent conflicts around "model cities" on the Gulf of Fonseca coast (Mackey 2014); violence and intimidation of garment industry workers in the *maquiladora* sector (Brown 2015); the encroachment of foreign and national military forces into La Moskitia in escalation of the wars over drug profits (McCain 2012); the murder of Indigenous Tolupan activists defending their land from mining companies (Global Witness 2015); or the conflict at the site of a mine owned by the Canadian company Aura Minerals, which has upset a local community in Copán by expanding its operations into a community cemetery without permission (Rights Action 2016). These and many other cases suggest a mapping of violence in Honduras that connects violence to the expansion of capital. Below, I will offer greater detail on a few cases.

THE DAMMING OF THE GUALCARQUE

The biggest news story to come out of Honduras in 2016 was the assassination of Berta Cáceres, a world-renowned Indigenous environmental activist who had been a central figure of both the national resistance movement and her local struggle against a hydroelectric dam project. Cáceres was a co-director of the Consejo Cívico de Organizaciones Populares e Indígenas de Honduras (Civic Council of Popular and Indigenous Organizations of Honduras—COPINH) and received the Goldman Environmental Award the year before. She was the subject of harassment and death threats; she received as many as thirty-three threats in the years leading up to her murder, from sources including Blue Energy, owned in part by the Canadian firm Hydrosys. Still, she seemed too prominent a figure to actually be targeted for assassination ("Berta Caceres Received Death Threats" 2016). Her death sent the terrifying message that no one in the Honduran social movement was safe should they oppose the will of the oligarchy and its foreign investors. In the context of much international attention and massive protests in Honduras, the Honduran police arrested four men for the assassination; two of them were explicitly linked to the Honduran company trying to build the dam, Desarrollo Energético S.A. (DESA), one a company engineer and the other private security. The other two men were former and active members of the Honduran military, and a former member of the Honduran military police has claimed that his unit was trained by the US military and received a "hit list" of activists to be killed, which included Cáceres (Lakhani 2016a). Her assassination was quickly followed by the murder of another COPINH leader, Nelson García, and, his case having drawn far less international attention, authorities claimed the murder had no connection to his political work.

Cáceres and García were among the leaders of a struggle at Rio Blanco, a Lenca Indigenous community in the southern department of Intíbuca near the Gualcarque River. That river became the source of much conflict after DESA declared its intention to build a series of hydroelectric dams called Agua Zarca, which would significantly disrupt the river and the communities that depend on it. DESA claimed the dam was a development tool that would provide energy for rural households. This played well to its investors, especially the Inter-American Development Bank and the state-funded investment agencies of Finland and the

Netherlands, among other foreigners who provided more than half of the financing for the project (Bosshard 2016). Nevertheless, the claim that Agua Zarca would power Honduran households was quite misleading: DESA's primary customer would not have been the Honduran state, which was gutting social provisions, privatizing public institutions, and pouring what was left of its resources into the military and police. Rather, the project was designed to support private—mostly foreign— extractive industry investors, who needed energy for mining operations in the region. Indeed, a quick look at a map of the region shows several mining concessions in the immediate vicinity.

The Gualcarque River in Rio Blanco falls on territory guaranteed to the Lenca under agreements dating back to 1911. This communally held territory is both a sacred cultural space and a crucial component of the survival of Lenca communities in Intíbuca. It is the primary source of water for drinking, fishing, washing, cooking, cleaning, and irrigating land, and it is carefully protected by the community, which has "lived on this land for generations and wisely [stewarded] it" (Gynther 2013). The Agua Zarca project would cause irreparable harm to the river and the communities that depend upon it, blocking the flow of accessible water for local use and disrupting the flow of fish, while the flooding of huge tracts of farmland would not only destroy arable agricultural land, it would also wreak havoc with pristine forested areas, produce greenhouse gases, and contaminate the surviving land and water (Nichols 2013).

As the Lenca organized to protect their territory from the proposed dam, their actions were increasingly met with violence. The last time I spoke to Berta Cáceres, about a year before she was killed, she explained to me that the police were focusing on community leaders and targeting them with trumped-up charges, subjecting them to violent arrests and dragging them through the courts in order to drain their energy and resources. Widely respected leaders like Tomás Membreño, Aureliano Molina, and Berta herself were all among those targeted; in Berta's case, police planted weapons in her vehicle in order to charge her with a variety of crimes (Berta Cáceres, interview, February 18, 2015). The goal was to tie up community leaders in the judicial system and disrupt the process of resistance, but it was also a warning to cease their activities. In fact, two of these three activist leaders have since been killed; only Molina is still alive (Charles 2014a).

Still, the community maintained a well-organized network of resistance to DESA's project. When the company went to Rio Blanco to try to buy the land, it was very explicitly rejected. The company then turned to the local mayor, Martiniano Dominguez, who in 2011 began surreptitiously transferring legal title of the land to the wealthy, non-Lenca, Pineda Madrid family, who were using violence and intimidation to take control of the land. The family's hired thugs—presumed to be ex-police and military and/or connected to organized crime—harassed Lenca community leaders and would release their cattle onto locals' agricultural land right around harvest time to destroy an entire season's worth of food crops on communal Lenca lands. For each bit of land the operatives of the Pineda Madrid family seized, the mayor would grant the family legal title, which allowed them, in turn, to sell the land to DESA (Bird 2013). As such, the Pineda Madrid family essentially did "dirty work" for DESA, which could later claim to know nothing about the violence and intimidation that occurred before its arrival in the territory. The foreign-owned mining companies that would purchase energy from DESA would appear even further removed from the coercive and violent tactics necessary to construct Agua Zarca, assuming it goes ahead, even though it is clear the violence in Rio Blanco is directly connected to the interests of capital in the region (Pedro Landa, interview, May 4, 2012).

Indeed, in April 2013, DESA attempted to proceed with construction, but the community organized physical blockades of the road to the river using "their bodies, a stick-and-wire fence, and a trench" (Bell 2014). After several attempts by the company to evict the protesters, the Honduran National Police set up a permanent encampment near the company office. After that time, direct violence against the community significantly increased. At a July 15, 2013, gathering of over two hundred community members to dialogue with the company, Honduran military Sergeant Jasser Sarabia shot community leader Tomas García three times at point-blank range in front of the crowd. Tomas's seventeen-year-old son, Alan García, was also shot, though he survived (Global Initiative for Economic, Social, and Cultural Rights 2014, 3). The sergeant was charged with murder in self-defence, but witnesses to the killing were, themselves, systematically targeted for violence to prevent them from testifying. It is clear, then, that the company has the full violent apparatus of the state behind it, if it needs to draw from that resource. In April 2014, Tomas García's sister, María Santos Dominguez, was attacked, with her family, by men with machetes who were recognized to be connected to the Honduran police, leaving three people hospitalized and María's twelve-year-old son with a fractured cranium (Gynther 2014).

Indeed, even after international attention was drawn to this case by the murder of Berta Cáceres, the violence has continued: as recently as July 2016, another COPINH leader, Lesbia Janeth Urquía, was murdered in a machete attack. Honduran police claimed it was a domestic familial dispute (Carasik 2016). However, it is clear that much of the violence taking place in this region is connected to the conflict between the hydroelectric companies and the affected communities, and attempts to obscure this fact serve the interests of those whose profits are dependent on this violence. As Greg Grandin poignantly noted in the immediate aftermath of her assassination, "The names of Berta Cáceres's murderers are still unknown. But we know who killed her" (Grandin 2016).

THE BANANA COAST

Though Honduras's north coast was the heart of the banana industry, the plantations themselves were built on swampy inland territory and, as a result, displaced far fewer communities than one might have expected. Today, however, this region has become one of the major sites of conflict in the country, both in the fertile inland Aguán Valley and along the many connected north coast villages of the Afro-Indigenous Garífuna people. The ancestors of the Garífuna arrived in the Caribbean on a slave ship that wrecked near St. Vincent and were later displaced to the northern coast of Central America. UNESCO has declared the communal Garífuna culture one of nineteen "Masterpieces of the Oral and Intangible Heritage of Humanity." The survival of the Garífuna people and culture is being directly threatened by the seizure of the territory and resources upon which that cultural life depends. The once peaceful region has been beset by violence since the early 1990s, as the tourist industry moved in and attempted to seize Garífuna land for resorts, cruise ports, and retirement homes. Garífuna communities have been displaced, sacred spaces have been razed and converted into shopping centres and other tourist-oriented developments, and fishing, shipping, agriculture, and transportation corridors have all been disrupted by the development of new ports, roads, bridges, and complexes. In sum, the invasion of foreign "development" has made the concrete practices of maintaining Garífuna life increasingly difficult (Rodriguez 2008).

This escalating problem reached a crisis since 2014, when the Honduran state began parcelling off pieces of Garífuna territory as "model cities," or Zonas de Empleo y Desarrollo Económico (Zones of Employment and Economic Development—ZEDE), wherein foreign corporations can essentially govern their concessions as independent fiefdoms (Carasik 2015). Their only oversight is a panel of twenty-one individuals, mostly made up of foreign far-right ideologues, including the son of former US President Ronald Reagan and an Austrian general secretary of the Friedrich Hayek Institute (Mackey 2014). Since the ZEDE projects began—there are now five concessions on Garífuna land—community resistance has become ever more defiant, at the same time as many Garífuna, especially young people, have abandoned their homes to undertake the dangerous journey to the United States to find work (Garsd 2014). Violence has become an ever more typical consequence of this crisis; in Nueva Armenia, for instance, community resistance to the ZEDE elicited mass arrests and detentions of community members and the burning to the ground by armed men of the entire village ("UN to Set Up Human Rights Office" 2015). Around the same time, in 2014, a community of nearly five hundred people in Barra Vieja was subjected to an attempted violent eviction by military and police. No one was killed and the community was firm in its refusal to leave, but many homes and buildings were destroyed, and the threat of future violence was made explicit ("Garifuna Take On Mega-Tourism" 2014).

Perhaps the most emblematic case on the north coast is the community of Triunfo de la Cruz, which has been struggling against new encroachments on its territory since 1993, especially since the mid-2000s. After the municipal government of nearby Tela rezoned the land to complicate the picture of land titling, parcels of Garífuna territory were sold to a Honduran company called Inversiones y Desarrollo El Triunfo S.A. (IDETRISA), which set off a long battle between the community and the company over its plan to develop a tourist resort called "Club Marbella." That conflict got bloody as early as 1997, when company thugs killed three community leaders (Kersson 2013, 76). Though IDETRISA is a Honduran company, the majority of the tourist industry is foreign-owned, particularly by Canadian firms, which make up the dominant proportion of north coast tourist investment and call the area "Little Canada" (Cuffe 2014). Smaller Honduran companies will often do the initial heavy lifting to establish the project, with an understanding that it will be sold to larger transnational firms once the project is close to completion. This has been the case for many of the tourist developments in the north coast and Roatán Island, the majority of which are owned by North American capital (Spring 2011). The most noteworthy example here is the "Banana Coast" development, which welcomed its first cruise ship to the port of Trujillo in 2014; the land was originally procured on behalf of Canadian tycoon Randy Jorgensen by a *testaferro*—a Honduran buyer who acts as a front for foreign capital—named Joel Ortiz (Guillen Mejía 2014). For his part, Jorgensen dismisses Garífuna land claims as "extortion," despite his having purchased their land after it was sold illegally (Paley 2010).

It is hardly surprising that the Garífuna are resisting this form of "development." But resistance in Honduras has become a dangerous business. Companies like IDETRISA, or Jorgensen's Life Vision Properties, can avail themselves not just of direct police and military support but can easily find local agents—former police or military, sometimes connected to organized crime, and always with violent reputations—to intimidate activists. This was precisely the strategy employed in Triunfo de la Cruz, where local thugs created a parallel community leadership whose interests conveniently coincided perfectly with tourism entrepreneurs; Garífuna communities are led by the elected *patronato* traditional leadership, but this second *patronato* tried to assert itself to Honduran authorities as the real leadership in order to sell the land in question. This alternate group was comprised of well-known locals and used violence and intimidation to try to cement its position ("Crean patronato" 2010). Having accepted the legitimacy of the fake *patronato*, Honduran authorities facilitated the transfer of land to the company, but the local activist network Organización Fraternal Negra Hondureña (Fraternal Organization of Black Hondurans—OFRANEH) intervened and took direct action against the company, dismantling the walls it had begun building while denouncing the fake *patronato*, describing "the illegal sale of land...authorised by the parallel council created within the community by the municipality—a council currently led by the intimidating brothers, Martínez y Braulio Martínez" (Triunfo de la Cruz Garífuna 2011).

The violence of contemporary Honduras, then, has been brought to Garífuna territory as a by-product of the growth of profitable industries for foreign capital there. Threats and intimidation—violent in themselves—are always backed by the possibility of more serious attacks. OFRANEH leaders are constantly threatened and some, like Gregoria Flores Martínez and Jesús Alvarez, have been killed (Rights Action 2005). Nonlethal attacks are commonplace: in 2015, six children were hospitalized after security forces used "indiscriminate violence" against members of the community of Puerto Castillo (Charles 2014b). Arson and other destruction of homes, offices, radio stations, and other significant community buildings are reported regularly. In some cases, entire villages have faced eviction and demolition, and this tactic has also been prominent in the Aguán Valley, south of Garífuna territory but mired in very similar—and even deadlier—struggles. The campesinos of the Aguán have been struggling for decades over their access to land, and they have been met with violence from large landowners, most notably the estate of the late Miguel Facussé. Hundreds of campesinos connected with the Movimiento Unificado Campesino del Aguán (Unified Campesino Movement of the Aguán) have been assassinated in the past decade, and especially since the coup of 2009, and entire villages—like Rigores in 2011—have been razed to the ground (Joni Rivas, interview, May 3, 2012).

CONDEMNED TO DEATH

I conclude by briefly addressing one of the most notorious extractive industry disasters in Honduras, the now closed (but rumoured to be re-opening) San Martín mine, owned by Canadian gold mining giant Goldcorp. Medical brigades in the region around the mine consistently demonstrated that the mine was creating a health catastrophe. When the mine opened in 2000, 8 percent of people living in the region suffered from skin diseases; by 2010, the rate was 80 percent (Juan Almendares, interview, May 4, 2012). Local environmental activist Carlos Amador described the Siria Valley, where the mine is located, as having been "condemned to death." He testified at Goldcorp shareholder meetings in Canada, describing health disasters that had resulted from lead and arsenic poisoning: skin disease, diseased hair follicles such that women in their thirties were losing their hair, high levels of lead in people's blood, even a case where a woman lost twin babies as a result of arsenic poisoning (Carlos Amador, interview, May 8, 2012).

In 2007, responding to pressure from social movements, the Honduran public health ministry took a series of blood samples from sixty people in the Siria Valley and discovered their blood was laced with dangerously high levels of arsenic, lead, mercury, cadmium, magnesium, chromium, and nickel. The results of the study, however, were not released until 2011, at which point two executives from Goldcorp were taken to the Honduran courts. The judge ruled in favour of the company, despite the fact that one of the people tested in 2007—five-year-old Lesly Yaritza—died in 2010 after suffering from a degenerative muscle condition in her legs that left her barely able to walk at the time of her death (Carasik and Russell 2011).

The violence Goldcorp inflicted through the process of heap leaching, using cyanide and poisoning the earth and water in the Siria Valley, was matched by a willingness to employ direct physical violence against the well-organized community movement against the mine. As elsewhere, Goldcorp's opponents were often subject to criminalization, and many activists faced arrests and detention for their involvement in peaceful blockades of mining operations. Many others faced death threats and intimidation: Carlos Amador was regularly followed by men on motorcycles when he travelled to Tegucigalpa. At home in the Siria Valley, where he is a teacher and radio broadcaster, he often noticed two grey vehicles with tinted windows parked outside the radio station while he was there; an unmistakable threat in Honduras. On one occasion, fifteen armed police officers approached his school with guns raised in attack position; when they did not find him, they proceeded to his house to interrogate his two daughters (Spring 2010). These threats of violence came just days after private security guards killed one and injured two members of the same community that was blockading a logging operation on lands claimed by the community of El Porvenir (Carlos Amador, interview, May 8, 2012).

While most of the casualties of the San Martín mine are related to contamination rather than bullets, the ever-present reality for people living in the Siria Valley is that opposition to the poisonous mining projects brings the possibility of extreme violence, as it does in the Aguán, in Garífuna territory, in Rio Blanco, or anywhere else where profits are being extracted from Honduras. For them, Honduras is indeed the most dangerous country in the world. This same can be said for lawyers trying to advocate on behalf of these communities, journalists trying to tell their stories, or trade unionists trying to help people protect themselves; all three vocations carry alarming rates of assassination (Gies 2016).

With such a vast array of armed forces in Honduras—almost all connected to circuits of capital that intensely exploit people and resources—it should be no surprise that violence has become part of daily life. From official Honduran state forces—the military, the police, and the military police—to the networks of private security companies employed by businesses and large landowners, to the paramilitary organizations that represent the criminal gangs, to the foreign forces like the US DEA and the US Army operating in Honduras, the country is increasingly ruled by violence on behalf of overlapping—though sometimes conflicting—networks of capital.

None of the above analysis should imply that all violence in Honduras is explicitly political and directly connected to the profits of one company or another. The extreme poverty created by neoliberalism in Honduras reinforces existing patterns of petty crime, street gang violence, and domestic violence, to name a few, which are only indirectly linked to the expansion of foreign capital in Honduras. Furthermore, there are forms of daily violence—extortion of taxi drivers by localized criminal gangs, for instance—which are not always or necessarily directly linked to any particular member of the Honduran oligarchy or a foreign corporation. In cases like these, it is more fruitful to think of the violence as part of a cascading set of consequences of the use of the Honduran state as a protection racket for capital; while the state may not sanction or carry out this violence, its inability and unwillingness to govern on behalf of the greater social good opens up space for such forms of violence. Nevertheless, it is abundantly clear that much of the violence that plagues contemporary Honduras is, in fact, directly related to the mounting confrontations between capital and communities, and that any starting point in trying to address this crisis would have to begin by addressing both the overwhelming power and impunity with which foreign capital operates, and the network of official and unofficial support it receives from the coup government in Honduras.

REFERENCES

Alvarado, Fred. 2015. "El proceso de remilitarización estadounidense y el fracaso de la guerra contra las drogas." *El Debate*, June 11. http://www.revistadebate.net/el-proceso-de-remilitarizacion-estadounidense-y-el-fracaso-de-la-guerra-contra-las-drogas/.

Barahona, Marvin. 2005. *Honduras en el siglo xx*. Tegucigalpa, Honduras: Editorial Guaymuras.

Bell, Beverly. 2014. "One Year of Resistance in Rio Blanco." *Foreign Policy in Focus*, April 1. https://fpif.org/one-year-resistance-rio-blanco/.

"Berta Caceres Received Death Threats from Canadian Company." 2016. *Telesur*, March 4. https://www.telesurtv.net/english/news/Berta-Caceres-Received-Death-Threats-from-Canadian-Company-20160304-0027.html.

Bird, Annie. 2013. "The Agua Zarca Dam and Lenca Communities in Honduras." *Rights Action Report*, October 3. http://rightsaction.org/sites/default/files//Rpt_131001_RioBlanco_Final.pdf.

Booth, John A., Christine A. Wade, and Thomas W. Walker. 2010. *Understanding Central America: Global Forces, Rebellion, and Change*. Fifth edition. Boulder, CO: Westview Press.

Bosshard, Peter. 2016. "European Funders Suspend Support for Agua Zarca Dam." *Huffington Post*, March 16. https://www.huffingtonpost.com/peter-bosshard/european-funder-suspend-s_b_9479642.html.

Brown, Kimberley. 2015. "Women's Rights and Textile Factories in Central America." *Telesur*, March 7. https://www.telesurtv.net/english/analysis/Womens-Rights-and-Textile-Factories-in-Central-America-20150307-0017.html.

Carasik, Lauren. 2015. "There Are No Peasants Here." *Foreign Policy*, October 23. https://foreignpolicy.com/2015/10/23/there-are-no-peasants-here-honduras-zedes-land-grabs/.

———. 2016. "Blood in Honduras, Silence in the United States." *Boston Review*, August 16. http://bostonreview.net/editors-picks-world-us/lauren-carasik-blood-honduras-silence-united-states.

Carasik, Lauren, and Grahame Russell. 2011. "Goldcorp and the Death of Lesly Yaritza." Faculty publications, Western New England University School of Law, December 24.

Charles, Jeanette. 2014a. "The Human Rights Crisis in Honduras." *Telesur*, November 6. http://rac-wp02.telesurtv.net/english/telesuragenda/teleSUR-Investigation-The-Human-Rights-Crisis-in-Honduras-20141023-0023.html.

———. 2014b. "Violence in Honduras since the 2009 Coup." *Telesur*, July 17. https://www.telesurenglish.net/analysis/Violence-in-Honduras-Since-the-2009-Coup-20140717-0132.html.

"Crean patronato paralelo para seguir vendiendo tierras comunitarias garífunas." 2010. *Red Morazánica de Información*, January 17. https://redsolhonduras.blogspot.com/2011/01/informaciones-honduras-nr-649-19-enero.html.

Cuffe, Sandra. 2014. "'Little Canada' Displacing Afro-Indigenous Communities in Honduras." *Ricochet*, December 5. https://ricochet.media/en/243/little-canada-displacing-afro-indigenous-communities-in-honduras.

Edelman, Marc, and Andrés León. 2013. "Cycles of Land Grabbing in Central America: An Argument for History and a Case Study in the Bajo Aguán, Honduras." *Third World Quarterly* 34 (9): 1697–1722.

Frank, Dana. 2012. "Honduras Gone Wrong." *Foreign Affairs*, October 16. https://www.foreignaffairs.com/articles/americas/2012-10-16/honduras-gone-wrong.

Gagne, David. 2014. "Is Honduras Faking Its Falling Homicide Rates?" *Insight Crime*, August 13. https://www.insightcrime.org/news/brief/honduras-faking-falling-homicide-rates/.

"Garifuna Take On Mega-Tourism, Displacement and Organized Crime in Honduras." 2014. *Telesur*, November 6. https://www.telesurtv.net/english/analysis/teleSUR-Investigation-Garifuna-Take-on-Mega-Tourism-Displacement-and-Organized-Crime-in-Honduras-20141023-0025.html.

Garsd, Jasmine. 2014. "Garifuna: The Young Black Latino Exodus You've Never Heard About." *Splinter News*, April 6. https://splinternews.com/garifuna-the-young-black-latino-exodus-you-ve-never-he-1793841871.

Gies, Heather. 2016. "Honduran Democracy Still in Crisis 7 Years after Coup." *Telesur*, June 28. https://www.telesurtv.net/english/analysis/Honduran-Democracy-Still-in-Crisis-7-Years-After-Coup-20150520-0052.html.

Global Initiative for Economic, Social, and Cultural Rights. 2014. *Joint Parallel Report to the Committee of Economic, Social, and Cultural Rights*. February 13.

Global Witness. 2015. "Honduran Hitmen Kill Fifth Indigenous Land Activist amid Protests against Mining and Illegal Logging." Press Release, June 23. https://www.globalwitness.org/fr/press-releases/honduran-hitmen-kill-fifth-indigenous-land-activist-amid-protests-against-mining-and-illegal-logging/.

Gordon, Todd, and Jeffery Webber. 2013. "Post-Coup Honduras: Latin America's Corridor of Reaction." *Historical Materialism* 21 (3): 16–56.

Grandin, Greg. 2016. "The Clinton-Backed Honduran Regime Is Picking Off Indigenous Leaders." *The Nation*, March 3. https://www.thenation.com/article/the-clinton-backed-honduran-regime-is-picking-off-indigenous-leaders/.

Guillen Mejía, Celso. 2014. "Consultoría investigativa sobre situación actual de tierra y territorio Colon uno." Organización Fraternal Negra de Honduras, February 27. https://www.scribd.com/document/213550621/Investigacion-tierra-celso-guillen-pdf.

Gynther, Brigitte. 2013. "Defending Rio Blanco: Three Weeks of the Lenca Community Roadblock." *Upside Down World*, April 23. http://upsidedownworld.org/news-briefs/news-briefs-news-briefs/defending-rio-blanco-three-weeks-of-the-lenca-community-roadblock-in-honduras/.

———. 2014. "Who Should Really Be On Trial for the Rio Blanco Dam?" *Upside Down World*, March 19. http://upsidedownworld.org/archives/honduras/honduras-who-should-really-be-on-trial-for-the-rio-blanco-dam/.

Kerssen, Tanya. 2013. *Grabbing Power: The New Struggles for Land, Food and Democracy in Northern Honduras*. Oakland, CA: Food First Books.

Lakhani, Nina. 2016a. "Berta Cáceres's Name Was on Honduran Military Hitlist, Says Former Soldier." *The Guardian*, June 21. https://www.theguardian.com/world/2016/jun/21/berta-caceres-name-honduran-military-hitlist-former-soldier.

———. 2016b. "Did Hillary Clinton Stand By While Honduras Coup Ushered in Era of Violence?" *The Guardian*, August 31. https://www.theguardian.com/world/2016/aug/31/hillary-clinton-honduras-violence-manuel-zelaya-berta-caceres.

Lapper, Richard. 1985. *Honduras: State for Sale*. London: Latin America Bureau.

Mackey, Danielle Marie. 2014. "I've Seen All Sorts of Horrific Things in My Time. But None as Detrimental to the Country as This." *New Republic*, December 14. https://newrepublic.com/article/120559/ive-seen-sorts-horrific-things-time-none-detrimental-country-this.

———. 2017. "The Election Fraud in Honduras Follows Decades of Corruption Funded by the U.S. War on Drugs." *The Intercept*, December 23. https://theintercept.com/2017/12/23/honduras-election-fraud-drugs-jose-orlando-hernandez/.

MacLeod, Murdo J. 2008. *Spanish Central America: A Socioeconomic History, 1520–1720*. Austin: University of Texas Press.

McCain, Greg. 2012. "The DEA and the Return of Death Squads." *Counter Punch*, June 15. https://www.counterpunch.org/2012/06/15/the-dea-and-the-return-of-the-death-squads/.

Mejía, Joaquín A., Victor Fernández, and Omar Menjívar. 2009. *Aspectos históricos, conceptuales y sustanciales sobre el proceso contituyente en Honduras*. Tegucigalpa, Honduras: Movimiento Amplio por la Dignidad y la Justicia.

Meza, Victor, ed. 2014. *El manejo politico de la inseguridad publica*. Tegucigalpa, Honduras: Centro de Documentación de Honduras..

Nichols, Joshua. 2013. "Rio Blanco Communities Take Action to Defend Rivers, Territory, and Life." *Intercontinental Cry*, April 9. https://intercontinentalcry.org/indigenous-peoples-begin-anti-hydro-dam-action-in-honduras/.

North, Liisa, and CAPA (Canadian-Caribbean-Central American Policy Alternatives). 1990. *Between War and Peace in Central America*. Toronto: Between the Lines.

de Ochoa, Margarita Oseguera. 1987. *Honduras hoy: Sociedad y crisis política*. Tegucigalpa, Honduras: Centro de Documentación de Honduras.

Paley, Dawn. 2010. "Snowbirds Gone Wild! Canadian Retirees and Locals Clash in Honduras." *This Magazine*, November 4. https://this.org/2010/11/04/canada-snowbirds-honduras/.

Pine, Adrienne. 2008. *Working Hard, Drinking Hard: On Violence and Survival in Honduras*. Berkeley: University of California Press.

Robinson, William I. 2003. *Transnational Conflicts: Central America, Social Change and Globalization*. London: Verso.

Rodriguez, James. 2008. "Garífuna Resistance to Mega-Tourism in Tela Bay." *Upside Down World*, August 6. http://upsidedownworld.org/archives/honduras/honduras-garifuna-resistance-to-mega-tourism-in-tela-bay/.

Rights Action. 2005. "The Tourist Industry and Repression in Honduras." *Upside Down World*, October 16. http://upsidedownworld.org/archives/honduras/the-tourist-industry-and-repression-in-honduras-83105/.

———. 2016. "Aura Minerals Preparing to Illegally Remove Cemetery in Honduras, with Military Support." February 12. https://miningwatch.ca. nmsrv.com/blog/2016/2/12/community-fears-toronto-based-aura-minerals-preparing-illegally-remove-cemetery.

Shipley, Tyler. 2013. "The New Canadian Imperialism and the Military Coup in Honduras." *Latin American Perspectives* 40 (5): 44–61.

———. 2016. "Genealogy of a Social Movement: The Resistencia in Honduras." *Canadian Journal of Latin American and Caribbean Studies* 41 (3): 348–65.

Spring, Karen. 2010. "Threats against Carlos Amador, Member of the Siria Valley Environmental Committee, Which Has Opposed Goldcorp Gold Mining in Honduras since 2000." *Aqui Abajo*, April 29. http://www. aquiabajo.com/blog/2015/11/20/threats-against-carlos-amador-member-of-the-siria-valley-environmental-committee-which-has-opposed-goldcorp-gold-mining-in-honduras-since-2000.

———. 2011. "Canadian Porn Kings, Tourism 'Development' Projects, Repression and the Violation of Indigenous-Garifuna Rights in Honduras." *Aqui Abajo*, February 14. http://www.aquiabajo.com/blog/2015/11/20/canadian-porn-kings-tourism-development-projects-repression-the-violations-of-indigenous-garifuna-rights-in-honduras.

Torres-Rivas, Edelberto. 1993. *History and Society in Central America*. Austin: University of Texas Press.

Triunfo de la Cruz Garífuna, Pro-Improvement Community Council. 2011. "Public Statement." Tela, Atlántida, Honduras, August 2.

"UN to Set Up Human Rights Office in Violence-Marred Honduras." 2015. *Telesur*, January 14. https://www.telesurtv.net/english/news/UN-to-Set-up-Human-Rights-Office-in-Violence-Marred-Honduras-20150114-0056.html.

Weisbrot, Mark. 2013. "Why the World Should Care about Honduras' Recent Election." *The Guardian*, December 3. https://www.theguardian.com/commentisfree/2013/dec/03/honduras-election-eu-oas-observer-fraud-violence.

Wilkinson, Tracy. 2015. "A Honduran Coup Comes Full Circle." *Los Angeles Times*, April 27. http://www.latimes.com/world/mexico-americas/la-fg-a-honduran-coup-20150427-story.html.

CHAPTER 3

UNDER SIEGE

PEACEFUL RESISTANCE TO TAHOE RESOURCES AND MILITARIZATION IN GUATEMALA

Luis Solano

Translated from Spanish by members of the Network in Solidarity with the People of Guatemala (NISGUA) and MiningWatch Canada[1]

Almost from the moment Canadian-US mining company Tahoe Resources acquired the Escobal silver project from Goldcorp in 2010, the company and the Guatemalan government have used repression, criminalization, and, ultimately, militarization to try to silence peaceful resistance to mining activities in the area. Instead of

---

1   This chapter is a summary of a report written by Luis Solano and published in 2015. Research for the report was commissioned by the International Platform against Impunity in Central America and MiningWatch Canada, and was carried out with assistance from NISGUA and local residents in the departments of Santa Rosa and Jalapa, Guatemala. MiningWatch originally distributed an earlier version of this summary, and the full report is available online at http://miningwatch.ca/sites/default/files/solano-underseigereport2015-11-10.pdf. It is used here with permission.

treating local residents as people peacefully defending their lands from the negative impacts of mining on their health, water, and agriculture, Tahoe Resources' militarized security strategy seemed designed to face an insurgency.

In 2011, Tahoe Resources hired a US security and defence contractor, International Security and Defense Management, LLC (ISDM), which boasts experience with corporations working in war zones such as Iraq and Afghanistan, to develop its security strategy. With ISDM's help, Tahoe Resources hired the Golan Group private security company and Alberto Rotondo, now under arrest for his role in a shooting attack on peaceful protesters in April 2013 when he was Tahoe's head of security. Tahoe Resources itself is now being sued for negligence and battery in British Columbia courts in connection with this attack (related documents and updated information can be found at tahoeontrial.net).

For over five years, agricultural communities affected by Tahoe Resources' Escobal mine, both Indigenous and non-Indigenous, have been peacefully defending their lands and livelihoods. Far from being treated with respect as defenders of the environment, community leaders and peaceful protesters have been labelled as terrorists and targeted by counter-insurgency tactics aimed at silencing and quashing their opposition to mining activities.

Throughout the southeastern departments of Jalapa and Santa Rosa, local organizers have carried out multiple *consultas*, or local plebiscites, in which roughly fifty-five thousand people in seven municipalities have voted against the silver mine and proposed expansion plans. More than two hundred complaints were also submitted in opposition to Tahoe Resources' final permit for mineral extraction. All of these were dismissed without consideration on the same day that the Guatemalan government announced approval of the final mining permit, giving rise to more protests. Despite the communities' clear message, the company and the Guatemalan government have continued to force the project on the communities, making use of both private and public security forces. This imposition culminated in May 2013, with the government decreeing a "state of siege," or a localized period of heavily militarized martial law. The state of siege was imposed in municipalities surrounding the mine, since which time the military presence has continued in the region through the installation of two new army posts and an inter-institutional pilot project developed by Guatemala's National Security Commission.

The Escobal mine case is rooted in the capital accumulation model adopted by the Guatemalan government and business elites after the signing of peace agreements in 1996. The model is based on extractive industries, agribusiness, the privatization of the electric system, the transformation of the electric grid to prioritize hydroelectric dams, and massive investment in telecommunications. The end of the armed conflict generated a wave of investment in these areas that deepened conflicts over territory and the use of natural resources. With many of these areas inhabited by Indigenous peoples, many communities have organized themselves into movements of resistance and territorial defence. The response by powerful groups and local and international investors has been to turn once again to the police and military in order to protect their interests and consolidate their extractive model. People affected by this approach have been repressed and their human rights have been violated (Solano 2009).

TAHOE RESOURCES' CONNECTION TO LOCAL, NATIONAL, AND INTERNATIONAL ELITES

Tahoe Resources built its underground silver mine on the 19.99-square kilometre Escobal mining concession, an area equivalent to about one-fifth of the territory of the municipality of San Rafael Las Flores in the department of Santa Rosa, which has a total area of eighty-five square kilometres. The Ministry of Energy and Mines granted the final permit for mineral extraction at the Escobal mine on April 3, 2013. Tahoe Resources announced that it put the mine into commercial operation in January 2014. The company estimates that mine operations will last approximately eighteen years, however, this could be extended if the project expands. The Escobal mine forms part of a much larger project that includes over twenty mining concessions that have been requested and that are in different stages of development, from exploration to extraction, located in the departments of Guatemala, Jalapa, Santa Rosa, and Jutiapa. The total area of these concessions is approximately 1,290 square kilometres.

Locally, Tahoe Resources' close connections with the Crowe family were important to initiate mineral exploration and extraction in the municipality of San Rafael Las Flores. The Crowe family have historic links to mining activities that took place in the area in the 1920s and owned lands in this area until 2013. From 2007 onward, landowner Carlos

Crowe Santis served as manager of community relations for Tahoe
Resources. Previously, he worked for Goldcorp's Guatemalan subsidiary,
Montana Exploradora, which operates the controversial Marlin mine in
the northwestern highlands.

Nationally, one key actor is Guatemalan lawyer Jorge Asencio Aguirre.
Asencio Aguirre registered Tahoe Resources' Guatemalan subsidiary,
Minera San Rafael, S.A. (MSR), in 2010 and continues to act as one of its
legal representatives. Asencio Aguirre also represents subsidiaries of
Goldcorp and Kappes, Cassiday, and Associates in Guatemala, whose
mine projects are also focal points of enduring and at times violent con-
flicts. As he once stated on the Guatemalan television program, *Libre
Encuentro*, Asencio Aguirre helped develop Guatemala's 1997 Mining Law.

Guatemala's National Director of Mining, Fernando Castellanos
Barquín, is responsible for awarding Tahoe's mineral extraction licence
in April 2013, at which time he dismissed without consideration over two
hundred complaints that local residents had filed, given worries over
potential mine impacts on water and health. Before taking up his government post in 2012, Castellanos Barquín worked for Kluane Guatemala,
S.A. This drilling company did contract work for MSR between 2007 and
2010. His controversial decision to dismiss the residents' complaints
has been subject to an ongoing series of legal appeals that residents feel
should have suspended mining operations.

Internationally, top executives of the Canadian mining companies
Glamis Gold and Goldcorp founded Tahoe Resources in 2009. Registered
in Vancouver, with offices in Vancouver and Nevada, Tahoe acquired the
Escobal project for US$505 million from Goldcorp in 2010. Goldcorp
was the top shareholder in Tahoe until June 2015, when it sold all of its
shares for approximately C$1 billion. To date, four of eight board mem-
bers have current or past experience with Goldcorp or its predecessor
Glamis Gold. Tahoe Resources CEO Kevin McArthur was once president
of Glamis Gold and of Goldcorp, and currently advises Goldcorp's CEO.

CRIMINALIZATION OF COMMUNITY LEADERS
AND MILITARIZATION OF PEACEFUL PROTEST

As soon as peaceful resistance began in late 2011, the Guatemalan government and MSR's private security forces began to criminalize, stigmatize,
and defame local Catholic priests, leaders of the Committee in Defense

of Life and Peace in San Rafael Las Flores, organized residents from the municipality of Mataquescuintla, members of the Comisión Diocesana de Defensa de la Naturaleza (Diocesan Commission for the Defense of Nature), and leaders of the Parlamento del Pueblo Xinca de Guatemala (Parliament of the Xinca People of Guatemala).

A very important characteristic in this process is that all but one of the more than one hundred cases of criminalization against local residents and community leaders have been dismissed for lack of evidence, or for including false evidence and/or statements. In the one case that went to trial, the accused community leader was eventually acquitted. In some cases, numerous charges were made against the same movement leader over a period of years and, while no one remains in prison, several people have spent days or months in preventative prison while their situation was clarified.

Despite police repression of their protests and the large number of cases of criminalization, local organizations continued to hold local plebiscites. Between 2011 and 2013, twelve municipal- and community-level *consultas* were held in San Rafael Las Flores and surrounding municipalities in which tens of thousands of people voted against Tahoe's Escobal project and any mining activities on their lands. Another two municipal consultations and one community consultation have been held since then.

The company and the Guatemalan Chamber of Commerce unsuccessfully filed several injunctions against these processes between 2011 and 2013. The consultation processes were ultimately held up by a Constitutional Court decision, which ruled them legitimate and vital to local decision making.

When the state granted Tahoe Resources its final mineral extraction permit in April 2013, protests intensified. Four community plebiscites were held in the municipality of San Rafael Las Flores that same month and almost daily demonstrations took place. Police repressed peaceful protesters on April 6, wrongfully detaining twenty-six people for four days without warrants signed by a judge. On April 27, private security guards fired on a peaceful protest in front of the mine site, injuring seven men.

On April 30, 2013, the public prosecutor captured Tahoe Resources' then security manager, Alberto Rotondo, at La Aurora International Airport and indicted him on May 7, 2013, on charges of causing grave and minor injuries and obstruction of justice. Rotondo escaped house arrest and fled to Peru in 2015. Interpol captured him in early 2016, but, as of a year later, an ongoing extradition process had still not returned Rotondo to Guatemala for trial (Lakhani 2017).

On June 18, 2014, the seven injured men sued Tahoe Resources Inc. for negligence and battery in the British Columbia Supreme Court. The company requested that the case be rejected, and BC Supreme Court Justice Laura Gerow agreed, suspending the case in November 2015 and suggesting that the claimants present their case in Guatemala. The decision was then appealed, and on January 26, 2017, the British Columbia Court of Appeal rejected Tahoe Resources' original request to suspend the case. In the judgment, the Court of Appeal overturned a lower court decision that had found Guatemala was the more appropriate venue for the case. The Court of Appeal ruled that several factors, including evidence of systemic corruption in the Guatemalan judiciary, pointed away from Guatemala as a preferable forum, thereby keeping the case in British Columbia. The court concluded, "There is some measurable risk that the appellants will encounter difficulty in receiving a fair trial against a powerful international company whose mining interests in Guatemala align with the political interests of the Guatemalan state" (CCIJ 2017).

Rotondo, however, has still not faced trial in Guatemala. Having fled in 2015 to Peru, where he was eventually arrested, Rotondo is currently awaiting a decision on extradition. Rotondo's escape from Guatemala was an important factor in the 2017 judgment from the BC Court of Appeal.

On May 2, 2013, the Guatemalan government declared a state of siege for thirty days in four municipalities around the mine site. This was downgraded to a "state of prevention" eight days later. During this time, the homes of community leaders active in the anti-mining resistance were raided and five people were jailed for months. Two military outposts have remained in the area ever since.

Key to the escalation of local conflict was a decision by the National Security Commission to categorize the Escobal mining project as a "strategic natural resource," characterizing those opposed to it as a threat to national security. This led to the establishment of a pilot project in the municipality of San Rafael Las Flores, which was called the Inter-Institutional Commission for Integrated Development. The stated purpose of this project was to "[develop] policies, strategies, projects and recommendations that would enable the Committee to holistically address security and development issues toward the betterment of the quality of life of the population and to ensure environmental protection." It was justified based on "attacks and kidnappings of members of the National Police, and robbery of explosive material and munitions belonging to the mining company and the National Police" that had taken place months prior and were blamed on members of the resistance to the mining project (Secretaría Técnica del Consejo de Seguridad Nacional 2013).

According to residents, the real aim was to silence social protest against MSR and interrupt municipal and community plebiscites underway. Local plebiscites effectively came to a halt for six months once the state of siege was declared and have only gradually resumed since late 2013.

Tahoe Resources directly assisted in establishing this office, as reported in its 2013 Annual Information Form and recorded by the National Security Commission. The inter-institutional group includes participation from the Ministry of Energy and Mines (the lead institution), the Ministry of the Environment and Natural Resources, the Ministry of the Interior, the Technical Secretary of the National Security Commission, the Secretary for Strategic State Intelligence, the National Commission for Protected Areas, and the Presidential Committee of the National Dialogue System.

The creation of this inter-institutional commission demonstrates the influence of military security and intelligence in the area.

REVELATIONS ABOUT TAHOE RESOURCES' QUASI-MILITARY SECURITY STRATEGY

Filings in the case against Tahoe Resources in British Columbia include important revelations about the company's militarized security strategy, beginning in 2011 with the hiring of a major US security contractor and Alberto Rotondo.

The sworn testimony of Donald Paul Gray, vice-president of Tahoe Resources, demonstrates links between a conglomerate of companies and individuals tied to military and intelligence services, contracts with private security companies with large military projects, and companies with mining and construction operations in Guatemala.[2]

---

2   *Garcia v Tahoe Resources Inc.*, 2015 BCSC 2045. Gray's affidavit can be found online at https://tahoeontrial.files.wordpress.com/2015/04/affadavit-donald-paul-gray-24nov14.pdf.

According to Gray, in 2011, MSR "engaged International Security and Defense Management, LLC ('ISDM')," a company founded by veterans of the US Armed Forces and based in California, "to assess its security needs and requirements during the construction phase of the Escobal project." ISDM is listed among the most important private military companies in the world, and boasts experience providing security operations for corporations working in war zones, including Iraq and Afghanistan.

Through ISDM, "MSR came to contract with [the Golan Group], formally called Alfa Uno, and retained it to develop and implement MSR's security plan." Golan Group is an Israeli private security company founded in 1983 by members of the Israeli special armed forces. Notably, between 2005 and 2009, the Golan Group provided security services to Glamis Gold and Hudbay Minerals at their Marlin and Fénix mining projects, respectively. The Golan Group has also worked for Kappes, Cassiday, and Associates at its conflict-ridden El Tambor project near Guatemala City. It had provided security services for MSR before, during, and after the incidents of April 27, 2013.

Also through ISDM, Alberto Rotondo was contracted as head of security and came to manage the contract with the Golan Group. Rotondo claims on his LinkedIn profile page that he has military training in counter-insurgency. He graduated in 1974 from the Peruvian Naval Academy and, between 1980 and 1981, received training at the United States Naval Special Warfare Command, headquartered in Coronado, California. Between 1985 and 1986, he received training in psychological operations, civil affairs, and low-intensity terrorism at the John F. Kennedy Special Warfare Center and School in Fort Bragg, North Carolina, the location of the US Army Center and School for Psychological Operations. According to community members interviewed, from 2011 until the state of siege, Rotondo designed and oversaw plans to criminalize the opposition to the mine. Rotondo worked for Tahoe Resources until shortly after the shooting on April 27, 2013.

Also revealing is wiretap evidence against Rotondo, authorized by the Lower Court Penal Judge for Narcotrafficking Activities and Crimes against the Environment of Guatemala, which was translated and submitted to the BC Supreme Court as part of the legal proceedings against Tahoe Resources.

In the wiretaps, Rotondo orders guards to open fire against protesters during the events of April 27, 2013, using criminal and racist language.

These recordings include conversations between Rotondo and Juan Pablo Oliva Trejo. Oliva Trejo was taken into police custody on May 4, 2013. He is a legal representative of Counter Risk, S.A., a company contracted by Tahoe Resources to carry out risk consultancy and to track media coverage. Oliva Trejo's father is retired Colonel Juan Guillermo Oliva Carrera, president and director of the Asociación de Estudios Políticos Militares (Association of Military Politics Studies—AEPM). Oliva Carrera was prosecuted for being one of the supposed intellectual authors of the high-profile assassination of anthropologist Myrna Mack in 1990. AEPM houses Counter Risk, S.A., and Supervivencia Urbana, S.A., a shooting range. Oliva Carrera is the director of political risk analysis for Supervivencia Urbana, S.A., and Oliva Trejo is a shooting instructor. General Alfredo Augusto Rabbé Tejada also works for Supervivencia Urbana, S.A., and is an associate of Mayaquímicos, S.A. (MAQUISA). MAQUISA is in charge of the explosives MSR uses for its mining operations, some of which were stolen in November 2012. The explosives theft was believed to be a set-up used to criminalize community leaders opposed to the Escobal mine and to justify the state of siege in May 2013.

Tahoe Resources has now changed security firms. It hired a relatively new company, Centurion Security, S.A., which received its licence to operate as a private security company in early 2014. Centurion's roots began with another security firm originally founded by British soldiers in 2006 that had past experience providing security in Guatemala's oil sector, where its services included "comprehensive advice on every aspect of security—from corporate operations, commercial risk and foreign investment to counter-terrorism and espionage and support to regional governments."

CONCLUSION

As long as Tahoe Resources and the Guatemalan government continue to treat communities affected by the Escobal project—or any other mine project in the country—as insurgents instead of people peacefully standing up for their land, water, and in defence of their existing ways of life, the kind of conflict and violence observed to date can be expected to continue.

If these conditions persist, the anti-mining resistance will continue to be rated on a scale ranging from "a controllable threat" to a "terrorist threat." These categorizations have already led to a counter-insurgency-style response with the aim of dismantling the resistance movement. The ongoing militarization of communities and militarized security detail in Santa Rosa and Jalapa, thanks to the installation of the inter-institutional commission in San Rafael Las Flores and two military outposts in the region, is troubling evidence of this.

The effect in recent years has been the creation of a state of terror through military and police persecution, criminalization and persecution of leaders, as well as the arrest of leaders based on false accusations and massive raids on the homes of key people within the opposition movement. The processes to criminalize and persecute dozens of community members were never based on any real evidence. Not a single accusation for which people involved in the peaceful resistance to mining in Santa Rosa and Japala were detained was ever proven. These arbitrary detentions were more punitive in nature, with the purpose of demobilizing anti-mining protests. Furthermore, since 2013, two leaders in the local resistance, including sixteen-year-old Topacio Reynoso and Telésforo Pivaral, have been murdered, while others have been shot and wounded, including Topacio's father, Edwin Alexander Reynoso, who has been shot twice and survived. Those responsible for these murders and attacks have still not been brought to justice.

Despite a lower profile under these conditions, the struggle of local communities continues. Municipal plebiscites on mining continue, and there was strong electoral support for several mayors in San Rafael Las Flores and surrounding areas who campaigned on anti-mining platforms.

It is time for the company and the Guatemalan government to stop the resource wars and respect the clear message the local population has been sending: an end to mining, and the protection of their land and water from the mining harms they are already suffering.

REFERENCES

CCIJ (Canadian Centre for International Justice). 2017. "In Milestone, BC Court Clears Guatemalans' Lawsuit against Vancouver Mining Company to Go to Trial." January 26. http://www.ccij.ca/news/milestone-bc-court.

Lakhani, Nina. 2017. "The Canadian Company Mining Hills of Silver—and the People Dying to Stop It." *The Guardian*, July 13. https://www.theguardian.com/

environment/2017/jul/13/the-canadian-company-mining-hills-of-silver-and-the-people-dying-to-stop-it.

Secretaría Técnica del Consejo de Seguridad Nacional. 2013. *Cronología para la consitución del Grupo Interinstitucional de Recursos Naturales*. May.

Solano, Luis. 2009. "La transnacionalización de la industria extractiva: La captura de los recursos minerales e hidrocarburos." *El Observador* 19: 3–36.

CHAPTER 4

DEADLY SOY
THE VIOLENT EXPANSION OF PARAGUAY'S AGRO-EXTRACTIVE FRONTIER

Arturo Ezquerro-Cañete

On June 15, 2012, eleven peasant activists and six police officers were killed in a shootout during a botched security operation by 324 police to evict sixty members of the organization Movimiento por la Recuperación Campesina de Canindeyú (Movement for the Peasant Recovery of Canindeyú), which had occupied land near Curuguaty, in northeastern Paraguay. The tragedy was the country's worst incident of political violence for decades, igniting criticism from peasant movements and opposition leaders, albeit for very different reasons. The official version stated that the campesinos, or small peasant farmers, fired at police first, but this view was strongly contested by human rights and activist organizations (CODEHUPY 2012; PEICC 2012; FIAN International and Vía Campesina 2014). In fact, an independent examination of audio footage by Spanish ballistics experts found the police were killed by automatic fire, incompatible with the rudimentary hunting rifles captured from the occupying campesinos. The presence of children suggested they were not expecting violence. Many believed the shootout was orchestrated by hidden marksmen, a view detailed by the Plataforma de Estudio e Investigación de Conflictos Campesinos (PEICC 2012), which argued that the police, who were wearing bulletproof vests, were all killed by shots to the head and neck. In the immediate aftermath of the Curuguaty massacre, a medley of conservative social forces saw its opportunity and converged around the impeachment and removal of moderately left-of-centre President Fernando Lugo (see Ezquerro-Cañete and Fogel 2017), bringing to an end the country's halting democratic experiment, underway since 1989.

The above episode is reflective of the intensification of efforts by imperialism and the Latin American Right to turn back the clock on the progressive cycle of the 2000s. In this sense, the Paraguayan case—along with the 2009 military coup in Honduras—signalled, perhaps, the earlier stages of a receding "pink tide," which has intensified in recent years (Petras and Veltmeyer 2018; see also Chapter 2). For one thing, the Paraguayan case inaugurated an emerging regional shift towards "smart coups...whereby Left governments are forced out of office and a new Right-orientated government put in place, with, preferably, relatively little bloodshed and an element of popular and institutional legitimacy" (Cannon 2016, 119).

Against this backdrop, this chapter will explore the role of organized violence within Paraguay's agro-export development model. Drawing from a wide array of existing research, news reports, activist blogs, and analysis of data from the Coordinating Committee for Human Rights in Paraguay's 2014 report on extrajudicial and arbitrary executions of rural and Indigenous inhabitants (CODEHUPY 2014), it is argued that the current agrarian extractivist project in Paraguay is reinforced by, and even contingent on, violence perpetuated by the state to protect private agribusiness interests. Granovsky-Larsen and Paley began this volume with the observation that criminalization and repression work to undermine resistance. The analysis of the predatory practices and repressive nature of agro-extractivism in Paraguay substantiates this assertion and reveals how this current development strategy runs on the "blood of extraction" (Gordon and Webber 2016).

Following this introduction, I describe the context of soybean production in Paraguay, framing this model within the resurgent extractive imperative throughout the region. From there I tie the country's agricultural boom in genetically modified (GM) soy production to the neoliberal militarization of the countryside and the associated criminalization of resistance (Palau 2006). I then explore some illustrative instances where state security forces have violently repressed peasant protests, while mercenaries and paramilitary organizations have carried out arbitrary executions. At the end of the chapter, I briefly reflect on the theoretical implications of the violence inherent within the soy sector in Paraguay.

CONTEXTUALIZING THE EXPANSION OF AGRO-EXTRACTIVE CAPITAL

In Paraguay, like elsewhere in Latin America (Kay 2001, 2007), conflicts over land and territories are largely rooted in a country's unequal and exclusionary agrarian system (Nagel 1999). Indeed, Paraguay's shameful land distribution, calculated as a 0.94 Gini coefficient (Guereña 2013), is widely recognized as being among the most unequal in the world. In recent years, however, land conflicts have also revolved around the social and environmental conflicts provoked by the expansion of GM soy (Semino, Joensen, and Rulli 2006; García-López and Arizpe 2010). Semino, Joensen, and Rulli (2006, 18) estimate that half of all land conflicts in Paraguay, and particularly the most violent ones, are attributed to the "soy boom."

GM soy production was introduced into Paraguay shortly after its approval and commercialization in Argentina in 1996. Initially, transgenic seeds were smuggled and planted illegally in Paraguay until being legalized in 2004. Since the mid-1990s, the production of GM soybeans in Paraguay has skyrocketed. In 1996–1997, 2.77 million tonnes of soy were produced; by 2013–2014, that production rose to 8.19 million tonnes. The land dedicated to soy also increased correspondingly: between 2000 and 2012, the soy sector grew at an average rate of almost 150,000 hectares per year, more than doubling from 1.2 million hectares in 2000 to more than 2.9 million hectares in 2012. By 2015, more than 3.2 million hectares were being used for soy production. Moreover, while soy production originated in the frontier area of the eastern region (i.e., Itapúa, Alto Paraná, and Canindeyú)—which in 1979 accounted for 80 percent of the country's land area devoted to this crop (Baer and Birch 1984, 787)—during the 1990s and 2000s, the soybean frontier has been making its way from east to west into the fast-growing departments of Caaguazú, Caazapá, and San Pedro (see Table 4.1).

Table 4.1: Land Surface Dedicated to Soy Production by Department (Hectares), 1991–2015

Department	1991	2001	2015	% Change 1991–2015
Alto Paraná[a]	228,504	530,308	896,053	292.1
Itapúa[a]	210,523	356,173	632,236	200.3
Canindeyú[a]	49,030	238,112	619,524	1,163.6
Caaguazú	21,799	85,204	396,169	1,593.5
Caazapá	8,931	71,580	176,552	1,876.8
San Pedro	17,367	33,840	288,022	1,558.4
National Total	552,657	1,350,568	3,264,453	490.7

Source: Ezquerro-Cañete (2016). [a] eastern frontier region

The consolidation of this agro-export development model in Paraguay is best understood by locating it within the emergence of a neoliberal food regime (Otero 2012), which is most clearly manifested in South America's Southern Cone as a so-called soy republic. More broadly, the model should be situated within the wider debates around the renewed extractive imperative in Latin America (Veltmeyer and Petras 2014; Gudynas 2015; Svampa 2015). As Veltmeyer summarizes, the most serious contradiction of the new extractivism is that "a large part of the benefits of economic activity are externalized, i.e. appropriated by groups outside the country and region, while virtually all of the costs— economic, social and environmental—are internalized and disproportionately borne by the Indigenous and farming communities contiguous to the open pit mines and other sites of extraction" (2016, 779). From this perspective, I argue that Paraguay has witnessed and experienced all of the contradictory developments and pitfalls of agro-extractivism. As a researcher at the Buenos Aires-based group Grupo de Reflexión Rural declares, "Paraguay could be viewed as the country in which agri-business show their most brutal side, by evicting and attacking people with complete impunity. The militarization and para-militarization of the countryside are linked to the increase of soya cultivation and the security systems of the agribusiness" (Rulli 2007, 221).

MILITARIZED NEOLIBERALISM AND THE
CRIMINALIZATION OF RESISTANCE

In terms of the interrelated political, military, and economic components of imperialism, several authors have argued that Paraguay, because of its geostrategic position in the "heart of South America," cannot escape US influence (Ceceña and Motto 2005; Schünemann 2008; Zibechi 2012). Chomsky (2007, 10) points out that Paraguay has maintained its position as "one of the few remaining reliable land bases for the U.S. military" in Latin America. In the context of US geopolitics, the 1990s saw the advent of a new militarized form of imperialism that, with the spread of military and paramilitary forces across the country, was already being compared to an extension of Plan Colombia in Paraguay (Palau 2009b). In 2004, a military agreement between the United States and Paraguayan governments came into effect. Under the cloak of strengthening the democratization process, the government of Nicanor Duarte Frutos (2003–2008) decreed as legal the presence of US military forces in the countryside, guaranteeing the immunity of 499 members of the military for any violation of the country's laws that might occur in the process of their "humanitarian assistance" (counter-insurgency training) provided to Paraguayan troops (Schünemann 2008, 258, 273–76; Petras and Veltmeyer 2015, 85). The blurring of foreign policy and military and development goals of US organizations in Paraguay is not unlike the extension of US hegemony described by Granovsky-Larsen and Paley in the Introduction to this volume, wherein elite politics are subsumed to the political interests of Washington. At the same time (and again for geographic reasons), Paraguay is also vulnerable to the worst manifestation of Brazilian subimperial interests, particularly as related to soybean agribusiness (Vuyk 2014; Zibechi 2014; Oliveira 2016).

Elsewhere, I have documented the exclusionary and socially problematic nature of what we might call the "transgenic soyization" of Paraguay's agriculture (Ezquerro-Cañete 2016). However, the model of rapacious agrarian capitalism maturing in Paraguay today not only involves the increased concentration of landholdings, dampened overall employment and accelerated forced expulsion of the peasantry, deforestation, and a growing dependence on agrochemicals that compromise environmental quality and human health (Ezquerro-Cañete 2016). It also necessarily and systematically involves what Paraguayan sociologist Marielle Palau (2006) refers to as "militarized neoliberalism": the increasingly repressive role of military and security forces in policing the inevitable conflicts, struggles, and explosions of resistance that occur in response to the expansion of the agro-extractive frontier. Indeed, by the mid-2000s, under legislation passed during the Nicanor Duarte Frutos administration (2003–2008), eighteen new military bases were established in the most conflictive areas. Armed paramilitary Neighbourhood Committees for Citizen Security, often with state funding and training, began to guard soy fields to prevent peasants from taking action against fumigation machines, despite allegations of torture and extrajudicial killings (Semino, Joensen, and Rulli 2006, 18; Lambert 2012). In December 2008, the Ministry of the Interior withdrew the legal status of such groups, although in practice some continue to operate with impunity (Lambert 2012).

At the same time, a fundamental part of militarized neoliberalism is the ideological attempts by the Paraguayan state and media to demonize social movement opponents as criminals. With regard to the latter, "hyperbolic public outrage against *campesinos* in the wake of the Curuguaty shooting, including overtly racist diatribes in the mainstream and alternative media, shows that the event confirmed many urbanites' fear of the dark, inscrutable masses believed to be a constant threat to the social order" (Hetherington 2012, 10; see also Nagel 1999). Criminalization in this context is characterized not so much by the overt use of force by police or armed militias to repress social protest (Palau 2009a), as it is by judicialization (*judicialización*), subjecting various acts to the criminal code using a widening repertoire of accusations (Areco and Palau 2016).

A prime example of criminalization was the sentencing of eleven peasants (eight men and three women) for the killings of six police officers during the Curuguaty massacre. On July 11, 2016, a Paraguayan court sentenced Rubén Villaba, who was identified as the leader of the campesino occupation, to thirty years in prison. Luis Olmedo was sentenced to twenty years as the main co-author of the crime, and two other men, Arnaldo Quintana and Néstor Castro, were given eighteen years each for the same charge. Seven other peasants received sentences of between four and six years for criminal association and invasion of private property ("Court Rules on 'Curuguaty Massacre'" 2016). Concerns over the lack of impartiality and independence in the investigations into

the events in Curuguaty are captured in a press release from the United
Nations Commissioner for Human Rights, Zeid Ra'ad Al Hussein:

> The conviction of 11 peasants in the Curuguaty case following
> a trial that allegedly did not respect judicial guarantees is deeply
> troubling...[also concerning is] the fact that, up to now, the deaths
> of 11 peasants, killed in the same incident, have not been investi-
> gated by Paraguayan authorities, nor have the allegations that
> some were summarily executed after being subjected to torture
> and other human rights violations. (OHCHR 2016)

Investigations have been cast in a shadow of doubt due to what Al
Hussein identifies as "allegations of serious irregularities in the actions
of the Public Prosecution Service, the judiciary, and the security forces
in relation to the police raid in Curuguaty in June 2012" (OHCHR 2016).
Accusations have also been made regarding the involvement of hidden
marksmen, planted to spark a political crisis in order to oust President
Lugo from office. In such a climate of suspicion, conspiracy theories
abound (for example, see PEICC 2012). The combined factors of repression and criminalization of peasant protest have further served to
defuse resistance to the penetration of agribusiness capital (Palau 2012;
Guereña 2013; Areco and Palau 2016).

"LA SOJA MATA": A PANORAMA OF VIOLENCE

"Soy = Glyphosate + Paramilitary" (*Soja = Glifosato + Paramilitares*) was
written on the banner at the forefront of a demonstration staged by
peasant and Indigenous organizations on August 31, 2006, to protest
against the Second Round Table on Sustainable Soy Conference held
at the Hotel Yacht Golf Club in Asunción (Maeyens 2006). The march
brought together the largest and most important peasant organizations
in Paraguay, including the Federación Nacional Campesina (National
Peasants Federation), Coordinadora Nacional de Mujeres Trabajadoras
Rurales e Indígenas (National Coordination of Rural and Indigenous
Working Women), Movimiento Agrario y Popular (Agrarian and Popular
Movement—MAP), and the umbrella organization Mesa Coordinadora
Nacional de Organizaciones Campesinas (National Coordinating
Committee of Peasant Organizations). The banner encapsulates the

twin forces of violence and dispossession faced by the peasant and Indigenous communities who live near soy operations. On the one hand, the transgenic soyization of land in Paraguay has engendered a regime of dispossession driven by new agro-industrial practices associated with this model. Specifically, I suggest the process might be termed "accumulation by fumigation and dispossession" (Ezquerro-Cañete 2016), that is, the forced displacement from land by the intensive use of agrotoxins, when crops are planted next to population centres (i.e., agrochemical drift as a new instrument in displacement). Here, the weak, absent, or conniving nature of the Paraguayan state is central to an understanding of how the application of highly globalized capital and chemically intensive agro-industrial practices has recast the dynamics of the historical process of primitive accumulation. Weak state capacity for policy making often means private actors are likely to bypass the state and design and implement rules by themselves, leading to the rule-making pattern of "state capture and abstention."

> Under state capture and abstention, powerful individuals, firms, or groups are able to influence the regulatory activity of the state to their own advantage (state capture) or to entirely substitute for the state in the design and implementation of rules that apply to their respective policy domain (state abstention)...powerful interest groups mobilize informal links to the state to obtain particularistic benefits; rule-making within the state is *ad hoc*; and important rules are formulated by private actors bypassing the state but later obtaining its endorsement. (Filomeno 2014, 441, 450)

This framework exemplifies how genetically modified soy came to be legalized in Paraguay. Monsanto's Roundup Ready soy (RR), a GM variety engineered to resist the herbicide glyphosate (Roundup), had been cultivated in Paraguay since 1999, when it was smuggled from Argentina before the Paraguayan state had approved its cultivation (Ezquerro-Cañete 2016, 704). In 2004, a private agreement was reached between Monsanto and a set of local agribusiness organizations, spearheaded by the Unión de Gremios de la Producción (Union of Producer Associations—UGP), whereby soy growers would pay a substantial royalty (4 percent) directly to the company for the use of RR soy, despite the fact the corporation did not have a patent in the country (Filomeno 2014,

252, 254). One month later, the government passed a special law legalizing the cultivation of GM soybeans in recognition of a material fait accompli in the countryside. Yet, another month later, the government created the National Plant and Seed Health and Quality Service (Servicio Nacional de Calidad y Sanidad Vegetal y de Semillas—SENAVE), an agency within the Ministry of Agriculture and Livestock (Ministerio de Agricultura y Ganadaría) for the regulation of biotechnology, biosafety, and intellectual property on plant varieties, which could certify for exporters that the royalty had been paid (Hetherington 2014, 70). In practice, however, SENAVE remained a weak state agency affected by capture by private actors (Filomeno 2014, 451). The UGP controlled policy making in the boardroom, while on-farm inspections were widely acknowledged as opportunities for illicit means of influence, such as bribery. In both legitimate and illegitimate ways, the UGP was said to "own" SENAVE (Hetherington 2014, 73), indicating once more the long legacy of oligarchies treating the state as their private property (Nickson and Lambert 2002).

On the other hand, national military and paramilitary groups connected to large agribusinesses and landowners in Paraguay have repressed, coerced, and murdered the ranks of an expanding landless peasantry with complete impunity (Guereña 2013; CODEHUPY 2014). Such arbitrary evictions of peasant and Indigenous communities from land occupations have led to numerous accusations against the police— and increasingly private forces—of violence, unjustified arrests, and extrajudicial executions. In this regard, as FIAN International and Vía Campesina claim, "The unstoppable expansion of soya crops is the cause of the harassment, attacks, and assassinations at the hands of the police, the paramilitary, and private armed groups who are antagonistic towards the rural leaders" (quoted in Rulli 2007, 221). The following sections outline emblematic cases of arbitrary executions, violent land evictions, and fumigation of people and their crops.

Fumigation

The expansion of transgenic soybean production has been accompanied by a steep increase in agrochemical use in Paraguay, in particular related to the adoption of the Monsanto-engineered, glyphosate-resistant Roundup Ready seed. Between 2009 and 2015, annual agrochemical use increased from 9.2 million kilos and 15.6 million litres to 30.8 million kilos and 20.5 million litres (Franceschelli 2015, 43). By 2015, 13.3 million litres of glyphosate, 9.1 million litres of paraquat, and almost 2 million litres of 2,4-D were being imported into Paraguay (Franceschelli 2015, 44). The increasing use of agrochemicals has taken place hand in hand with an alarming rise in pesticide-related illnesses and deaths among workers and residents. Indeed, a number of important clinical studies conducted at the Regional Hospital of Encarnación (department of Itapúa) have documented the harmful effects of occupational exposure to agrochemicals on human health, including associated risk factors for congenital malformations (Benítez-Leite, Macchi, and Acosta 2007) and a significant increase in the frequency of karyorrhexis and pyknosis (Benítez-Leite et al. 2010; see also Chapter 1). Furthermore, Palau et al. (2007, 332–46, appendix 2) provide a database of registered cases of human, animal, and vegetable contamination associated with the agrochemical drift of fumigations. This matrix reveals there were a total of ninety-six cases of pesticide-related intoxication as a result of agrochemical drifts between 2003 and 2006. Perhaps the case to garner the most public outrage against the soy sector was the 2003 poisoning death of Silvino Talavera, an eleven-year-old boy who was sprayed by a crop duster on his way home from school (Hetherington 2013). While cases like this were widely rumoured to have occurred throughout the countryside, this was the first one in which a team of activists and lawyers managed to get medical proof, in the form of tests on the boy's blood, that pesticides caused his death (Hetherington 2014).

Arbitrary Executions

The Chokokue report, published in 2014 by the Coordinadora de Derechos Humanos del Paraguay (Coordinating Committee for Human Rights in Paraguay—CODEHUPY) (2014), documents 115 victims of extrajudicial executions within a census from February 3, 1989, to August 15, 2013. Since the "parliamentary coup" of 2012, the format of assassinations has shifted from assassinations within the context of land conflicts—occupations and displacements—to assassinations carried out by hired gunmen (sicarios), either in the homes of peasant leaders or in public. Some examples follow.

On September 1, 2012, peasant leader Sixto Pérez was murdered in his home in the district of Ex-Puentesiño, Concepción. On December 1, 2012, two men on a motorbike shot Vidal Vega, another peasant leader, at his home near Curuguaty. Vega was a leader of the movement of landless farmers whose Curuguaty land invasion precipitated the June 15th shootout that left seventeen dead and led to the impeachment of former President Fernando Lugo. For decades, Vega had lobbied the government to redistribute part of a 135-square-mile landholding illegally occupied since 1964 by Blas Riquelme, a former president of the Partido Colorado. Vega was a leader of the Comisión Sin Tierra de Naranjaty (Landless Commission of Naranjaty) and secretary of the recently formed Comision de Familiares de Victimas de la Masacre de Curuguaty (Committee of Relatives of Victims of the Curuguaty Massacre). He had regularly taken food and clothing to the twelve imprisoned peasants pending the trial arising from the June killings, and was well known to the authorities. He himself had not been charged because he was away buying supplies when the violence erupted. As one among the few leaders not to be killed in the clash or jailed afterwards, he was expected to be a witness at their trial. According to the Inter-American Commission on Human Rights, on December 1, 2012, two hired gunmen arrived on motorcycle at the home of Vidal Vega. Police information quoted in news reports indicates the victim's spouse, María Cristina Argüello, answered the door and the two unknown men asked for Vidal Vega and shot him with 12-caliber rifles, in the presence of his family ("Human Rights Commission Demands Urgent Investigation" 2012; "Paraguay Politics" 2012; CODEHUPY 2014).

On February 19, 2013, Benjamín "Toto" Lezcano, a leader of the Coordinadora de Organizaciones Campesinas "José Gaspar Rodríguez de Francia" (José Gaspar Rodríguez de Francia Coordination of Peasant Organizations), was murdered in his home by a *sicario* in the district of Horqueta, Concepción; in March 2013, Dionisio González, a peasant leader, was murdered in the district of Alfonso Kue, Concepción. On April 21, 2013, in a case of mistaken identity, police shot Francisco Denis, a grassroots member of a peasant movement, on his way back from voting in the general elections in Kurusu de Hierro, Concepción. On May 31, 2013, Antonio Carlos Moreira, a Brazilian colonist with ties to the Movimiento Campesino Paraguayo (Paraguayan Peasant Movement) in the Laterza Kue land conflict, was shot in his home in the Caaguazú department by *sicarios*. On August 14, 2013, Lorenzo Areco, a member of the Organización Campesina Regional de Concepción (Regional Peasant Organization of Concepción), was murdered by *sicarios* on the streets of Yvy Ya'u, Concepción. Beyond these cases of cold-blooded killings, grassroots members of peasant organizations have also faced the frequent harassment and intimidation of thugs hired by agribusiness (CODEHUPY 2014).

Of the 115 executions recorded, 77.4 percent occurred in just five departments—Canindeyú (twenty-five killings), San Pedro (twenty-one), Concepción (sixteen), Caaguazú (fifteen), and Alto Paraná (twelve). These executions thus manifest a marked regional concentration. Not coincidentally, four out of these departments are also the country's most *sojero*, or soy-intensive, departments.

The Chokokue report also highlights a complete lack of accountability with respect to the extrajudicial executions of campesinos, which has been extraordinary during the fourteen-year period. In fact, not a single person has been charged for any one of the 115 executions investigated in the report. In the few instances in which the negligible actions of judges and prosecutors have reached the Jurado de Enjuiciamiento Magistrados (Special Jury of Judges), the result has been absolute impunity without exception (CODEHUPY 2014, 171).

Violent Land Evictions

Land conflicts in Paraguay result from a large number of overlapping factors, where historical injustices (i.e., *tierras malhabidas*, or ill-gotten lands) often blend with the agro-extractive shift in the development model. When communities refuse to leave their property or attempt to take disputed territory through land occupations, they often face heavy repression. The case discussed in this section—Tekojoja—is an example of violent dispossession, whereby communities in regions where agribusiness corporations are seeking to expand production suffer displacement at the hands of police and paramilitary forces.

Tekojoja is a campesino camp located in the eastern department of Caaguazú. Between 2002 and 2006, a group of several hundred campesinos in Tekojoja from MAP were embroiled in a violent struggle with a handful of Brazilian soy producers from the nearby community of Santa Clara. Approximately two hundred hectares were in dispute between peasants and soy producers attempting to purchase the land for GM soy production. The lands in dispute had been bought illegally by Brazilian migrants: the land in Santa Clara had been purchased from speculators in the 1970s, while land in Tekojoja had recently been bought from land-reform beneficiaries against the citizenship requirements codified in the land-reform law (Hetherington 2011, 70). The National Institute for Rural and Land Development (Instituto Nacional de Desarrollo Rural y de la Tierra) made a shady contract granting thirteen agricultural lots in the region to a group of Brazilian soy producers. In response, peasants began a recuperation process and occupied those two hundred hectares in June 2003. Meanwhile, MAP initiated legal action to recognize the land as property of Tekojoja. Brazilian *sojeros* (soy farmers) carried out two violent evictions—in December 2004 and again in June 2005—displacing fifty-six families, burning their houses, and stealing their possessions. During the last eviction, two people were shot dead.

On December 3, 2004, Judge Gladis Escobar ordered the eviction of the peasant settlement, an action that left forty-six houses burned and twenty hectares of crops destroyed. The peasants then reoccupied their lands. The people of MAP related that

> after the tractors had destroyed our crops, they came with their big machines and started immediately to sow soy while smoke was still coming out from the ashes of our houses. Next day we came back with oxen and replanted all the fields over the prepared land. When the police came, we faced them with our tools and machetes, we were around 70 people and were ready to confront them. In the end they left. (Maeyens 2008)

The soy producers took action again. On June 24, 2005, the attorney of Vaqueria headed another eviction of the land reoccupations, despite the fact that no decision had been taken by the Supreme Court on the case of the illegal sale of land rights (*derecheras*) in the region. This time, soy farmers, aided by heavily armed men, evicted fifty-six families (four hundred people, including 223 children), and eventually shot Ángel Cristaldo (twenty years old) and Leoncio Torres (forty-six years old), without any provocation. The second eviction is bitterly depicted by Canadian anthropologist Kregg Hetherington, who bore witness to the event during his doctoral fieldwork. Hetherington writes,

> Two truckloads of riot police showed up at five o'clock in the morning and began pulling people out of bed. They loaded the trucks with over a hundred campesinos, including Joel and his wife (who was then eight months pregnant), and drove them to the regional

jail while Opperman's gang drove through the community on tractors, demolishing houses and setting them on fire. Then, as Opperman was leaving the location, he spotted a group of about fifty campesinos, some of whom had hidden during the evictions, some of whom had gathered in solidarity to discuss a reaction. As his convoy drove past, men in the trucks opened fire on the campesinos with shotguns, killing two young men and severely wounding another. (2011, 119)

The above episode is far from an isolated case. Countless examples of this process have been documented, often linking state and paramilitary violence to the expansion of the agro-industrial sector (Semino, Joensen, and Rulli 2006; Rulli 2007; Fogel 2013).

THEORETICAL IMPLICATIONS AND FINAL REFLECTIONS

This chapter has sought to trace the increasingly aggressive insertion of agribusiness capital into the Paraguayan countryside. In so doing, it has linked the ascendancy of agro-industrial monocropping in Paraguay over the past two decades to a larger national phenomenon of "militarized neoliberalism" (Palau 2006). That is to say, the rapid transformation— or transgenic soyization—of agriculture could not have succeeded without the role of the state and paramilitary forces in suppressing peasant organizations that sought to challenge the predatory expansion of agribusiness capital. As illustrated in the above case studies, the expansion of the agro-extractive frontier has often used violence and coercion to appropriate lands, resulting in the erosion of human rights. In this light, the expansion of the soy sector in Paraguay reflects an acute tendency towards *extrahección* (or "extrahection" in English), a concept coined by Gudynas (2015, 127–28), which refers to instances when extractive activities are involved in the violation of human rights (e.g., threats, intimidation, outright repression, and assassination). In Paraguay, this has involved murder, death threats, assaults, arbitrary detention, and the systematic repression of peasant organizations seeking land and more favourable conditions.

In sum, the cases of arbitrary execution, violent land evictions, and fumigation of people and their crops mentioned in this chapter are just a few examples of the "other face" of the agro-export model in Paraguay

(Riquelme and Vera 2013), or the "dark side of the boom," of the recent expansion of agribusiness in South America (Lapegna 2013). Any honest assessment of the rural development model in Paraguay must thus move beyond a tunnel vision focus on increased agricultural production to include a focus on the negative "externalities" associated with the neoliberal food regime, particularly the impact on social exclusion and marginality. Failure to do so will result in a continuation of growing explosiveness in the countryside, such as the Curuguaty massacre of eleven peasants in 2012.

REFERENCES

Areco, Abel, and Marielle Palau. 2016. *Judicialización y violencia contra la lucha campesina (2013–2015).* BASE Investigaciones Sociales.

Baer, Werner, and Melissa Birch. 1984. "Expansion of the Economic Frontier: Paraguayan Growth in the 1970s." *World Development* 12 (8): 783–98.

Benítez-Leite, Stela, María Luisa Macchi, and Marta Acosta. 2007. "Malformaciones congénitas asociadas a agrotóxicos." *Pediatría (Asunción)* 34 (2): 111–21.

Benítez-Leite, Stela, María Luisa Macchi, Virginia Fernández, Deidamia Franco, Esteban Ferro, A. Andrés Mojoli, Fabiola Cuevas, Jorge Alfonso, and Luciana Sales. 2010. "Daño celular en una población infantil potencialmente expuesta a pesticidas." *Pediatría (Asunción)* 37 (2): 97–106.

Cannon, Barry. 2016. *The Right in Latin America: Elite Power, Hegemony, and the Struggle for the State.* New York: Routledge.

Ceceña, Ana Esther, and Carlos Ernesto Motto. 2005. "Paraguay: Eje de la dominación del Cono Sur." *OSAL* 17 (May–August): 275–88.

Chomsky, Noam. 2007. "Imminent Crises: Threats and Opportunities." *Monthly Review* 59 (2): 1–19.

CODEHUPY (Coordinadora de Derechos Humanos del Paraguay). 2012. *Informe de derechos humanos sobre el caso Marina Kue.* Asunción, Paraguay: Coordinadora de Derechos Humanos del Paraguay.

———. 2014. *Informe Chokokue 1989–2013: El plan sistemático de ejecuciones en la lucha por el territorio campesino.* Asunción, Paraguay: Coordinadora de Derechos Humanos del Paraguay.

"Court Rules on 'Curuguaty Massacre.'" 2016. *Latin American Weekly Review,* July 14.

Ezquerro-Cañete, Arturo. 2016. "Poisoned, Dispossessed and Excluded: Towards a Critique of the Neoliberal Soy Regime in Paraguay." *Journal of Agrarian Change* 16 (4): 702–10.

Ezquerro-Cañete, Arturo, and Ramón Fogel. 2017. "A Coup Foretold: Fernando Lugo and the Lost Promise of Agrarian Reform." *Journal of Agrarian Change* 17 (2): 279–95.

FIAN International and Vía Campesina. 2014. *Conflictos Agrarios y Criminalización de Campesinos y Campesinas en Paraguay: El Caso Marina Kue y la "Masacre de Curuguaty."* Oakland, CA: Food First/Institute for Food and Development Policy and Transnational Institute.

Filomeno, Felipe Amin. 2014. "Patterns of Rule-Making and Intellectual Property Regimes: Lessons from South American Soybean Agriculture." *Journal of Comparative Politics* 46 (4): 439–58.

Fogel, Ramón. 2013. *Las tierras de Ñacunday, Marina Kue y otras calamidades.* Asunción, Paraguay: Centro de Estudios Rurales Interdisciplinarios/Servi Libro.

Franceschelli, Inés. 2015. "Pobre Paracelso." In *Con la Soja al Cuello: Informe sobre Agronegocios en Paraguay 2013–2015*, edited by Marielle Palau, 42–45. Asunción, Paraguay: BASE Investigaciones Sociales.

García-López, Gustavo A., and Nancy Arizpe. 2010. "Participatory Processes in the Soy Conflicts in Paraguay and Argentina." *Ecological Economics* 70 (2): 196–206.

Gordon, Todd, and Jeffery R. Webber. 2016. *The Blood of Extraction: Canadian Imperialism in Latin America.* Halifax: Fernwood Publishing.

Gudynas, Eduardo. 2015. *Extractivismos: Ecología, economía y política de un modo de entender el desarrollo y la naturaleza.* Cochabamba, Bolivia: Centro de Documentación e Información Bolivia.

Guereña, Arantxa. 2013. *The Soy Mirage: The Limits of Corporate Social Responsibility: The Case of the Company Desarrollo Agrícola del Paraguay.* Oxford, UK: Oxfam.

Hetherington, Kregg. 2011. *Guerrilla Auditors: The Politics of Transparency in Neoliberal Paraguay.* Durham, NC: Duke University Press.

———. 2012. "Paraguay's Ongoing Struggle over Land and Democracy." *NACLA Report on the Americas* 45 (3): 8–10.

———. 2013. "Beans before the Law: Knowledge Practices, Responsibility, and the Paraguayan Soy Boom." *Cultural Anthropology* 28 (1): 65–85.

———. 2014. "Regular Soybeans: Translation and Framing in the Ontological Politics of a Coup." *Indiana Journal of Global Studies* 21 (1): 55–78.

"Human Rights Commission Demands Urgent Investigation into Killing of Paraguayan Peasant Leader." 2012. *Mercopress*, December 5. http://en.mercopress.com/2012/12/05/human-rights-commission-demands-urgent-investigation-into-killing-of-paraguayan-peasant-leader.

Kay, Cristóbal. 2001. "Reflections on Rural Violence in Latin America." *Third World Quarterly* 22 (5): 741–75.

———. 2007. "Land, Conflict, and Violence in Latin America." *Peace Review: A Journal of Social Justice* 19: 5–14.

Lambert, Peter. 2012. "Countries at the Crossroads 2011: Paraguay." In *Countries at the Crossroads 2011: An Analysis of Democratic Governance*, edited by Jake

Dizard, Christopher Walker, and Vanessa Tucker, 487–506. Lanham, MD: Rowman & Littlefield Publishers.

Lapegna, Pablo. 2013. "The Expansion of Transgenic Soybeans and the Killing of Indigenous Peasants in Argentina." *Societies without Borders* 8 (2): 291–308.

Maeyens, An. 2006. "Paraguay: Soja = Glifosato + Paramilitares." *Biodiversidad en América Latina*, September 5. http://www.biodiversidadla.org/Noticias/ Paraguay_soja_glifosato_paramilitares.

———. 2008. "The Battle of Tekojoja, Paraguay." *La Soja Mata*, August 16. http:// lasojamata.iskra.net/en/node/15.

Nagel, Beverly Y. 1999. "'Unleashing the Fury': The Cultural Discourse of Rural Violence and Land Rights in Paraguay." *Comparative Studies in Society and History* 41 (1): 148–81.

Nickson, Andrew, and Peter Lambert. 2002. "State Reform and the 'Privatized State' in Paraguay." *Public Administration and Development* 22 (2): 163–74.

OHCHR (Office of the United Nations High Commissioner for Human Rights). 2016. "Zeid 'Deeply Troubled' by Outcome of Paraguayan Land Killings Case." http://www.ohchr.org/EN/NewsEvents/Pages/DisplayNews. aspx?NewsID=20289&LangID=E.

Oliveira, Gustavo de L. T. 2016. "The Geopolitics of Brazilian Soybeans." *The Journal of Peasant Studies* 43 (2): 348–72.

Otero, Gerardo. 2012. "The Neoliberal Food Regime in Latin America: State, Agribusiness Transnational Corporations and Biotechnology." *Canadian Journal of Development Studies* 33 (3): 282–94.

Palau, Marielle. 2006. "El lado militar de la ofensiva neoliberal en Paraguay." *OSAL* 20 (May–August): 339–50.

———. 2009a. *Criminalización a la lucha campesina*. Asunción, Paraguay: BASE Investigaciones Sociales.

———. 2009b. "Los Intentos del Plan Colombia por seguir Avanzando en Paraguay." In *Criminalización a la lucha campesina*, edited by Marielle Palau, 23–34. Asunción, Paraguay: BASE Investigaciones Sociales.

———. 2012. "Los Intentos del Plan Colombia por seguir Avanzando en Paraguay." In *Criminalización a la lucha campesina*, edited by Marielle Palau, 23–34. Asunción, Paraguay: BASE Investigaciones Sociales.

Palau, Tomás, Daniel Cabello, An Maeyens, Javiera Rulli, and Diego Segovia. 2007. *Los refugiados del modelo agroexportador: Impactos del monocultivo de soja en las comunidades campesinas paraguayas*. Asunción, Paraguay: BASE Investigaciones Sociales.

"Paraguay Politics: Quick View–Peasant Leader's Murder Adds to Social Tens[ion]." 2012. *The Economist Intelligence Unit*, December 7.

PEICC (Plataforma de Estudio e Investigación de Conflictos Campesinos). 2012. *Informe masacre de Curuguaty*. Asunción, Paraguay: PEICC.

Petras, James, and Henry Veltmeyer. 2015. *Power and Resistance: US Imperialism in Latin America*. Leiden, Netherlands: Brill.

———. 2018. "The Return of the Right." In *The Class Struggle in Latin America: Making History Today*, edited by James Petras and Henry Veltmeyer, 250–65. London: Routledge.

Riquelme, Quintín, and Elsy Vera. 2013. *La otra cara de la soja: El impacto del agronegocio en la agricultura familiar y la producción de alimentos*. Asunción, Paraguay: Proyecto Acción Ciudadana contra el Hambre y por el Derecho a la Alimentación.

Rulli, Javiera. 2007. "Soya Expansion and the Paramilitarisation of the Countryside." In *United Soya Republics: The Truth about Soya Production in South America*, edited by Javiera Rulli, 194–216. Buenos Aires, Argentina: Grupo de Reflexión Rural.

Schünemann, Anke. 2008. "Hidden Agenda in Paraguay: The Dilemma of External Democratization through Military Co-Operation." In *Armed Forces and Conflict Resolution: Sociological Perspectives*, edited by Giuseppe Caforio, Gerhard Kümmel, and Bandana Purkayastha, 257–82. Bingley, UK: Emerald Group Publishing Limited.

Semino, Stella, Lilian Joensen, and Javiera Rulli. 2006. "Paraguay Sojero: Soy Expansion and Its Violent Attack on Local and Indigenous Communities in Paraguay: Repression and Resistance." Buenos Aires, Argentina: Grupo de Reflexión Rural. http://www.munlochygmvigil.org.uk/FINAL_PARAGUAY_REPORT.pdf.

Svampa, Maristella. 2015. "Commodities Consensus: Neoextractivism and Enclosure of the Commons in Latin America." *South Atlantic Quarterly* 114 (1): 65–82.

Veltmeyer, Henry. 2016. "Extractive Capital, the State and the Resistance in Latin America." *Sociology and Anthropology* 4 (8): 774–84.

Veltmeyer, Henry, and James Petras, eds. 2014. *The New Extractivism: A Post-Neoliberal Development Model or Imperialism of the Twenty-First Century?* London: Zed Books.

Vuyk, Cecilia. 2014. *Subimperialismo brasileño y dependencia del Paraguay: Los intereses económicos detrás del golpe de estado de 2012*. Asunción, Paraguay: Cultura y Participación.

Zibechi, Raúl. 2012. "Introducción: Paraguay en el tablero geopolítico regional." In *USAID en Paraguay: La asistencia como estrategia de dominación*, edited by C. Coronel, R. Doughman, E. Duré, A. Irala, and M. Palau, 15–21. Asunción, Paraguay: BASE Investigaciones Sociales.

———. 2014. *The New Brazil: Regional Imperialism and the New Democracy*. Edinburgh, Scotland: AK Press.

CHAPTER 5

"AND THEN THE PALM FARMERS CAME"
VIOLENCE AND WOMEN'S RESISTANCE IN THE COLOMBIAN AFRO-PACIFIC REGION

Paula Balduino de Melo

Translated from Spanish by Simon Granovsky-Larsen

In Colombia's southern Pacific region, criminal gangs, guerrillas, para-militaries, and the country's armed forces intervene systematically in Afro-Colombians' ancestral collective territories. The Afro-Pacific population as a whole lives in a state of dramatic suffering, loss, and restrictions. This chapter addresses the forms of violence that have been established within this context, from a position that seeks to share the perspective of Afro-Pacific women. It begins with a historical reflection on the development of organized violence in the municipality of Tumaco, from the 1980s through to today.[1] Capital itself has been the driving force

---

1   This chapter is based on anthropological research carried out in Colombia's southern Pacific region and Ecuador's northern Pacific between 2012 and...

of war in this context, considering the ways in which the United States has been involved in bringing investments to this region of Colombia.

Over the following pages, territoriality will be presented as a central reference point for socio-political conflict, especially when considering the dispute over Afro-Colombians' ancestral collective territories. The chapter also considers organized violence from the perspective of ethnic and racial relations. The narratives of Afro-Pacific women hold within them a possible ethnic-racial reading of the actors involved in this scenario. Race and geography form a binomial: "white" people, or *paisas*, from Colombia's northwest, arrive in Tumaco to sow African palm, illegal crops, and violence; they represent the Afro-Pacific peoples' other.

Finally, the chapter presents Afro-Colombians' female-centred approaches to resisting organized violence. Within this context, women are the anchor of Afro-Pacific resistance. The *matronaje* female leadership system points to a condition of plural existence, a kind of female leadership based in the family and the community. Women resist violence by insisting on maintaining networks of reciprocity, affective and political ties, and intra-ethnic solidarity.

CAPITAL AS WAR FACTORY

In the municipality of Tumaco, situated within the Colombian department of Nariño, socio-political forms of violence are related to the entrance of big capital in the 1990s, whether its arrival came alongside illicit crops, African palm plantations, or shrimp farms. Here, war is rooted in a context of dispute over the ancestral territories of Afro-Colombians, who hold collective land titles along the banks of the rivers of the Pacific region. Organized acts of violence established a systematic process: as soon as collective titles were issued, violent actors connected to the plantations would emerge.

...2014. As such, the research does not systematically address Colombia's post-conflict scenario, which began to take shape in 2016. A brief update is included in the text, however, and this chapter is also complemented by the work of Rosalvina Otálora Cortés (Chapter 6), which considers the post-conflict scenario in light of the expansion of transnational coal extraction and minerals mining in Colombia.

Here, the notion of organized violence is used as suggested by Granovsky-Larsen and Paley in the Introduction to this volume: "violence as organized not only due to the formal structure of armed groups but also organized in its relationship to capitalism." In this case, the acts of violence are directed at the Afro-Pacific people, apparently to dispossess populations from ancestral collective territories in the interests of big capital.

The Pacific region was long referred to as a "peaceful backwater."[2] During the 1980s, this changed along with the arrival of new sociopolitical forms of violence. The incorporation of the region into the war was marked by a neoliberal developmentalist gaze, which conceived of the Pacific as a "promised land," as "geostrategic," and as a key region for national modernization. New forms of violence arrived alongside big capital, materializing in state-based and private economic enterprises that began first in the northern department of Chocó and later in the southern Pacific region covered in this chapter. As Oslender explains, paramilitary groups are associated with this dynamic:

> Paramilitary groups empty the land and prepare it for intervention by capital. This is the logic of the "great neoliberal nightmare": the destruction and cleansing of future intervention zones for capital in its thirst for new spheres of exploitation and appropriation, carried out by state and non-state agents. (2004, 37)

In the late 1990s, the narco-trafficking industry took a turn, disguising itself behind other socio-economic projects, such as mining, agro-industry (especially African palm), and tourism.

Tumaco is a coastal city in the extreme south of the Colombian Pacific, along the Ecuadorian border. The Black or Afro-descendant population makes up 88.8 percent of the city's population, according to the national census of 2005. Illustration 5.1 shows the location of Tumaco, along with the most important surrounding cities and the rivers flowing to Tumaco's coastal inlet, where I carried out my fieldwork.

In Tumaco, the war dates back to the mid-1990s. As in other regions, the beginning of the war is associated with the arrival of *sicario* hit men

---

2   Throughout this chapter, terms that appear within quotation marks are part of the regional vocabulary of Afro-Pacific women.

and other "groups on the fringes of the law," alongside the systematic planting of coca crops. These groups are considered a virus: they invade the Black collective, infect their territories, and cause ruptures in the social fabric of the Afro-Pacific people.

Illustration 5.1: Location of Tumaco, Colombia, and Surrounding Rivers

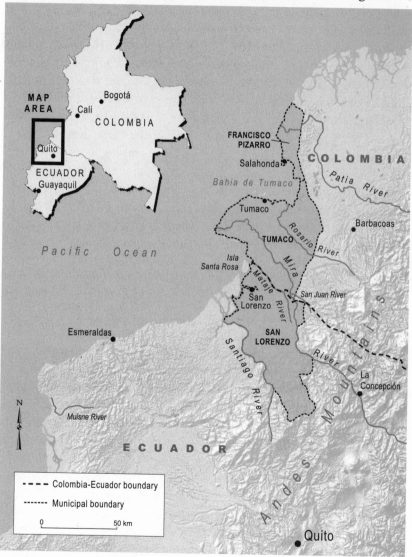

Source: Copyright ©2009 Esri.

The arrival of paramilitaries to the far southern region of Colombia opened the doors to violence and fear. We can glimpse the roots of socio-political violence in their actions. The paramilitary presence changed the behaviour of guerrilla groups in the region, with the two beginning to confront one another militarily towards the end of the 1990s. Jhon Antón Sanchéz (2005) writes that 2002 was a year of constant clashes between the 29th Front of the Fuerzas Armadas Revolucionarias de Colombia (Revolutionary Armed Forces of Colombia—FARC), which controlled the coastal area of Nariño, and the Southern Liberation Block of the paramilitary group Autodefensas Unidas de Colombia (United Self-Defence Forces of Colombia—AUC) (see Chapter 6 for further discussion of paramilitary activity in Colombia). These confrontations made Tumaco the second most dangerous city of the Pacific region after Buenaventura. The AUC formed at the end of the 1990s during a period when the various paramilitary groups were beginning to present themselves as self-defence groups. These same paramilitary groups then organized themselves as a confederated national entity characterized by selective assassinations and massacres, as Álvarez (2013) explains. As a result, the worst hit areas of the war began to spread outwards: to the Chocó department in the north, and to the departments of Cauca and Nariño in the south.

At the national level, the Colombian government began to take controversial measures to combat drug trafficking. These were funded intensively by the United States, one of the main destination countries for Colombian drugs leaving Tumaco and Buenaventura. Plan Colombia was launched in 2000 during the government of Andrés Pastrana and strengthened under the subsequent administration of Álvaro Úribe Velez. The anthropologist and activist Carlos Rosero (2002, 554) defines the plan as "a disputed anti-drugs strategy that, far from eradicating illicit crops, has managed to spread these to other areas, including the departments of Nariño, Cauca, Valle, Chocó, Antioquia, and other parts of the Amazon."

It is necessary to understand the nuances of North American intervention in Colombia in order to understand socio-political violence in the southern Pacific region. One of the branches of American financial support is delivered as humanitarian assistance; it is important to pay attention to the relationships that develop between transnational actors, governments, and Black civil society organizations. International organizations began to arrive in the Pacific region only in the context of anti-narcotics campaigns. A country receiving international cooperation is expected to offer some form of comparable assistance, and, in this case, it was delivered in the form of the first structural support the Colombian state had provided to the historically forgotten Pacific region. The Pacific, we could say, was brought into the Colombian nation through processes linked to the conflict.

The United States Agency for International Development (USAID) deserves special attention within this explanation. Agustín Laó-Montes (2010) explains that USAID works together with the US State Department, a branch of government that adopted neoconservative and imperialist positions over the period of the Clinton and Bush administrations, positions that were maintained by the Obama administration.

Some of the community leaders I spoke with expressed a critical reading of this approach to international cooperation. They say the financial support given by development agencies barely considers the topic of organization, meaning the agencies are not directly involved in strengthening the institutions that represent the Afro-Pacific people. Rather, financing is commonly directed towards productive projects, which are more timely actions. Within the complex scenario of the armed conflict, decisive intervention in economic production would require the decisions and actions of high-ranking officials of the Colombian government, as well as a change in the state's conceptualization of development. Furthermore, the productive projects financed by international cooperation between Colombia and the United States allow for genetically modified seeds produced by large American corporations to enter ancestral Black territories. The seeds arrive alongside other corporate products, all of which points to the deepening of a harmful relationship between Black politics and neoliberalism.

A vicious cycle is thus created, centred around capital and materialized in forms of violence. The United States injects resources to militarize Colombia. The Colombian military provokes war in the countryside, combating guerrillas and inviting the participation of paramilitaries, criminal gangs, and *sicarios*. Black collectives, and especially women, find themselves affected by these dynamics in numerous ways, including through sexual violence, exile, and other forms of violence. Humanitarian aid then arrives, offering assistance to the Afro-Pacific people. Cellular phones and other electronic equipment reach the hands of community leaders through international cooperation projects, and these open access to privileged information about the war, especially information on territorial management.

This dynamic is present across Tumaco. Militarization is heavy there: walking through the streets of Tumaco, one would cross paths with armed soldiers on every street corner. In the first decade of this millennium, the war was taken up within the city. In May 2003, as part of Plan Colombia, a police anti-narcotics base was built near the airport and was used for planes leaving to fumigate coca crops. The base takes up nearly half of the urban area of Tumaco, and has become iconic of the conflict in the surrounding area.

Since the early 2000s, Tumaco has been the municipality with the greatest area dedicated to coca crops in all of Colombia, according to figures published in a report co-written by the United Nations Development Program and the Government of Nariño (2006). The crop was grown on 7,128 hectares in 2006, and every indication was that the amount under production would grow. As the departmental government of Nariño reported in its Bi-National Border Forum in 2012, Nariño produces 26 percent of Colombia's coca crops.

Sanchéz (2005) views the increase in illicit crops as the main driver of the war in Nariño. Armed groups associated with narcotics growing seized territorial and social control over the Afro-Pacific people. This is the origin of displacement, or exile, as we prefer to call it. One of the contemporary expressions of exile is that in which "war and racism intertwine in order to convert determined minorities—segments of the population with distinctive features and non-dominant positions—into majority subjects of horror" (Rosero 2002, 555).

Tumaco experienced various violent episodes during the years of my fieldwork, between 2012 and 2014. In February 2012, ten people were killed and seventy were wounded in an attack on a police patrol in downtown Tumaco. Between October and November 2013, the entire municipality had no electricity for around thirty days, and people believed the FARC were destroying electrical towers throughout the month.

In July 2015, the FARC blew up an oil pipeline, and the spill contaminated the Mira River that provides water for Tumaco's population. The event was considered one of Colombia's worst environmental tragedies in a decade. The people of Tumaco were left without water, and women who make their living from shellfishing could not work and so their families could not eat. Some areas of the Mira River were left lifeless.

Meanwhile, in Havana, Cuba, the official "peace" negotiations between the FARC and the Colombian government were underway. The negotiations took place between 2012 and June 23, 2016, when the two parties signed a "bilateral and definitive ceasefire," including a maximum of 180 days for the FARC to disarm (see Chapter 6). On January 26, 2018, however, a police unit was attacked in San Lorenzo, Esmeraldas, in the far north of Ecuador on the border with Tumaco. According to the *matronas*, the attack was carried out in the style of the FARC. Organized violence is the expression of a complex web, one that cannot easily be dismantled in full. It would seem as though the national peace agreement has not yet been capable of transforming the situation in Tumaco and its surrounding areas.

TERRITORIALITY: THE HEART OF THE CONFLICT

In Colombia's southern Pacific region, socio-political violence takes place within a context of disputes over the ancestral territories of Afro-Colombians, and various groups carry it out. Afro-Pacific women's narratives hold that African palm plantations, shrimp farms, paramilitaries, and guerrillas are all connected. All of these are agents that exploit ancestral territories, and the Afro-Pacific collective believes it is losing power to them.

The war cut directly through the Black territories along the banks of rivers running to the Pacific, which had been recognized through collective titling under Law 70, passed in 1993. Law 70 regulates transitional Article 55 of the Constitution of 1991, which directs Congress to create a law that would recognize the Black communities that have occupied state owned land in rural riverbank areas of the Pacific Basin according to their traditional productive practices, and demarcate their right to collective property in these areas (Constitución Política de Colombia 1991).

The Afro-Colombian people celebrate Law 70 as a victory, as I have seen through my ethnographic research in the southern Pacific region.

Legal recognition of ethnic territories is produced through community councils. According to Law 70, these councils are "the legal entities [that] exercise maximum administrative authority within Black Community Lands" (Article 8, Law 70). These councils are also charged with the management of ethnic territories. The formation of a community council is a prerequisite to receive collective title as a Black ancestral territory.

The process was unravelled by the time war arrived. As one community leader says, "We have had status as a Community Council since 2000, fifteen or sixteen years now. But soon after we won Law 70, just a few years later, [the war] began" (Interview, 2013).

The war put into motion a systematic process: as soon as collective title was received, violent groups would appear, groups that were aligned with large plantations, especially of African palm. This brings back the words of Carlos Rosero (2002, 552) regarding a double movement: one, a logic of recognition and the other a logic of "forced internal displacement."

As I understand it, violence grew throughout the first decade of the 2000s, alongside the pattern of political mobilization of the Afro-Pacific people. And so the war arrived first to those rivers where the struggle for collective territorial title had begun.

I believe there is a dispute between the territorial understandings and experiences lived over time by the Black communities and, more recently, by armed actors. The ties between armed actors, plantation projects, and illicit crops have generated deep changes in ancestral territorial management and pushed the Black collective into exile. Anyone who decides to stay within the territory experiences the consequence of absolute paralysis, whether due to explicit restrictions imposed by armed groups, implicit restrictions, or sheer fear.

I understand that socio-political violence in the region reveals the existence of different periods of time related to the behaviour of armed groups, especially the FARC. There is a polarization between the national and local levels, which points to a regionalization of the FARC.

At the national level, the FARC's command carried on with a discourse based on the campesino struggle and the right to land, which was reflected in the peace negotiations in Havana. However, this discourse is anchored in a conception of the campesino reality that is stripped of its ethnic and racial dimensions. Black ancestral territories did not count among the guerrilla vocabulary, and neither did Indigenous territories. For example, in the Havana negotiations, the FARC's demands related to agrarian reform called for a series of actions to democratize agrarian networks in Colombia. This was a discourse structured around the

"Campesino Reserve Zones." It did not mention Black territories; it was as if they did not exist.

In Tumaco, the discourse around campesino land rights is far removed from the actual dynamics of guerrilla groups. In general, as far as I can tell from the opinion of the Afro-Pacific people, the FARC is just one more armed group fighting over territorial control.

I suggest that armed groups entered Black collective territories without respecting ancestral forms of territoriality. The FARC also entered these territories without recognizing the secular territorial authority the Afro-Colombian people hold over the riverbanks of the southern Pacific region. In her analysis of political systems, Hannah Arendt (2004) distinguishes between violence and power, the essence of which is effective domination. Violence, for Arendt, is characterized by its eminently instrumental quality, while power is an end in and of itself. Authority, in her view, is characterized by its recognition by others, without the use of coercion or persuasion. Nevertheless, power, violence, and authority are dimensions that commonly appear together. Power and violence are frequently found together, but they are inversely proportional. "Domination through the use of pure violence occurs when power is on its way to being lost" (Arendt 2004, 33–34). When violence dominates, power is lost.

In the case of the south Pacific region of Colombia, armed groups ignoring Afro-Pacific authority are left with the use of violence. It is the method of domination that becomes possible. Since violence and power are inversely proportional, as armed groups employ pure violence, the ancestral power of the Black collective along the banks of Pacific rivers loses strength.

THE COLOUR OF VIOLENCE

The narratives of the conflict recounted by Afro-Pacific women offer a possible ethnic-racial reading of the actors involved in violence. The regionalization of race, as Peter Wade (1997) understands it, is a key analytical element for understanding chronic violence: its configuration as organized acts of war and as a network of social relations. Race and geography form a binomial. The region becomes a powerful language of social differentiation. The geography of culture thus frames the racial order and the republican national imagination. In this sense, space or region are metaphors for race and culture at the same time as they constitute a medium for the construction of social relations.

It is necessary to contend with the distinct territorial experiences associated with different ethnic and racial groups. Historically, people living on these riverbanks have combined multiple small- and medium-scale productive activities: fishing, agriculture, mining, silviculture, hunting, and gathering. These activities are all carried out along the rivers, distributed according to a division of communities along the high, medium, and low sections of a river.

As I understand from my ethnography, the low river zone of beaches and mangroves is dedicated to fishing and shellfishing. Medium and high river zones are mainly dedicated to agriculture. That is where *fincas*, or farms, are found: small plots of agricultural land used for subsistence but which can also produce for market sales. Contrasting with the *fincas*, the *monte*, or mountain, refers to a series of plots across various sites, where wood and other products are collected. The *monte* is found within forests. Artisanal mining, or *playada*, is carried out in the high river zone. This map of river production does not depict any of these activities as exclusive to one zone, but it does point to the prevalence of activities in particular areas. There is a simultaneous occurrence of productive activities associated with particular cultural practices, which also form part of a territory. In other words, the Afro-Pacific use of rivers, beaches, and forests together constructs territoriality.

The people that traditionally live on the riverbanks of the Pacific region are Afro-descendant; they are Black, while those who come with African palm, coca, and violence are white, the people commonly referred to as *paisas*. Once again, territoriality is at the heart of the question. The *paisas* brought *sicario* hit men with them to defend their economic interests. In that sense, the war is tied to territorial control. Armed actors connected to institutional actors (both state and private), with their violent practices, are drawn to empty out the Pacific region through the exile of Black people along the riverbanks. It is important to keep in mind that this zone is a strategic area for global commerce, since the rivers and oceans have ample capacity to ship products.

Traditional Black tasks in the city have also shifted under the contemporary war scenario. I have heard many stories from Afro-descendants who had to sell their small businesses due to extortion by armed groups, the so-called vaccine of mandatory payments to both paramilitaries and guerrillas. This extortion is usually directed at urban sellers and business owners, but it also affects rural people. Attacks such as those targeting electrical towers also interfere with small businesses, which cannot survive without electricity. When it becomes difficult to maintain businesses, Afro-descendants sell them to the *paisas*, who arrive in Tumaco with financial power. And so the war has a direct impact on the lives of Black people, whether in the countryside or the city. Contemporary armed groups dominate rural and urban zones, and disarticulate the organizational processes of the Afro-descendent people in their ancestral territories.

As such, I understand violence to be racialized. Whites arrive in Tumaco spreading plantations, illegal crops, and violence. They represent the Other of the Afro-Pacific people. They initiated a war fuelled by a productive logic that runs counter to the multifaceted territorial management traditionally practised along the banks of the Pacific rivers.

THE SENSE OF VIOLENCE AND WOMEN'S RESISTANCE

When I first arrived in Tumaco, I was not tuned in to the complicated scenario of local violence. I travelled in order to carry out anthropological research together with Afro-Pacific women, and especially female leaders from riverside communities. As soon as we connected, they began to share stories with me about the violence they had experienced. Listening to them, the conflict began to materialize in front of me. I had known it was there, but up until that moment I had not seen it, felt it, or noticed it, since I was not familiar with the local rules of violence.

Through my immersion in these stories, I came to understand that the eruption of socio-political violence represented a rupture within the Afro-Pacific social system, a break in the social ties whose construction and maintenance had been carried forward mainly by women. As leaders, I understand these women are involved in interwoven relationships. They are the leaders, the wise women, the shamans, the Elders. Acting as midwives, healers, priests, and folk singers, they shine light on the paths of life. The Afro-Pacific cosmovision is understood and practised through them. Their hands bring people into the world; their words pray and cure sickness from the body, mind, and heart; their songs feed the soul. In other words, it is through them that the cycle of birth-life-death is produced. *Matrona* women make possible an abundance of relations.

The contemporary war scenario established a new social state that has been placed alongside the long-standing values of the riverside world: solidarity. The new social reality restored and disseminated fear and terror. In the final part of this chapter, I attempt to interpret the feelings associated with violence, through the lived experiences of Afro-Pacific women and their lives of staying in or leaving their ancestral territories. I understand territory to be a platform where various planes related to the lives of these women intersect.

As I understand it, women feel that the presence of armed actors blocked territorial management, impeded mobility, and threatened or ended people's lives. For some women, pressure from paramilitaries was so dramatic that the only alternative was to leave the territory. This exit would be accompanied by silence, a silence that was configured as its own law with the war, a path leading to survival that some people would find. They would not talk, since talking makes you vulnerable and can even lead to death. As I heard once along a path, "He who talks is left alone." This is how you learn to not talk. Silence becomes the law. As Álvarez explains (2013, 140), the rules of war are made up of conventions that are hidden by discretion, distrust, and silence.

At the same time, there is a kind of suffering associated with silence. It is something imposed, even something intended to discipline. The women I spoke with long to transform it. Silence is formed through pain. Their stories reveal a desire to subvert the law of silence. Nevertheless, the climate of terror that has been established seems to rob them of that possibility. To share Tzvetan Todorov's (1995) definition, terror is a condition imposed by a context of socio-political violence, through which an erasure of people's autonomy is attempted. Armed actors in the war—whether paramilitaries, *sicarios*, murderers, soldiers, or guerrillas—impose a form of living that causes pain and suffering. They use physical violence, but they also pressure people with the implicit laws of silence, distrust, and fear.

The feeling of belonging to territory leads women to confront threats, especially against their lives, but also to live with those threats and continue living in their ancestral territory. As Álvarez (2013) says, to belong to territory means having a metonymical relationship with it. It is better to live a threatened life within your territory than to leave and stop feeling like a full person. That is the path taken by some women, but it is not the only one, and sometimes it is not even possible.

Those who are able to remain in their ancestral territories live a life of uncertainty. There is the unpredictable possibility of an attack, which can happen while they carry out routine activities like walking to their *fincas*. They can never know when the ordinary could be interrupted, when their lives could be taken from them. On the other hand, despite the constant threats, life's rhythms cannot be stopped. The intense sensation of fear—a paralyzing fear—lives together with the imperative to carry on with life. And so, in this interim condition, people can be surprised by attacks from armed actors.

"Displacement," as the exit from ancestral territory is commonly called, is a fact that has been consolidated. According to Sanchéz (2005, 283), "Colombia, Sudan, and the Congo are the top three countries on the list of those responsible for the displacement of millions of people." According to the United Nations High Commissioner for Refugees, around 7.2 million people have been forced off their land in Colombia, with 10 percent of these being Afro-descendants (Spindler 2017). I understand displacement to be a strategy of resistance, since leaving the rural area does not mean abandoning ancestral cultural practices. In the end, territory is the place where women, men, animals, and life all walk. It is in constant flux, and its existence is only extended by the footsteps of these women.

As I understand it, to leave or to stay within the territory are complementary strategies. The struggle takes place within this double movement. The women who go leave their contributions and their example for those who stay. And, for their part, those who stay carry on the organizational work to honour the legacy left by their *compañeras*.

Political activism also carries with it an ambivalence: while it makes some women even more vulnerable, it also maintains the connection of those women to territory. The war implodes a network of social connection, care, affect, and political activism the women build around themselves. Armed groups co-opt their children, kill their husbands and brothers, and separate their friends from their land. Still, these women find the strength to resist, whether by staying in place or straying from the course of their lives like rivers. *Matrona* female leaders are key to the Afro-Pacific people's resistance. They evoke the spirit of returning the Pacific to a state of "peaceful backwater."

REFERENCES

Álvarez, Silvia M. 2013. *El presente permanente: Por una antropografía de la violencia a partir del caso de Urabá, Colombia.* Bogotá, Colombia: Editorial Universidad del Rosario.

Arendt, Hannah. 2004. *Da violência.* Translated by Maria Claudia Drummond. First published 1969–70. http://www.sabotagem.revolt.org.

Constitución política de Colombia. 1991. http://www.corteconstitucional.gov.co/inicio/Constitucion%20politica%20de%20Colombia.pdf.

Government of Nariño, United Nations Development Program. 2009. "Política pública para la equidad de las mujeres nariñenses desde su diversidad étnica, social y cultural, en un territorio en construcción de paz." http://xn--nario-rta.gov.co/2012-2015/dependencias/files/POLITICA_PUBLICA_DE_GENERO_DE_NARIO.pdf.

Láo-Montes, Agustín. 2010. "Cartografías del campo afrodescendiente en América Latina." In *Debates sobre ciudadanía y políticas raciales en las Américas Negras,* edited by Claudia R. Mosquera, Agostín Láo-Montes, and César R. Garavito, 281–328. Bogotá: Universidad Nacional de Colombia, Facultad de Ciencias Humanas, Centro de Estudios Sociales, Universidad del Valle.

Oslender, Ulrich. 2004. "Geografías de terror y desplazamiento forzado en el Pacífico colombiano: conceptualizando el problema y buscando respuestas." In *Conflicto e (in)visibilidad: Retos en los estudios de la gente negra en Colombia,* edited by Eduardo Restrepo and Axel Rojas, 35–52. Popayán, Colombia: Editorial Universidad del Cauca.

Rosero, Carlos. 2002. "Los afrodescendientes y el conflicto armado en Colombia: la insistencia en lo propio como alternative." In *Afrodescendientes en las Américas: Trayectorias sociales e identitarias (150 años de la abolición de la esclavitud en Colombia),* edited by Claudia R. Mosquera, Mauricio Pardo, and Odile Hoffmann, 547–59. Bogotá: Universidad Nacional de Colombia, ICANHIRD-ILAS.

Sanchéz, Jhon H. A. 2005. "Comunidades negras del Pacífico: conflicto, territorio y región." MA thesis, Universidad Nacional de Colombia.

Spindler, William. 2017. "Forced Displacement Growing in Colombia Despite Peace Agreement." *United Nations High Commissioner for Refugees,* March 10. http://www.unhcr.org/afr/news/briefing/2017/3/58c26e114/forced-displacement-growing-colombia-despite-peace-agreement.html.

Todorov, Tzvetan. 1995. *Em face do extremo.* Campinas, Brazil: Papirus Editora. First published in 1994.

Wade, Peter. 1997. *Gente negra, nación mestiza, dinámicas de las identidades raciales en Colombia.* Bogotá, Colombia: Siglo del Hombre Editores.

CHAPTER 6

COAL AND CONFLICT

TRANSNATIONAL INVESTMENT, VIOLENCE, AND THE EXTRACTION OF MINERAL RESOURCES IN COLOMBIA

Rosalvina Otálora Cortés

Translated from Spanish by Dawn Paley

O ver a year has passed since the ratification by the Congress of the Republic of the final text of the Peace Accords, which came out of negotiations in La Havana (Cuba) between the Colombian government and the FARC (Revolutionary Armed Forces of Colombia) guerrillas. This agreement has as its objective the end of the armed conflict that has brought Colombia to its knees for over sixty years. The first text of the agreement was the object of a plebiscite on October 2, 2016, and Colombian society, which is heavily polarized and divided, voted "no" to the Peace Accords. In addition to low participation in the plebiscite (there was an abstention rate of 63 percent), the no vote won, with 50.21 percent of the votes, against 49.78 percent of the votes for "yes" to peace. This outcome was unexpected in a country that has been bled out by armed conflict for decades. Colombia was even characterized as a country that is gravely ill; only a society that is extremely fragmented could choose to stay at war. The negative result of the plebiscite can be explained by the government's inability to educate the public with respect to the Peace Accords, by a public relations campaign based on the lies of the no side, and by the role that clergy from evangelical and Catholic churches played with regard to sensitive issues like gender and the inclusion of LGBTI people in the first version of the Peace Accords.

Following the no vote in the plebiscite, the national government entered into talks with the no side, which was headed up by former presidents Álvaro Uribe Vélez and Andrés Pastrana (who, in the 1990s, was unable to arrive at an agreement with the FARC through the Caguán process), who represented the Democratic Center political party. This group presented more than five hundred modifications to the Havana texts, which were, according to the government, organized and brought to the negotiating table for revisions. The final agreement came out of this process, it was signed in the Colón Theatre in Bogotá, on November 24, 2016, and was later approved by the Congress of the Republic, the highest body of popular representation. There are many challenges that lay ahead for Colombia in terms of the implementation of the Peace Accords, which include new legislation, some of which has already been published (amnesty, special jurisdiction for peace, modification of the regulations of Congress, etc.), as well as pending legislation on sensitive issues like the problem of land ownership, which is a key structural axis of the conflict. In the midst of election season (during which some candidates promised, for example, to destroy the peace agreement), the implementation of the Peace Accords has met with various setbacks, including the decision of the Constitutional Court to limit the fast-tracking of peace laws by Congress, pessimism on the part of the FARC, and holdups in the disarmament timeline, both in the process of reincorporation of guerrillas into society and in the construction of zones and mechanisms to help make these things happen.

As debate and opposition to the Peace Accords continues, the task we face as Colombians is to think through how to move towards a benign post-agreement phase. In this new phase, the issue of mining is fundamental. The management of mining resources and the role transnational corporations (TNCs) have played in the armed conflict will remain a relevant variable.

This chapter presents the case of coal mining by two of the sector's most important TNCS (Drummond and Cerrejón Zona Norte S.A., a consortium made up of Glencore, BHP Billiton, and Anglo American), cases that give weight to the concept of organized violence as understood through one of its facets: transnational violence. Coal mining in Colombia allows us to observe some of the mechanisms of organized violence used to obtain economic benefits for transnational corporations and local elites. Among these mechanisms are the dynamics of "dispossession in multiple dimensions" (physical dispossession from land and goods, as well as political and social dispossession), the role of armed actors that provide security for TNCS (paramilitarism), corruption, and lobbying connected to regulation (Navarro Trujillo 2012; see also the Introduction to this volume). The continuation of colonial relationships is also evident in the coal sector, with resource extraction based on economic dependence and clientalist relationships, which benefit economic interests and further weaken the Colombian state.

The model of economic development that Colombia consolidated over the past two decades is highly dependent on the export of minerals and hydrocarbons, similar to what has taken place elsewhere in Latin America. The growth of the extractive industries in the region has generated various conflicts involving organized violence and forced changes in national legislation. It has also contributed to abuses in communities where mining projects are developed (no consultation of affected populations, torture, extrajudicial assassination, etc.), which have led to social protest and acts of resistance, sometimes expressed through violence (Fundación para el Debido Proceso 2011).

Mining projects in Latin America are often developed in remote areas where there is minimal state presence and little capacity to guarantee that TNCS respect basic norms regarding human rights. This situation is complicated further in the presence of armed conflict, which, as in Colombia, means public and private security forces are contracted by TNCS to protect corporate installations, or deployed by governments to disperse protests. In addition, the lack of capacity or will on the part of governments to demand that TNCS be accountable for the abuses that result from their activities feeds violence and conflicts in the sector (Fundación para el Debido Proceso 2011).

THE CONCEPT OF TRANSNATIONAL VIOLENCE

Chesnais says that the term *violence*, according to its original meaning, refers to the "abuse of force" (Chesnais 1982, 438). However, there are various conceptualizations of violence, like moral or symbolic violence and economic violence (attacks on property or those that result in losses to the economic system).

Oquist defines *violence* as an instrument with a rational character, as "it is the means used to achieve an end that is potentially feasible and which, in addition, has the potential to attain it," as compared to *irrational violence*, which is "physical aggression or a clear threat of the same which doesn't pursue a goal, rather, violence itself is the goal" (1978, 37).

Catherine LeGrand posits that the United Fruit Company in Colombia was able to erect a state within the state in which laws were imposed (through violence) by the US corporation, while peasants who worked for the company did so in inhuman conditions (LeGrand 1989). These kinds of violence by a TNC, as a means for further profit, is what we are referring to. In the context of armed conflict, this all becomes more complex, because TNCS can be implicated in rights violations and/or have relations with armed actors through a host of different mechanisms (extortions by groups, financing those groups, and so on). Transnational violence can thus be understood as one of the possible facets of the concept of organized violence advanced in this book. The transnational form of organized violence, which is deployed by TNCS taking advantage of their economic power in the face of a weak state and a nascent civil society, is presented as though its objective were the security of all, when, in reality, it benefits the interests of certain economic and political actors, including TNCS and local elites (see also the Introduction to this volume).

There is no doubt that transnational violence is linked to other forms of social violence and activities and illicit networks that operate across borders. Globalization creates a world market without borders that subordinates the role of the state to powerful economic interests. In this scenario, the TNC becomes one node of power that transforms life for local people. In addition, TNCS have been accused of using violence in territories where they extract resources, promoting and financing conflicts and generating state corruption at the local and national level that helps in the maintenance of authoritarian regimes, among other things (see OMAL 2016).

There are numerous well-documented cases of abuses by TNCS. Kamminga (1999) classifies these abuses based on the participation of the state, categorizing them based on whether they are committed with the concomitance of the state of origin, such as in the case of the participation of the United Fruit Company in the coup d'état in Guatemala in 1954, or the participation of ITT in the overthrow of Salvador Allende's government in Chile in 1973 (see Martín-Ortega 2008, 67). Within this category, corporations in the mining sector are regularly accused of practices including forced work, displacement, and disappearance (especially of union members and social leaders), extrajudicial executions, torture, and so forth. The location of these companies depends on the location of the primary materials or natural resources that are found in areas where the internal conflict is active. Here, we see a "mutual dependence" between multinational corporations and host states, as well as the armed groups that control the conflict zones (Martín-Ortega 2008, 67).

One of the most complicated aspects of this scenario is the contracting of security and surveillance services by TNCS. Groups that carry out these services are often constituted by security forces (army or police; there have even been military bases detected in areas of mining exploitation). At times, the TNCS contract private companies, rebel militias, or paramilitary groups to keep control of their area of interest. Colombia provides us with clear examples of these practices. TNCS like Chiquita Brands[1] and Drummond are involved in legal processes after having

---

[1] Nearly a century has passed since the massacre at Ciénaga, Magdalena (December 1928), in which the transnational banana corporation United Fruit Company was implicated. Much more recently, this same corporation, now called Chiquita Brands, along with its subsidiary Banadex and its marketing company Banacol, were implicated in arms trafficking when they carried out payments to the AUC paramilitaries in Urabá Antioqueño between 1997 and 2004. In 2007, Chiquita was fined $25 million by a US court, an amount that does not line up either with the corporation's means or the number of victims. Strangely, the Colombian public prosecutor's office closed its own case on the same crime in 2012. The power of this corporation, which in the past acted as a "state within a state," according to LeGrand (1989), continues to be immense. The violence carried out in Urabá at the end of the twentieth century was stoked by the investments of this banana company, and by weapons that its banana export boats brought into the country. Together, these crimes produced thousands of victims in the region.

been accused of paying the paramilitary group, Autodefensas Unidas de Colombia (United Self-Defence Forces of Colombia—AUC), to carry out security functions in the areas they are exploiting (Francisco Ramírez Cuellar, interview, 2016). These situations have led to grave violations of human rights, including the disappearance and murder of union leaders, all to guarantee the security of foreign investment in Colombia.

THE ARMED CONFLICT IN COLOMBIA AND THIRD PARTY OPPORTUNISM

The causes of the armed conflict in Colombia are many, and there is great divergence in the focus of scholars on this subject. Among the root causes of the conflict are land tenure, institutional weakness, income inequality, and the tendency to use ballots and bullets simultaneously, as well as the precarious and sometimes absence of a state presence in some areas. The notion of an "armed conflict" has been used to talk about confrontations from the 1940s until today. These are often closely related to social conflict, especially in rural areas with regard to political violence (Pizarro 2015; Gutiérrez Sanín 2007; Wills 2015). The most recent moment of the armed conflict in Colombia is characterized by the presence of paramilitary groups with financial resources that—as never before—flow from drug trafficking, kidnapping, and extortion. Paramilitary groups have their origins in the self-defence groups that formed in the 1960s to oppose the extortion activities of the guerrillas.

By the mid-1980s, these self-defence groups had transformed into paramilitaries, and they were strengthened through state policies (including security cooperatives known as Surveillance and Private Security Agrarian Self-Defence Cooperatives, or CONVIVIR) that allowed civilians to usurp the monopoly over force and violence. The paramilitary phenomenon led the country into a period of brutal violence from the mid-1990s onwards (Romero 2003). "Colombia transitioned from a confrontation between insurgent movements and the state counterinsurgency apparatus towards a much more complex conflict in which paramilitary groups and 'opportunistic third parties' emerged, introducing a new dynamic into politics" (Pizarro 2015, 49). The paramilitaries that did not demobilize are today members of the so-called criminal bands (known in Colombia as BACRIM).

Pécaut (2015, 11) calls criminal organizations or political agents that participated in the conflict for personal benefit "opportunistic third parties." There are national and multinational corporations in this category. They aligned with paramilitary fronts in order to generate the displacement of the population, taking lands illegally or purchasing them for well under their market value (Fajardo 2015). In some cases, TNCS linked with paramilitary groups because these groups provided security against guerrilla extortions, or because the violent actions of paramilitaries (displacements, massacres, threats, etc.) were beneficial to business (Otálora 2006).

THE NEW DYNAMIC OF MINING IN COLOMBIA

The mining sector in Colombia was restructured at the end of the 1990s, and its legal framework is enshrined in the Mining Code (Law 685 of 2001, modified by Law 1382 of 2010), which provides incentives for mining exploitation by TNCS. The development plan, "Prosperity for All" (Law 1450 of 2011), which was introduced at the beginning of President Juan Manuel Santos's first term, established the mining energy sector as one of the five key sectors the federal government would rely on as a pillar to consolidate growth and employment.[2] With the changes carried out under these guidelines, the role of the state and its interaction with the private sector was redefined, limiting the government role to that of regulator and tax collector. At the same time, foreign investors in Colombia achieved important guarantees regarding legal certainty and financial protection. In addition, administrative reforms were introduced to dismantle "state entrepreneurship" and reduce government investments in the mining sector. The economic importance and dynamism of mining has been recognized, but there is also a consensus around the weakness of the Colombian state in terms of controlling the

---

2   The other four pillars mentioned in the "Prosperity for All" development plan, released by the Santos Government, are: infrastructure (construction of energy infrastructure and road networks facilitating the movement of goods); housing (emphasizing dignified housing and employment for the poorest Colombians); agriculture (stimulating agriculture for internal and foreign markets); and innovation (science and technology in the service of development) (Departamento Nacional de Planeación 2010).

derivative impacts of the mining industry (Garay Salamanca 2013). The relative microeconomic stability of the country is well established, even though Colombian institutions are fragile and corrupt.

The new dynamism in the mining sector has had three considerable impacts on Colombia's economy: first, exports were increasingly concentrated until three sectors (oil, coal, and coffee) made up the majority of exports, leading to the negative effects of an influx of money without proper planning; second, the country became an important area for foreign investment, with a focus on the exploration for and exploitation of minerals and hydrocarbons, to the detriment of development of industrial processes and financial modernization; and third, unemployment remains high, as mining does not contribute to a solution to this key macroeconomic problem (Bonilla 2011). Today, the commodity boom is coming to an end. Colombia has cost overruns in mining and energy exploration and exploitation, and consultation processes along with difficulties in acquiring environmental permits have made the country less attractive for foreign capital ("Sectores bajan giros" 2014).

THE CASE OF TRANSNATIONAL COAL EXTRACTION

The extraction of coal in Colombia began in the second half of the nineteenth century, as local deposits were located to supply the internal market. Key efforts were made in the exploitation of Cerrejón and the Isaacs concession, as well as the concession of the Pan American Investment Company (Otálora 2016).

Since the 1990s, coal has become Colombia's second most important export after oil. Today, coal extraction is carried out by the private sector, and 92.2 percent of this extraction takes place in the departments of Cesar (53.41 percent) and Guajira (38.79 percent), where the Drummond Ltd. and Cerrejón mines operate (Ministerio de Minas y Energía 2015). Colombia is the country in Latin America with the greatest reserves of bituminous coal, which is the highest-quality coal (calorific power, low humidity, ash, and sulfur) and is the most competitive.

Drummond Ltd. and Cerrejón are the two most important coal projects in the country, and they have profoundly transformed the environmental and institutional spaces where they operate. Interviews regarding the consequences of coal extraction reveal contradictory opinions, which range from deep concern for health and environmental impacts, as well as the links with conflict in the region, to those that affirm the positive aspects that transnational investment brings for development in Colombia (Otálora 2016). One union leader, for example, affirms, "The main impacts of multinationals are social impacts, impacts on human rights, on the environment and on culture, basically. Socially these companies are the main causes of poverty, of deepening the social divides; through violence and fraud they have provoked change in national legislation which favours these companies to the detriment of the social development of the country, and basically of the communities in which they develop their project" (Francisco Ramírez Cuellar, interview, 2016). In contrast, the interviews with white-collar Cerrejón workers revealed an emphasis on the positive impacts of transnational investment in the department of La Guajira (La Mina Cerrejón employees, interviews, 2012).

DRUMMOND AND VIOLENCE IN CESAR DEPARTMENT

Drummond Limited is a family-owned company with its head office in the United States. In 2013, the Japanese firm Itochu Corporation acquired 20 percent of the company's shares. Drummond's operations are located in Cesar department, which over the last many years has lived through the complex, intertwined dynamics of violence and mineral wealth. In 1995, the mine began extracting and producing coal, and since then Drummond has become increasingly important for the regional and national economy. Later, the company began a process of expanding its mining operations and its rail and seaports. In 2009, the company started exploitation at its second mine, El Descanso, and today it counts nearly two billion tons of coal reserves spread between La Loma, El Descanso, Rincón Hondo, Similoa, and Cerrolargo, the last three of which are currently in an environmental permitting process (Drummond Ltd. 2016). In addition, the company has gotten involved in exploration and development of methane gas in partnership with Ecopetrol (Colombia's state oil company).

In 2013, Drummond created more than 4,600 direct jobs in Colombia, paying over US$250 million in salaries and benefits. It also provides employment to more than eight thousand direct contractors and over twenty thousand indirect contractors. In addition to the annual payments of $180 million in royalties, the company has promised to pay an asset tax of $95.5 million over the next four years (Revista Dinero 2013).

The armed conflict and social conflict around the coal mine's activities have affected the population and impeded the strengthening of state institutions. Just by observing the social indices of poverty and access to basic services like water, health, and education, it is possible to affirm that though there are major profits being made in the region, this is not reflected in the quality of life of local residents (Observatorio del Caribe Colombiano 2015).

Sintramienergética, which is the mine workers' union, is represented by a group of US lawyers led by Terry Collingwood, who sued the company and its board of directors in the United States (in an Alabama court, as that is where Drummond is based). The company was accused of collaborating with paramilitaries that killed three union leaders at Drummond (Valmore Locarno, Víctor Hugo Orcasita, and Gustavo Soler) in March of 2001. During the second stage of proceedings, the judge ruled there was no proof the directors of Drummond in Colombia or in the United States were complicit in these crimes (Verdad Abierta 2012). Lawyers for the victims are evaluating the possibility of starting new cases linked to the displacements and homicides that have taken place as a result of the construction of the rail line that carries the coal from the mine to the port and has also caused illnesses (H.B. lawyers representing victims, interviews, 2015).

But these are not the only links with paramilitaries that Drummond is accused of. There is a third complaint related to the TNC's creation and financing of the Juan Andrés Álvarez paramilitary bloc to protect their mining operations from guerrilla incursions.[3] This paramilitary bloc was responsible for the killings of various Colombians. The legal complaint also asks that the mining company pay for its assumed complicity in the forced displacement and murder of peasants in Mechoacán, where the company bought lands. These legal cases are currently underway (Verdad Abierta 2012).

---

3   The Juan Andrés Álvarez paramilitary bloc emerged in 1996, financed by political and business leaders as a response to kidnappings and extortions by the FARC and ELN (National Liberation Army) guerrillas. It is derived from the ACCU (Córdoba and Urabá Self-Defence Groups) and carried out violent activity in the departments of Cesar and Magdalena, being foremost among those responsible for violence in this area. The Juan Andrés Álvarez bloc demobilized in 2006 in Chimila, together with the Northern Bloc.

Drummond Limited has defended itself in various instances through press releases and open letters against what it considers "propagandistic tracts" that muddy the good name of the company (Drummond Ltd. 2014). In an open letter directed at the readers of the report *The Dark Side of Coal*, published by Pax Christi, Drummond wrote, "Independent of the intentions behind the publication of this report, none of them is, as the report claims, to 'reveal the truth.' Rather the truth is as follows: Drummond has never paid or supported in any other way any illegal group in Colombia, be it guerrilla or paramilitary...Each of these cases that has gone before a tribunal has ended with a ruling in favor of Drummond" (Drummond Ltd. 2014, 13).

Drummond also shared testimonies that negate financing or relations between the company's directors and the self-defence groups of the Northern Bloc. The company affirms that Drummond has defended itself from false claims of collusion with paramilitaries since 2002, and states that it has been exonerated from all such charges in every case that was concluded (Drummond Ltd. 2014).

Drummond continues to deny its responsibility in the killings of unionists, and court cases in the United States have exonerated the company. In terms of ongoing cases against the TNCs in the US courts, we can affirm that the relation between companies and violence is not yet clearly defined judicially but that TNCs have access to political mechanisms like lobbying and otherwise that can allow them to obtain favourable decisions.

CERREJÓN AND VIOLENCE IN LA GUAJIRA

In 1995, Cerrejón celebrated one decade of operations and the accumulated extraction of one hundred million tons of coal in the Cerrejón North Zone. At the end of the 1990s, a new association contract was signed that allows twenty-five more years of extraction. This is a new step in the privatization of Cerrejón, in which Carbocol (the state coal company) sold its share in the project. In 2010, the mining project began to expand, and Cerrejón exported 444.9 million tons of coal and was one of the largest and most profitable corporations in Colombia (Gualdrón 2010).

In order to increase production, Cerrejón began rerouting the Ranchería River so as to be able to access the five hundred million tons of coal under the river's path. This project has faced resistance from many social sectors due to the environmental, social, and cultural impacts of diverting the river in La Guajira and among the Wayuu Indigenous people. The Ranchería River is one of the only rivers that flows in La Guajira, which is otherwise mainly desert. The project was suspended when coal prices reached historic lows. Bruno Stream, a key waterway of the Ranchería River, was also under threat of diversion to allow annual coal production, estimated at thirty-five million tons. The National Authority for Mining Licences granted permission for the river rerouting (Mejía 2015).

The report, *Digging Deeper: The Human Rights Impact of Coal in the Global South*, published in November of 2015, detailed the negative impact of coal mining on human rights. Over the past fifteen years, the expansion of El Cerrejón has displaced communities that had traditionally occupied territories near the mine. Two of the most important such cases are those of the municipalities of El Tabaco and Tamaquito.

The municipality of El Tabaco "was a hamlet founded by enslaved Cimarrones who, in 2001, had been removed through the order of a judge from the Municipality of Barrancas, who decided that the hamlet (population 1,100) could be expropriated. In 2002, the Supreme Court of Justice ordered the resettlement of the community in the municipality of Hatonuevo. Regardless, this has not been carried out" (Dejusticia and Business & Human Rights Resource Centre 2015).

Another community impacted by Cerrejón is Tamaquito, where people have not been displaced from their homes but have witnessed the mine growing around them, as the company buys lands, "leaving them without access to schools and health services, since according to community members the El Cerrejón security guards do not allow them to cross the lands belonging to El Cerrejón" (Dejusticia and Business & Human Rights Resource Centre 2015). The residents of Tamaquito were resettled at the end of 2013 in a hamlet called Tamaquito II, but they told members of the nongovernmental organization Dejusticia "the conditions of life are much worse in the new town" (Dejusticia and Business & Human Rights Resource Centre 2015).

According to Dejusticia, "Cerrejón...was given a deadline by the state to relocate the settlements of El Hatillo, Plan Bonito and El Boquerón... These communities are currently negotiating the conditions of their relocation, joining communities like Chancleta and Roche, which have already been relocated. For some activists, including those who are writing this report, this list of relocations constitutes a case of forced displacement" (Dejusticia and Business & Human Rights Resource Centre 2015, 13).

Lina Echeverri, the vice-president of public affairs for Cerrejón, told the *El Espectador* newspaper that the company decided to remove the communities because residents did not honour the agreements signed with El Cerrejón. Instead, residents refused to accept the farms the company gave them; rather, they opened a new round of negotiations and came with new demands the company could not fulfil (Noguera Montoya 2016).

Generally, the key issue for the communities in the struggle has been land, and, as peasants who produce food for their own sustenance, they are determined to survive. They cannot do so with one hectare of land per family, to be purchased for less than $2,000, which is what the company has offered, even though "it is impossible to find land with water in La Guajira for that price" (Noguera Montoya 2016).

In fact, the Constitutional Court has documented jurisprudence in cases where mining and criminal activities linked to narcotics have demonstrated functional relations. Among them, for example, is the following case: "In 2004 the massacre of 16 women leaders fighting megaprojects in La Guajira was recorded…It must be stated that in this respect there is a perception among Wayuu authorities that there is a link between mining megaprojects promoted by the state and paramilitary violence, especially in Bahía Portete…[with the] purpose…of taking over lands through terror and extermination" (Garay Salamanca 2013, 61).

The massacre at Bahía Portete, which took place in Alta Guajira in April of 2004, and the events prior to the massacre documented by the Group of Historical Memory of the CNRR (National Commission for Reparation and Reconciliation), show a relation between the massacre and the management of the Port of Bahía Portete, which was used by ships with important cargo, including contraband, drugs, and minerals (Grupo de Memoria Histórica 2010, 137). It is clear in this and other cases that paramilitary violence plays a particular role and is articulated to the economic interests of coal extraction.

THE LEGAL RESPONSIBILITY OF TNCs AND THEIR ROLE IN THE CONTEXT OF THE PEACE ACCORDS

In 2012, the United Nations Forum on Business and Human Rights took place in Geneva. The UN's High Commissioner for Human Rights, Navi

Pillay, stated that multinational corporations are actors that are just as important as states, if not more so, in a globalized world where money rules. For the same reason, she said, corporations are required to comply with laws: "the entire world is obligated to obey laws, including transnational corporations," said Pillay (UNHCR 2012).

Different initiatives like the Ruggie Framework,[4] or the use of national legislation like the Alien Tort Claim Act, can serve as a basis upon which to make legal claims to force corporations to answer for the crimes they are accused of having committed. The issue of the legal responsibility of corporations under international law is a topic that remains open. There have been steps taken forward and backward as this discussion carries on in various parts of the world. In addition, the implementation of human rights standards in the extractive sector presents great difficulties: there are powerful political forces with strong interests in maintaining the status quo. The power of TNCs to lobby for specific regulations is one part of this.

The issue of international human rights standards has generally gone in the direction of demanding responsibility from TNCs and corporations in the mining and extractive sector. As the Peace Accords are implemented in Colombia in the midst of diminishing hostilities on the ground, transnational mining companies could play a key role. In the last International Mining Exposition, which is held each year in Medellín, it was evident the mining sector could be important in the new economic and political life of the country, from the point of view not only of production but also as related to the problems that could arise if criminal activities related to illegal mining are not brought under control (Rueda 2016).

Massé (2016, 1) suggests that in an international scenario in which there are more rigorous standards with regard to the origin of the goods, products, and services that are exported by buyers and organizations like the OECD (Organisation for Economic Co-operation and Development),

---

4   The Ruggie Framework is based on three fundamental principles. First, it establishes the duty of the state to protect individuals from abuses committed by non-state actors. Second, it establishes that companies have the responsibility to respect human rights. The third principle is that adequate legal mechanisms should exist in the case of conflicts with regard to the impacts of corporations on fundamental rights (United Nations 2011, paras. 26, 82).

within which Bogotá is seeking a permanent seat, Colombian authorities maintain hope that the end of the armed conflict "will allow the advancement, healing and stimulation of the sector to put the train of mining and energy development back on track." Massé (2016) also suggests that TNCS are used to working in hostile territories and that the situation today is not as attractive for their operations. If we add to this the demands of international human rights standards like the Ruggie Framework, the OECD norms, and low mineral prices, there is a possibility international investment in this sector will decrease.

The reality is that the mining-as-locomotive economic vision has not been realized: production has fallen 10 percent and mining projects have become sites of financial loss and falling profits (Sarmiento 2016). The Colombian locomotive is in a process of deterioration and deceleration, heightened by the uncertainty generated by the political situation and the strong opposition of one segment of the Colombian Right to the Peace Accords.

The natural environment is another important element to think through in the post-accords period. It is clear the Colombian armed conflict has caused environmental harms, including the planting of land mines, occupations like that of the Gorgona Islands, impacts on the highlands like Sumapaz, the cutting of first-growth forests, and more (Silva Herrera 2016).

In addition, there are remote locations that have remained well preserved due to the armed conflict. Hochschild, the resident coordinator of the UN in Colombia, says violence has allowed for the preservation of environmental stability in some biologically rich and exuberant sites (Hochschild 2016). Julia Miranda, the director of Colombia's national parks, says the conflict has not necessarily functioned as a form of protecting biodiversity. She explains that parks like La Macarena (Meta), Nukak (Guaviare), Las Hermosas (Valle-Tolima), Puinawai (Guanía), and Los Churumbelos (Caquetá-Cauca-Huila) have been gutted by transnational mining, illegal mining, illegal crops, deforestation, and illegal traffic, while others have been sown with land mines (Silva Herrera 2016).

Finally, countries like Guatemala, the Democratic Republic of Congo, and Angola experienced the degradation of their environmental heritage in the post-conflict period. Keeping this in mind is relevant in terms of avoiding greater damage than has already been caused by the current model of mining in Colombia. It is of concern that the areas that have been determined priority locations for the implementation of the construction of peace are among the most biologically diverse regions on Earth (Orinoquia, Amazonia, and Chocó).

In 2016, Colombia's Constitutional Court made a series of crucial decisions regarding mining that were aimed at protecting the right of communities to decide what happens on their lands, and to have a healthy environment.[5] There remains a pending decision regarding the possible reversal of the protection of the high mountain tundra (*páramo*) of Santurbán, which has become one of the key symbols of ongoing conflicts between mining and environmental interests.[6] Boundary setting for the high mountain tundra of Santurbán is important for various reasons: this is a region where TNCs have interests in the extraction of oil and gold (there are twenty-eight mining concessions granted in the region), and traditional mining companies have extracted resources there for decades. Once the boundaries were set, many corporations sought titles, as it appeared there was sufficient legal certainty. If this situation shifts, it could negatively impact investment in the country. It also remains to be seen what economic alternatives the government can offer to the four thousand families that live inside the zone denominated as high mountain tundra.

5   The last legal rulings on this issue can be summarized as follows: The court decided that before granting a mining title, the state has the obligation to "establish a procedure that assures citizen participation, without prejudice towards different ethnic groups" (Silla Vacía 2016). The state is not only required to carry out consultation with Indigenous and African descendant communities but also with peasant and other communities that could be impacted by resource extraction. In February 2016, the court declared six articles of the mining policy contained in the National Development Plan of the current government to be contradictory to the Constitution. The argument in this decision was that the National Development Plan violated municipal autonomy regarding the use of land and territorial zoning laws. It is now clearly up to mayors and municipal councils to decide how land is used. In addition, the court prohibited mining in high mountain highlands, with serious implications for agrarian communities.

6   More than forty environmental organizations have demanded clear boundaries with regard to the designation of mountain highlands as set out by the minister of the environment, arguing the ministry violated the right of participation of citizens and that the current definition puts the right to water for 2.5 million people in Santander y Norte de Santander at risk.

Finally, the signing of the Peace Accords does not mean the Colombian conflict will end. The opposition from one segment of the Right, which has refused to recognize the agreement signed in the Colón Theatre in Bogotá, has created a climate of uncertainty and reinforced the radicalization of the Right and a rearrangement of paramilitarism in the countryside. In 2016, more than seventy social and peasant leaders (many of whom supported the Peace Accords and most of whom belonged to the Marcha Patriótica political movement) were assassinated in different parts of the country, five of them following the plebiscite, between October and December of 2016 (Fundación Nuevo Arco Iris 2016). In the first five months of 2017, thirty-two social leaders and human rights defenders were killed. "These crimes sounded the alarm bell in the international community and have brought a huge challenge forward for the state: to protect not only these people but also the guerrillas transitioning towards laying down their weapons as well as their families" ("Líderes sociales" 2017). If the government does not take the steps required of it to face this new wave of violence, it is possible we will see a repeat of what happened with the Unión Patriótica (Patriotic Union—UP), when its members (demobilized FARC leaders) were exterminated.[7] Unfortunately, the Colombian government has already showed its inability to protect the social forces that are in favour of peace.

The new text of the Peace Accords includes more than sixty changes and clarifications regarding reparations for victims using resources illegally obtained by guerrillas, the exclusion of foreign magistrates from participating in the Special Justice for Peace process, the explicit recognition of private property, reduced financing for the FARC's political party, and other adjustments sought by the no side. These changes were not enough for the Democratic Center party and the elites it represents, which continue to oppose the Accords in Congress. For its part, the FARC is taking advantage of this moment to present its political positions and to push forward on its quest to participate in politics via the ballot box, or so it appears from its recent interviews in the media. These same

---

7   The UP was formed in 1986 following peace agreements between the FARC and the government of Belisario Betancur. More than three thousand people were assassinated in the period following the agreement, including two presidential candidates, hundreds of local and regional leaders, and many UP members.

media have participated in nefarious ways in this process, deepening the polarization of Colombian society.

All of the above is taking place in a complex international context that has seen Donald Trump elected president of the United States. Trump's position on the Colombian Peace Accords is unclear. There was a meeting between Trump and President Santos in May of 2017, in which Trump lauded the Peace Accords with the FARC; however, US assistance in the post-conflict period will be concentrated on security and comes in at $28 million less than projected, which could lead to a re-narcoticization of relations due to an increase in coca production in Colombia and the fact that this is no longer a priority for the United States ("Esta es la carta que le envió Donald Trump" 2017). People close to Trump have shown concern because "Colombians could lose their homeland to terrorism and drug trafficking," and have taken public positions on the Right, close to the position of former President Álvaro Uribe Vélez ("Sectores bajan giros" 2014). In fact, the style of government that tends to advocate for free markets tends to cozy up to dictatorships and is at ease with the use of force. In this way, Trump is actually closer to the positions put forward by the Colombian Right.

Then there is assistance from the international community. Keeping in mind the difficulty of the situation that has led to the killings of many social leaders, the European Union has announced the disbursement of 2.3 million euros for the protection of human rights defenders towards strengthening the presence of the Office of the United Nations High Commissioner for Human Rights in key regions where the FARC is demobilizing, creating a specialized unit in the Attorney General's Office that will investigate conflict-related crimes, as well as promoting rural development and the economic reintegration of former FARC members and child soldiers ("Líderes sociales" 2017).

In a context as complex as Colombia today, corporations, and specifically TNCs, will have the chance to act more freely with regard to human rights. One would expect that the oversight and demands on these issues would decrease, and that advances relating to the Ruggie Framework of Social Corporate Responsibility would be reduced (Ostau De Lafont and Otálora 2018). This will likely lead to a weakening of human rights norms. The mining sector will remain important, but the fact that Trump is looking inwards and wants to move towards relying primarily on domestic supply for fuel will diminish the importance of its most faithful ally in Latin America, Colombia, which is an important exporter of oil. This could also lead to demands that the extraction of minerals be carried out in better conditions than those at TNCs today.

Corporations are another topic that has swirled around President Santos and the peace process. Corporate support for peace could be diminished in the future if paramilitary reactivation is not prevented. A good part of the corporate sector supported the yes vote, and those who supported the yes, in a country like Colombia—where McCarthyism is still alive and well—supported the FARC and could easily become targets of paramilitarism, which is currently on the rise. This could also lead to increased extortion attempts by paramilitaries.

What we can say for certain is that, following the Peace Accords and their adoption, there will still be many issues left to resolve: this post-agreement period includes complex issues, including the role of other armed groups like the ELN, which is also negotiating a peace agreement. There is no doubt the right wing and those who oppose the implementation of the Peace Accords will also play a role in determining how corporations will behave. The level to which TNCs observe international human rights agreements, and the capacity of the state to oblige compliance by TNCs and control the selective killings that are happening today—killings that especially target social leaders who supported the yes vote for peace—will greatly influence whether or not the next generation inherits a Colombia in peace.

REFERENCES

Bonilla, R. 2011. "Apertura y reprimarización de la economía colombiana: Un paraíso de corto plazo." *Nueva Sociedad* 23 (January–February): 46–65.

Chesnais, J. C. 1982. *Histoire de la violence*. Paris: 438.

Dejusticia and Business & Human Rights Resource Centre. 2015. *Digging Deeper: The Human Rights Impacts of Coal in the Global South*. https://www.business-humanrights.org/en/digging-deeper-the-human-rights-impacts-of-coal-in-the-global-south.

Departamento Nacional de Planeación. 2010. *Plan nacional de desarrollo "Plan Prosperidad para todos 2010–2014."* https://colaboracion.dnp.gov.co/CDT/Normatividad/ley14501606062011.pdf.

Drummond Ltd. 2014. "Carta abierta dirigida a todos los lectores del informe The Dark Side of Coal: Paramilitary Violence in the Mining Region of Cesar,

Colombia." https://studylib.es/doc/5498743/carta-de-pax-sobre-el-informe-de-el-lado-oscuro.

———. 2016. "¿Quiénes somos?" http://www.drummondltd.com/quienes-somos/drummond-en-colombia/Drummond.

"Esta es la carta que le envió Donald Trump al Presidente Santos." 2017. *El Heraldo*, October 27. https://www.elheraldo.co/colombia/esta-es-la-carta-que-le-envio-donald-trump-al-presidente-santos-416171.

Fajardo, D. 2015. "Estudio sobre los orígenes del conflicto social armado, razones de su persistencia y sus efectos más profundos en la sociedad colombiana." In *Contribución al Entendimiento del Conflicto Armado en Colombia*, 1–55. Bogotá, Colombia: Comisión Histórica del conflicto y sus víctimas. https://www.verdadabierta.com/.../1180-contribucion-al-entendimiento-del-conflicto-y-sus-victimas.

Fundación Nuevo Arco Iris. 2016. *Informe especial, second term*. Report presented by Noticias Uno. http://noticiasunolaredindependiente.com/2016/12/18/noticias/informe-lideres-asesinados.

Fundación para el Debido Proceso. 2011. "Empresas y derechos humanos: Una relación compleja." *Aportes DPLF*, September 15. http://www.dplf.org/sites/default/files/1317248743_1.pdf.

Garay Salamanca, L. J., ed. 2013. *Minería en Colombia: Fundamentos para superar el modelo extractivista*. Bogotá, Colombia: Contraloría General de la República.

Grupo de Memoria Histórica de la Comisión Nacional de Reparación y Reconciliación. 2010. "La masacre de Bahía Portete: Mujeres Wayuu en la mira." Bogotá, Colombia: CNRR.

Gualdrón, R. 2010. *Cerrejón: Hacia la rehabilitación de tierras intervenidas por minería a cielo abierto*. Bogotá, Colombia: Panamericana Formas E impresos.

Gutiérrez Sanín, F. 2007. ¿Lo que el viento se llevó? Los partidos políticos y la democracia en Colombia, 1958–2002. Bogotá, Colombia: Editorial Norma.

Hochschild, F. 2016. *Consideraciones Ambientales para la Construcción de una Paz Territorial Estable, Duradera y Sostenible en Colombia*. Bogotá, Colombia: United Nations Development Program and the Ministry of the Environment.

Kamminga, M. T. 1999. "Holding Multinational Corporations Accountable for Human Rights Abuses: A Challenge for the EC." In *The EU and Human Rights*, edited by Philip Alston, 558–65. Oxford: Oxford University Press.

LeGrand, Catherine. 1989. "El conflicto de las bananeras." In *Nueva Historia de Colombia*, volume 3, edited by Alvaro Tirado Mejía, 183–217. Bogotá, Colombia: Planeta.

"Líderes sociales deben tener máximo nivel de protección." 2017. *El Espectador*, May 28. https://colombia2020.elespectador.com/politica/lideres-sociales-deben-tener-maximo-nivel-de-proteccion-eamon-gilmore.

Martín-Ortega, Olga. 2008. *Empresas multinacionales y derechos humanos en el derecho internacional*. Barcelona, Spain: Bosch.

Massé, F. 2016. "¿Es posible de una minería del oro libre de conflicto en Colombia?" Presentation at the third meeting of Mining, Territory and Post-Accords, May 26. https://www.academia.edu/22753281/Miner%C3%ADa_y_post_conflicto_es_posible_una_miner%C3%ADa_de_oro_libre_de_conflicto_en_Colombia.

Mejía, Eliana. 2015. "Polémica en la Guajira por desvío de un arroyo. La Autoridad Nacional de Licencias Ambientales, ANLA, habría dado permiso para la obra." *El Tiempo.* https://www.eltiempo.com/archivo/documento/CMS-15207895.

Ministerio de Minas y Energía. 2015. "Boletines análisis minero." https://www.minminas.gov.co/boletines?idBoletin=238.

Navarro Trujillo, Mina Lorena. 2012. "Las luchas socioambientales en México como una expresión del antagonismo entre lo común y el despojo múltiple." *Observatorio Social En América Latina* XIII (32): 149–72.

Noguera Montoya, Susana. 2016. "Los daños colaterales del Cerrejón." *El Espectador*, April 2. http://www.elespectador.com/noticias/nacional/los-danos-colaterales-del-cerrejon-articulo-625055.

Observatorio del Caribe Colombiano. 2015. http://www.ocaribe.org/?la=es.

OMAL (Observatorio de Multinacionales en América Latina). 2016. http://omal.info.

Oquist, P. 1978. *Violencia, conflicto y política en Colombia.* Bogotá, Colombia: Biblioteca Popular.

Ostau De Lafont, F., and R. Otálora. 2018. *Derecho internacional del mundo del trabajo.* Bogatá, Colombia: Universidad Libre Panamericana.

Otálora, R. 2006. "Economías de guerra: Recursos mineros y empresas multinacionales en el Sur de Bolívar." MA thesis, IEPRI, Universidad Nacional de Colombia, Bogotá.

———. 2016. "Empresas transnacionales y estándares de derechos humanos en contextos de conflicto: análisis de caso de la minería del carbón en Colombia bajo los Principios Proteger, Respetar y Remediar de Naciones Unidas (1998–2014)." PhD dissertation, Universidad del Salvador, Buenos Aires, Argentina.

Pécaut, D. 2015. "Un conflicto armado al servicio del statu quo social y político." In *Contribución al Entendimiento del Conflicto Armado en Colombia,* 1–53. Bogotá, Colombia: Comisión Histórica del conflicto y sus víctimas. https://www.verdadabierta.com/.../1180-contribucion-al-entendimiento-del-conflicto-y-sus-victimas.

Pizarro, E. 2015. "Una lectura múltiple y plural de la historia." In *Contribución al Entendimiento del Conflicto Armado en Colombia,* 1–94. Bogotá, Colombia: Comisión Histórica del conflicto y sus víctimas. https://www.verdadabierta.com/.../1180-contribucion-al-entendimiento-del-conflicto-y-sus-victimas.

Revista Dinero. 2013. "Se confirmó venta de Drummond." *Revista Dinero.* http://www.dinero.com/negocios/articulo/se-confirmo-ventadrummond/121522.

Romero, M. 2003. *Paramilitares y autodefensas (1998–2003).* Bogotá, Colombia: Editorial Planeta Colombiana, IEPRI.

Rueda, M. I. 2016. "El reto en el posconflicto." *Revista Mundo Minero*, May. http://mundominero.com.co/el-reto-en-el-posconflicto/.

Sarmiento, E. 2016. "La economía en trance." *El Espectador*, November 27. https://www.elespectador.com/opinion/opinion/la-economia-en-trance-columna-667578.

"Sectores bajan giros de multinacionales al exterior." 2014. *El Tiempo*, October 2. http://www.eltiempo.com/economia/sectores/bajan-giros-de-multinacionales-al-exterior/14626696.

Silla Vacía. 2016. "La corte reescribe la minería y tiene a santurbán pendiente." http://lasillavacia.com/historia/la-corte-reescribe-la-mineria-y-tiene-santurban-pendiente-57257.

Silva Herrera, J. 2016. "Qué le espera al medioambiente en el escenario del posconflicto?" *El Tiempo*, February. http://www.eltiempo.com/archivo/documento/CMS-15210177.

UNHCR (Office of the United Nations High Commissioner for Human Rights). 2012. *La responsabilidad de la empresas para respetar los derechos humanos: Guía para la interpretación*. https://www.ohchr.org/Documents/Publications/HR.PUB.12,2_sp.pdf.

United Nations. 2011. "Informe del Representante Especial del Secretario General para la cuestión de los derechos humanos y las empresas transnacionales y otras empresas, John Ruggie, Principios Rectores sobre las empresas y los derechos humanos: puesta en práctica del marco de las Naciones Unidas para 'proteger, respetar y remediar.'" Report A/HRC/17/31. http://www2.ohchr.org/spdocs/business/a-hrc-17-31_sp.doc.

Verdad Abierta. 2012. "Blanco Maya confiesa que fue el puente entre Drummond y Paras." *Verdad Abierta*, April 20. https://verdadabierta.com/contratista-de-la-drummond-acusa-a-la-empresa-minera-de-financiar-a-los-paramilitares/.

Wills, M. E. 2015. "Los tres nudos de la guerra colombiana." In *Contribución al Entendimiento del Conflicto Armado en Colombia*, 1–44. Bogotá, Colombia: Comisión Histórica del conflicto y sus víctimas. https://www.verdadabierta.com/.../1180-contribucion-al-entendimiento-del-conflicto-y-sus-victimas.

PART II
MEXICO

CHAPTER 7

OIL, GAS, AND GUNS
WAR, PRIVATIZATION, AND VIOLENCE IN TAMAULIPAS, MEXICO

Guadalupe Correa-Cabrera and
Carlos Daniel Gutiérrez-Mannix[1]

This chapter describes the current state of violence and conflict in the Mexican state of Tamaulipas. As massive conflict between criminal organizations—and between these organizations and the Mexican state—has developed in resource-rich regions of this resource-rich border state, it has become crucial to analyze the resulting violence under a framework of resource extraction. In Tamaulipas we can find many of the elements of state and non-state violence described in the Introduction to this volume by Granovsky-Larsen and Paley,

1   Excerpts and key arguments of this chapter appear in Guadalupe Correa-Cabrera's book, *Los Zetas Inc.: Criminal Corporations, Energy, and Civil War in Mexico* (University of Texas Press, 2017). We thank the publisher for granting permission to use this material. We also thank Dawid Wladyka, Xavier Oliveras, and Wendy Macías for their help with map making and design.

including forced displacements in communal lands, assassinations of activists, and extreme levels of brutality. These phenomena coincide with the recent passage of Mexico's energy sector reform, which further aligns Mexico with US policy and strategic interests, placing Tamaulipas at the forefront of the discussion of extractivism, structural violence, and the expansion of capital.

Three days after taking office as president of Mexico, Felipe Calderón Hinojosa began to use the word "war" to refer to what he argued was a righteous assault on organized crime and impunity. This, although crime rates were falling and government sources indicated homicides and kidnappings in Mexico were decreasing year after year (Escalante 2009). On December 11, 2006, following a week of violent events in the state of Michoacán, including the deaths of several police officers, Calderón announced the anti-drug trafficking strategy Operación Conjunta Michoacán (Joint Operation Michoacán). While the initial number of soldiers, marines, and Federal Police sent to combat drug-trafficking organizations in Michoacán was estimated at over five thousand (see Chapter 9), it is important to mention that, soon after, Mexico's president began dispatching many more soldiers to other states, including Tamaulipas. Today, the border state of Tamaulipas is among the most militarized in Mexico, and this militarization can be directly traced to the ongoing war on drugs. It is in this context that we can begin to analyze the effects of organized violence in the state.[2]

In looking at Mexican states and zones where violence has been extreme in recent years, and where the "anti-narcotics" operations of the federal government have been concentrated, it is possible to clearly identify important resource-rich regions. Much of the violence that has occurred in the past few years has been concentrated in regions that are rich in hydrocarbons. This chapter focuses exclusively on Tamaulipas, a northeastern Mexican state with high levels of violence and social instability that are the products of a violent confrontation between criminal paramilitaries (or criminal groups originated within, tolerated by, operating in

---

2 We here use "organized violence" as an umbrella term that includes three categories: state-based armed conflict, non-state armed conflict, and one-sided violence. See Human Security Report Project's website (http://www.hsrgroup.org/our-work/security-stats/Organized-Violence.aspx) and Melander (2015).

conjunction with, or supported by the Mexican state)[3] and Mexico's federal forces, as well as being home to important hydrocarbon reserves.

Hydrocarbon reserves in Tamaulipas can be found on the mainland and in the coastal regions of the Gulf of Mexico, which are considered part of the state as well. Mexico's energy sector reform has given way to the privatization of lands, as well as of oil and gas wells and reserves. It is possible to begin to make a link between violence and a greater potential for the development of extractive industries in Tamaulipas.[4] Large infrastructure projects, like the Los Ramones natural gas pipeline, the Mazatlán-Matamoros super highway, and important border crossings (such as the Anzaldúas international bridge and the West Rail Bypass Bridge[5]) in this Mexican border state have generally not been negatively affected by extreme violence. On the contrary, such projects have been expanding and they seem to be mostly geared towards future extraction and the transportation of energy resources. In other words, while organized violence in the state has continued to plague the day-to-day lives of local residents, it has not led to a decrease in the amount of public and private investment related to the exploration and extraction of hydrocarbons such as oil and natural gas.

In the state of Tamaulipas, organized violence has displaced communities, destroyed social organizations, and effectively crushed all sorts of dissent among the local population and authorities. This repression has been geared particularly towards landowners and small-town residents, especially in areas where rich oil and gas reserves can be found. However, violence has also been rampant in major border and coastal cities, where the construction of massive infrastructure projects has taken place. This has created an ideal situation for transnational corporations to enter and extract the resources they deem appropriate without any major popular opposition, all while apparently receiving protection from the federal government (Paley 2014).

---

3   For further details on this concept and the relationship between the state and transnational criminal organizations, see Paley (2014) and Correa-Cabrera, Keck, and Nava (2015).
4   On this association in other parts of the Americas, see Paley (2014).
5   The West Rail Bypass Bridge between Matamoros, Tamaulipas, and Brownsville, Texas, is the first new rail crossing built between the United States and Mexico in more than a century.

TAMAULIPAS: STRATEGIC STATE AND BATTLEFRONT

Sporting a boundary with Texas and an extensive coastline, the Mexican state of Tamaulipas has one of the most dynamic borders in Latin America (see Illustration 7.1). Nuevo Laredo's customs alone handles approximately 40 percent of land trade between Mexico and the United States, and the three main maritime ports of Tamaulipas accommodate more than half of the ships destined for the European market (Alvarado 2012). Given its location, the state is in a geographic position to play a key role in drug trafficking and human smuggling going north into the United States and in arms trafficking going south into Mexico and Central America. Its main border cities (Nuevo Laredo, Miguel Alemán, Reynosa, Río Bravo, and Matamoros) are the closest points of entry to the United States for traffickers that import illicit cargo through maritime ports in the states of Quintana Roo and Yucatán and along the Gulf of Mexico, as well as the important ports on the Pacific between Puerto Madero, Chiapas, and San Blas, Nayarit (Guerrero 2010). Tamaulipas has more border crossings into the United States than any other Mexican state, eighteen in total.

Given the state's strategic location, illegal trafficking activities have long developed and proliferated alongside legal business dealings. This not only generated violent land disputes but also rejuvenated "old and violent political confrontations for the control of everything...transported through this territory" (Alvarado 2012). As trade along the border grew, especially illicit trade, organized crime became well entrenched in the state. According to Guerrero (2014), "The shape and size of [the Tamaulipas] border encouraged smuggling activities, and thus there initially appeared a strong and cohesive organization with a strong leadership, the genesis of the Gulf Cartel." This criminal group "was not only a pioneer in drug smuggling on a large scale, but also a trailblazer in the development of an armed wing with military discipline and high firepower" (Guerrero 2014).

The history of violence in Tamaulipas is closely related to the smuggling routes dating back to the 1930s, initially organized around alcohol, beginning during Prohibition in the United States, that cross the state from south to north. However, contemporary levels of violence in Tamaulipas are unprecedented and are directly tied to the militarized enforcement of narcotics prohibition. Specifically, in the case of

Tamaulipas, the militarized approach adopted by the Mexican government and supported by the United States government has meant organized criminal groups must employ more violent means to survive and operate. For instance, the Zetas organization—which had its origin in elite special forces of the Mexican Army—was created as the armed wing of the Gulf Cartel to provide protection to then leader, Osiel Cárdenas Guillén, to enforce the group's presence and dominion over the smuggling routes of Mexico's Gulf Coast.

Illustration 7.1: Tamaulipas: A Strategic Mexican Border State

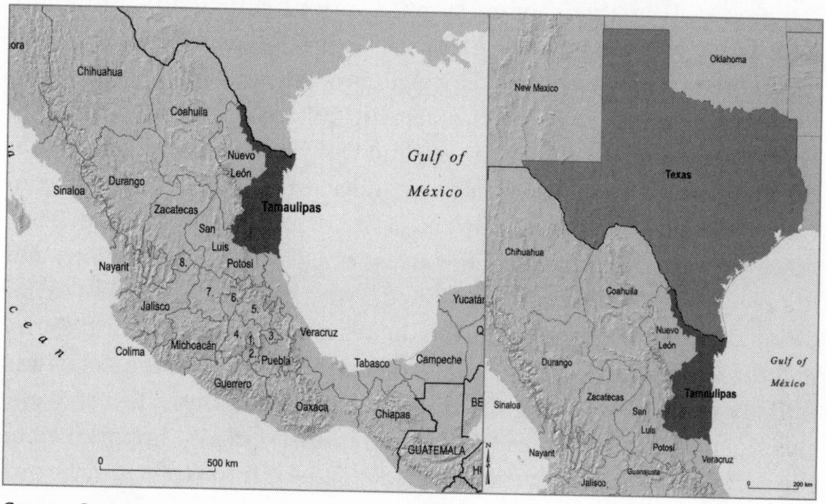

Source: Courtesy NASA/JPL-Caltech.

As a newly established "cartel" leader in 1999, Cárdenas Guillén sought to form a group around him that would both protect him and enforce his commands within the drug-trafficking organization. In order to do so, the Gulf Cartel leader employed thirty-one defectors from the Grupo Aeromóvil de Fuerzas Especiales (Mexican Special Forces Airmobile Group) under the command of Arturo Guzmán Decena. The newly created group was then named the Zetas, reportedly in reference to the radio frequency used to communicate when they were still army members.[6] Although the history of the early years of the Zetas remains

---

6 This is just one theory of the origin of this name, but it is probably the most popular.

blurry, it is clear the group soon gained the trust of Cárdenas and was quick to climb within the Gulf Cartel.[7]

Experienced in military tactics due to its members' backgrounds as elite special forces, the Zetas soon began training and equipping new recruits, creating a small but effective army. It overwhelmed other armed forces (including federal and state authorities) across the state by assembling in military-style convoys with high-powered machine guns, rocket-propelled grenades, and armoured vehicles. In January 2002, the first Zeta convoy or commando unit arrived in Nuevo Laredo, Tamaulipas (Pineda 2003). In this incident, a convoy of at least twelve SUVs entered the city freely and stopped at a local church (El Santo Niño). This date marks an era of clear expansion on the part of the Zetas. Not only would it come to control key regions of the state but it would grow to control criminal activities in states including San Luis Potosí, Nuevo León, Coahuila, Veracruz, Tabasco, and Quintana Roo. Nonetheless, at this moment in time, the Zetas were still an organization strongly controlled and guided from within the Gulf Cartel's high command. This, however, would change with the arrest of Osiel Cárdenas in 2003 and his eventual extradition to the United States in 2007. Cárdenas's extradition created serious problems in the relation between the Gulf Cartel and the Zetas due to the fact that the main objective of the Zetas was initially the protection of the Gulf Cartel's leader; once he was gone, the organization's new leadership was questioning its importance in the organization. This questioning soon turned into strained relations as it became obvious the Zetas controlled a great portion of the vital functions of the Gulf Cartel. For instance, a 2005 report by the Federal Bureau of Investigation (FBI) concluded,

> Los Zetas controls the major drug trafficking corridors along the south Texas/Mexico border for the Gulf Cartel and is involved in or linked to numerous criminal activities including kidnapping, murder, and alien smuggling. The group is undermining Mexican

---

7   It is significant that, in 2001, four important Mexican criminal organizations (the Sinaloa Cartel, the Juárez Cartel, the Colima Cartel [the Cartel of the Amezcua-Contreras family], and the Milenio Cartel [of Armando Valencia and his family]) met and formed La Federación as a response to the Zetas' greater influence and rapid advancement (De la O 2011).

law enforcement efforts in Nuevo Laredo, the primary location of recent drug-related violence. In June 2005, the Government of Mexico sent federal forces to Nuevo Laredo to restore order to the city. As Los Zetas has corrupted many Mexican public officials in the Nuevo Laredo-area, the government will likely achieve limited success at controlling their activities. (2005)

The same report suggests that, by 2005, the Zetas were completely capable of managing the cartel's main functions and were also strong enough to break away from the core of its "mother" organization; it amassed great profits from its own businesses, as well as Gulf Cartel stipends (FBI 2005). The Zetas also became increasingly powerful and were able to orchestrate several prison breaks in order to rescue Zeta members and gang members affiliated with the organization. Its increase in power and capabilities inevitably put pressure on the leadership of the Gulf Cartel, and relations between the two organizations became increasingly tense and dangerous. As the Zetas began to cleanse key positions from cartel members and replace them with its own members, it became evident the Gulf Cartel's leadership, then controlled by Eduardo Costilla, foresaw the possibility of losing control over the entire organization.

Although relations continued to deteriorate, it was not until 2010 that both organizations broke completely apart; this in turn increased violence to unprecedented levels. As both groups battled for control of the state, the violence created by this conflict rose to unimaginable levels, becoming especially gruesome when the federal government intervened in 2010–2011, sending thousands of soldiers and police officers to Tamaulipas. In total, around twelve thousand security force personnel were deployed to Tamaulipas in 2011, and two thousand more were sent in 2012 to combat and engage in the conflict between the Zetas and the Gulf Cartel.

Tamaulipas is today among the most violent and dangerous states in the Mexican republic and has continually ranked first in the number of disappearances and kidnappings registered by the Secretaría de Gobernación (Secretary of the Interior—SEGOB). The devastation created by the armed conflict initially between the Gulf Cartel and criminal paramilitaries, and subsequently between the army and these groups, has severely affected quality of life in Tamaulipas and has sparked internal displacements within the state towards other Mexican states and the United States. As mentioned, the violence has not hampered the massive infrastructure projects taking place within this border state, most of which are geared towards the extraction of oil and natural gas, which are abundant in this region of the country. Recent oil and shale gas discoveries underline that Tamaulipas has some of the largest reserves of strategic hydrocarbons and energy commodities (such as oil, gas, coal, and iron ore) in Mexico. The extraction of these natural resources has continued without interruption, as the war between criminal paramilitaries and the government of Mexico has and continues to wreak havoc among local people.

CASUALTIES OF THE WAR IN TAMAULIPAS

Mexico's Instituto Nacional de Estadística y Geografía (National Institute of Statistics and Geography—INEGI) has collected data provided by SEGOB in order to register the number of homicides that take place yearly in each state of the Mexican republic. This information shows a drastic increase in the number of homicides in Tamaulipas, spiking from 288 in 2009 to 1,016 in 2012 (see Table 7.1 and Figure 7.1), and, between 2011 and 2013, nearly one hundred clandestine graves containing hundreds of unidentified bodies were found in this state (Mendieta 2014).[8] A significant number of bodies were found in the municipality of San Fernando, showing signs of torture and belonging to migrants from different parts of Mexico or other countries who had been kidnapped and executed in Tamaulipas.

Also, SEGOB reported a total of 6,123 missing or disappeared people between 2006 and 2017 in Tamaulipas. This state has the highest number of *desaparecidos* (disappeared people) in the country (RNPED 2018). In a period of four years, between 2010 and 2014, a total of sixty-nine public officials were reported as disappeared, 90 percent of them belonging to law enforcement agencies (Mendieta 2014). Violence has not exclusively affected Mexican citizens and residents of this border state but also foreigners—particularly migrants in transit through Mexico intending to cross to the United States (RNPED 2018). In other words, violence has terribly affected the day-to-day lives of many people living in or moving through this Mexican state.

---

8   Numbers vary according to different sources.

Table 7.1: Homicides in Tamaulipas, 2000–2017

Year	Homicides	Year	Homicides
2000	222	2009	288
2001	165	2010	721
2002	165	2011	855
2003	244	2012	1,016
2004	225	2013	556
2005	357	2014	628
2006	346	2015	533
2007	265	2016	596
2008	308	2017	542

Source: INEGI *(2018), with data from* SESNSP *(Executive Secretariat of the National System of Public Security) of* SEGOB.

Figure 7.1: Homicides in Tamaulipas, 2000–2017

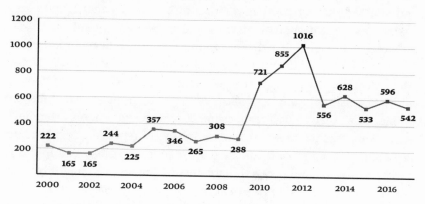

Source: INEGI *(2018), with data from* SESNSP *of* SEGOB.

The number of displaced people from certain key areas of the state has also been significant during the past few years. In Ciudad Mier, starting in November 2010, there was an exodus of hundreds of people, maybe more than half of the total population of the municipality (Casey and de Córdoba 2010). Approximately two hundred people left the town

of La Fé del Golfo in the municipality of Jiménez, and 250 people abandoned their properties and homes in the community of El Barranco—
located in the municipality of Cruillas (Mendieta 2014). Both La Fé del
Golfo and El Barranco were towns with fewer than three hundred inhabitants and thus the exodus registered in both places has, in fact, created
ghost towns. Situations like this seem to have become a pattern in some
regions of the state of Tamaulipas, where a number of localities were
abandoned by their afflicted inhabitants seeking shelter in a bigger and
safer town or city, or across the border in Texas.

Although levels of violence recorded in the state peaked in 2012, the
violent clash between criminal paramilitaries and Mexico's federal forces
continues today. In 2015, Tamaulipas registered the highest numbers of
kidnappings in the country—327, according to a report of the Executive
Secretariat of the National System of Public Safety (SESNSP 2018, 2). In
2004, there were no records of kidnappings in Tamaulipas. Part of the
reason for the very significant rise may be the fracturing of the Zetas and
the Gulf Cartel, which weakened these groups and forced them to search
for alternative sources of income, including extortion. As both groups
experienced a loss of leadership and control due to fighting each other
and dealing with government intervention, they further diversified their
activities and found alternative areas of operations that require less
logistical organization than international drug trafficking (Mejía 2014).

Violence in Tamaulipas has taken many shapes and gradations; this
is exemplified in recurrent mass executions of migrants and citizens.
Moreover, violence in the state has featured iconic dumping of bodies,
which consists of dumping dozens of dead, often mutilated, bodies in
public places such as parks, government offices, and schools (Mendieta
2014). This practice became common in several regions of Mexico, but
in Tamaulipas it almost became a daily practice, instilling fear into the
psyche of the Tamaulipecos (inhabitants of Tamaulipas) and migrants
alike. Another common practice at the height of the war was the use of
car bombs or targeted arson attacks in key cities of the state to scare both
authorities and residents. In *The Shock Doctrine*, Naomi Klein (2007)
refers to several cases in which shock tactics have been used against the
citizenry to spread fear and displace populations in order to create an
atmosphere in which governments or corporations could take advantage
of the situation and extract resources.

DIVERSIFICATION OF CRIMINAL ACTIVITIES

Initially, the violent confrontation between the Zetas and the Gulf Cartel broke out over control of the main trafficking routes, but very soon both groups weakened; this appears to be what led them to resort to other types of illegal activities. One of these activities was that of stealing and commercializing different types of hydrocarbons, such as natural gas condensate. However, organized crime groups were not completely new at profiting from the energy sector in Tamaulipas. Consider, for example, the case of the natural gas condensate extracted from the Burgos Basin when the Zetas and the Gulf Cartel collaborated and formed La Compañía (The Company). Recent investigations show how the condensate was transported from these vast reservoirs to the border with Texas. The shipments then crossed through formal customs by utilizing false documentation that classified them as NAFTA cargo. They were then taken to terminals and warehouses in Texas for temporary storage and later distribution to US buyers (Pérez 2011, 2012).

Another negative externality of organized violence in the state of Tamaulipas is the attack against civil society organizations. This type of violence has hindered civil society's ability to demand security and prosperity and has dampened all dissent and political opposition. Civil society in Tamaulipas has not been able to organize effectively after years of abuse and destruction by organized crime and government authorities. Unlike other states, the people of Tamaulipas have not been able to face violence in an effective way (Guerrero 2014). As Paley recognizes, in Tamaulipas, "there is a basic absence of advocacy." The state "doesn't have a proliferation of non-governmental advocacy, research or aid organizations devoted to assisting victims of the conflict and their family members" (Paley 2011, 23–24). This type of violence carries on; on May 10, 2017 (Mother's Day in Mexico), Miriam Rodríguez Martínez, a well-known activist in the state of Tamaulipas, was shot and killed at her home in San Fernando by an armed commando (Cedillo 2017). Rodríguez Martínez had initially become an activist in 2014 when she herself located the body of her daughter who had been kidnapped and killed in 2012.

Extreme violence and militarization are not the only factors present in this state in the past few years. Economic growth and the opening of the oil sector accompanied the brutal events already described (terror, forced displacements, and the government's failure to control organized crime and assure stability in this strategic region). During the most violent periods in Tamaulipas, important discoveries of oil and gas were made. At the same time, the Mexican government was able to provide the infrastructure that would promote trade and develop the energy sector after a historic reform.

TAMAULIPAS: A STATE RICH IN HYDROCARBONS

While violence in the northeastern part of the country continued to evolve, it soon became evident that Tamaulipas was experiencing a dire situation of terror and human rights violations. Decapitations, dismemberments, organized acts of terror, and the inability of the authorities to impose security and provide peace became evident, and this inevitably affected the livelihoods of residents, especially of those living in border and coastal towns and cities. Notwithstanding this complex situation, one cannot speak of a "failed state," due to the fact that the Mexican state was able to continue to create the conditions for private investment. Extreme violence and lack of government control over the security situation in Tamaulipas occurred at the same time that proven oil and gas reserves were found. Interestingly, a massive capital investment towards the extraction of hydrocarbons followed. Private and public investments poured into the state, but the already afflicted and embattled inhabitants of Tamaulipas felt few, if any, positive benefits. Tamaulipas has considerable oil and shale gas reservoirs (see Illustration 7.2), possibly the largest nationwide, which in turn have encouraged investment and the construction of offshore oil extraction wells (Daugherty 2015, 2).

A Wilson Center report identified Tamaulipas as one of "Mexico's most important states in terms of hydrocarbons development," which holds an important "portion of the country's oil and gas deposits, including offshore oil sites in the Gulf of Mexico and shale gas formations similar to those already being successfully developed in the [United States]" (Daugherty 2015). Hence, Tamaulipas will be an epicentre of energy production in Mexico after the country's recent changes in the constitutional framework.[9] The Government of Tamaulipas (2014, 10) has noted

9   On December 20, 2013, Mexico's Congress passed far-reaching constitutional reforms to open the energy sector to private participation and worldwide investment after seventy-six years of state monopoly. Subsequently, a series of new laws and amendments was passed to create the legal and regulatory...

Illustration 7.2: Hydrocarbons in Tamaulipas 1

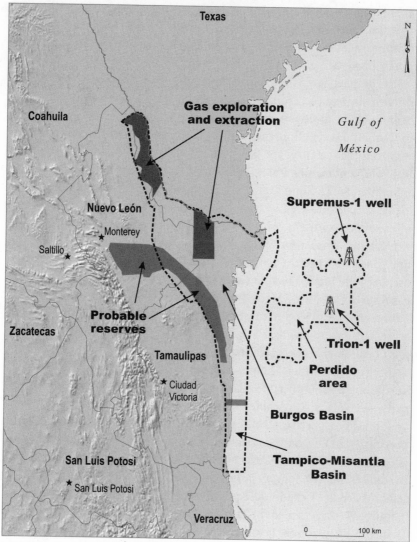

Sources: Courtesy NASA/JPL-Caltech.

...framework under which foreign energy companies would operate in Mexico. The overall reform that would fundamentally reshape Mexico's energy landscape includes twelve amended laws and nine new secondary laws, with changes governing the upstream, midstream, and downstream hydrocarbon sectors. Enabling or secondary legislation was approved in August 2014.

that the state contains "two important assets for the exploration and exploitation of hydrocarbons" in Mexico: the Burgos Basin in the north, and the Poza Rica-Altamira Asset, which is located in the Tampico-Misantla area and includes the southernmost region of Tamaulipas and northern Veracruz.

In the past few years, notwithstanding the violence and organized crime's control of certain regions of the state, important efforts have been made to discover, explore, and map all available energy resources in Tamaulipas. Oil and gas technicians have visited Reynosa and San Fernando in recent years and performed various geological, geochemical, and environmental studies in these hydrocarbon-rich regions (Dorantes 2014). Simultaneously, some key regions of Tamaulipas have experienced robust growth in gas and petroleum activity "in the form of incentive contracts with private foreign companies to engage in the exploration, extraction, and production activities of existing oil and natural gas fields" (Haahr 2015, 7). Particularly important are the developments in the Burgos Basin, where the country's most important natural gas reserves are located (see Illustration 7.3). It is worth mentioning that 26 percent of Mexico's natural gas production takes place in Tamaulipas, representing approximately "200 billion daily cubic feet and 18,000 barrels of condensed gas" (Haahr 2015, 7).

According to official figures, in 2014, approximately 65 percent of the 52.6 billion barrels of crude oil equivalent identified by the state oil company—Petróleos Mexicanos (Mexican Petroleum—Pemex)—as "conventional prospective resources" were located in Tamaulipas oil fields, specifically in Burgos, Tampico-Misantla, and the deep waters of the Gulf of Mexico (see Map 2) (Government of Tamaulipas 2014, 10). According to some estimates, four oil provinces concentrate a little more than sixty billion barrels of crude oil equivalent of "unconventional prospective resources" (Government of Tamaulipas 2014, 11).

In the early 2000s, Pemex identified five hundred oil fields located along the Tamaulipas coastal zone—between the mouth of the Rio Bravo in Matamoros and the locality of La Pesca in the municipality of Soto la Marina ("Hallan Yacimientos Frente a la Playa" 2011). During this time, Mexico's government also found important mineral resources in this state and mapped them as part of a serious effort to systematize the information related to all these findings (see Mexican Geological Survey 2011).

Illustration 7.3: Hydrocarbons in Tamaulipas II
Municipalities with large hydrocarbon reserves

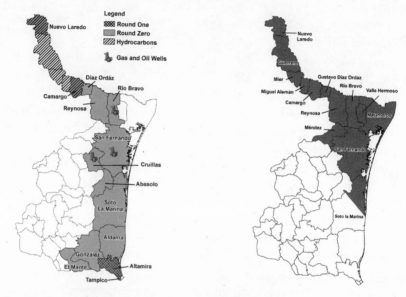

Sources: *Pemex (2014) (left map); Cartocritica (2014) (right map).*

VIOLENCE AND HYDROCARBONS IN TAMAULIPAS

Violence in Tamaulipas has technically dropped off over the past years, but symbolically it has not been visibly reduced. This has created a situation in which significant amounts of capital are still being mobilized to extract oil and gas while a violent and bloody armed conflict is taking place. Coexistence between legal and illegal corporations has become common, and the army or the Federal Police have secured high-risk areas in order to provide a sense of security for potential investors. This is considered necessary as armed groups have, on several occasions, targeted (kidnapped and killed) oil and gas field workers—mostly from Mexico's state oil company Pemex. These events have occurred as fuel theft has become rampant in the state. A report issued by the Mexican Senate states that illegal pipeline tapping went (in the entire nation) from 691 illegal taps in 2010 to 4,127 in 2014 (Gil Zuarth 2015). The same report states that the state of Tamaulipas—which accounts for a fifth of national gas production—registered the largest amount of illegal taps, with 539 out of the 4,127 registered nationwide in 2014. Lastly, it is believed that fuel theft in Mexico represents 4.4 percent of the overall oil and gas profits in the country (Gil Zuarth 2015).

Another focal point of organized violence was the city of San Fernando, which became infamous in 2010 as the site of the massacre of seventy-two migrants, who were most likely being smuggled towards Mexico's northern border with the United States. The city made headlines again in 2011, when several mass graves were uncovered. It was later reported these mass graves contained the bodies of around two hundred people, who had been travelling as bus passengers. The violence witnessed in this region was allegedly the direct result of the same violent conflict between the Gulf Cartel and the Zetas. The cities of the so-called Frontera Chica (Small Border) region between Nuevo Laredo and Reynosa experienced a similar situation;[10] violent and continuous confrontations among groups of criminal paramilitaries were registered here, bringing destruction, death, and fear to the inhabitants of these regions (Young 2013).

In the aforementioned places, one can also observe a pattern of coexistence between legal and illegal groups. In the case of San Fernando, this becomes obvious when we take into consideration that the city is among the most important in terms of hydrocarbon production (Manilla 2012). In this sense, we can conclude that San Fernando was at the time an energy-producing city under the control of the Zetas and one for which the federal forces, both the army and the Federal Police, fought tooth and nail to regain. This pattern of violence becomes even more evident when we look at how it affected other border cities, such as those that form the Frontera Chica, where the confrontation between criminal paramilitaries and government forces wreaked havoc. Specifically, for the city of Nueva Ciudad Guerrero, it is noteworthy to mention that, in 2010, members of a criminal paramilitary group (possibly the Zetas) overran the personnel working at Pemex's Gigante-1 gas well. Oil and gas theft also became common in this area, and this pattern and violence plagued most of Tamaulipas, but it was especially notorious in the northern part of the state.

As mentioned above, the immediate result of the weakening—or reconfiguration—of the two main criminal paramilitary groups operating

---

10 The Frontera Chica region includes Ciudad Camargo, Ciudad Miguel Alemán, Ciudad Mier, Nueva Ciudad Guerrero, and Díaz Ordaz.

in Tamaulipas was that they began to diversify their activities by resorting to kidnappings, extortion, and hydrocarbon theft. However, hydrocarbon theft became increasingly rampant in this border state and soon was a major source of income for crime organizations. It is estimated that organized crime groups may control up to 15 percent of the national production of gasoline (Gurney 2014; Mejía 2014). Although drug violence in Tamaulipas continues at alarming rates, it is now evident that oil and gas theft is central to the operation of the organized crime syndicates fighting for control of this Mexican state. This fact, in a sense, has created a deep interdependence between the need to obtain resources that can be used to purchase protection and the need to control the territory where natural resources are being extracted and transported.

The continuous theft of oil and gas, the targeting of energy field workers, and the control of swaths of territory very soon affected the viability of Mexico's oil giant, Pemex, which registered huge losses and lost the support of both the government and the public, as it was deemed unproductive and corrupt. This situation, however, has not stymied the flow of public and private capital towards oil and gas infrastructure; rather, this trend has steadily increased with the recent discoveries that demonstrate Tamaulipas is sitting on Mexico's largest oil and gas reserves. Energy in Tamaulipas, after all, is important for the local economy, and it is estimated that fifty-two thousand people in this state work for companies linked, in one way or another, to the energy sector. Even the embattled Pemex has announced the creation of large infrastructure projects for Tamaulipas that will further enable it to compete with private investment and will take advantage of the massive reserves located in this Mexican border state.

INFRASTRUCTURE FOR THE ENERGY SECTOR IN TAMAULIPAS

As mentioned above, infrastructure projects in Tamaulipas have not stopped nor has the speed of construction dwindled. To the contrary, the state is completely immersed in the Plan Nacional de Infraestructura 2014–2018 (National Infrastructure Plan), which encompasses several major infrastructure projects geared towards the energy sector (see Illustration 7.4). Most projects here are intended to further the pace of globalization in the region and to enable the extraction and transportation of hydrocarbons. Some key infrastructure projects in Tamaulipas are being developed in tandem with the gas pipeline being built towards the centre of the country (like the Los Ramones pipeline).

Illustration 7.4: New Infrastructure in Tamaulipas

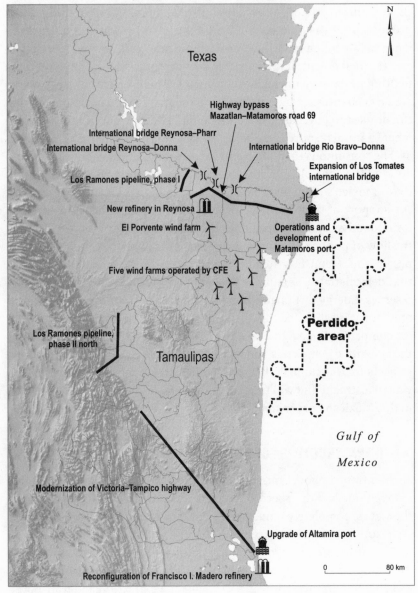

Sources: Courtesy NASA/JPL-Caltech.

Other projects such as the Mazatlán-Matamoros highway, the Tuxpan-Tampico highway, and the West Rail Bypass Bridge demonstrate the need to link the state with the rest of the country and the continent. Moreover, these projects make evident there is increasing interest in fulfilling promises made in the framework of the newly passed energy sector reform. They constitute a new energy paradigm for Mexico, a country where some strategic natural resources were exclusively owned and extracted by the state until very recently. Indeed, this reform has come to herald new market opportunities that have been exploited by both legal and illegal organizations.

Needless to say, private companies such as ExxonMobil, British Petroleum (BP), and Citgo have expressed interest in exploring and extracting the natural resources in this region—most of them in the energy sector. Among the most important energy projects proposed or underway in Tamaulipas are those related to the gas industry. If market conditions allow, future efforts will be centred on the development of the shale gas industry. Some of the companies that have expressed interest in this venture are BP, Citgo, ExxonMobil, and LyondellBasell Industries. All of these companies are already part of the Eagle Ford Shale Consortium, the Eagle Ford deposits in Texas that are contiguous with new gas deposits in Tamaulipas (Dorantes 2014).[11] Potential investment in Tamaulipas is not only geared towards exploration and extraction of hydrocarbons and energy resources but towards their storage and transportation. Future investments in this sector could be massive (Haahr 2015). As private companies begin to arrive to this state, the already mentioned coexistence between legal and illegal groups may become even more visible and alarming, since in many cases today they seem to work together.

International companies continue to eye the region for possible investment opportunities along the border with Texas (Young 2013). An example of this is the Los Ramones pipeline, which transports natural gas extracted from Texas to central Mexico, where it is used for the industrial plants located in the cities of San Luis Potosí, Querétaro, and Guanajuato. For Mexico's federal government, this pipeline constitutes the most important infrastructure project built in the past fifty years;

11 In 2014, Eagle Ford Shale Consortium's operations in Mexico were valued at more than ten billion dollars (Dorantes 2014).

this demonstrates its willingness to invest heavily in infrastructure, even as the profits of the oil and gas sector are increasingly privatized (Macías 2013). Indeed, the Los Ramones pipeline has become the centrepiece of the energy sector developments that have arrived with the newly implemented energy sector reform. This project will distribute natural gas from north to south and will, according to proponents, enable the unprecedented industrialization of central Mexico. Moreover, this pipeline will transport natural gas to the ports of Manzanillo and Altamira in order to enable exports of this hydrocarbon to Asian and European nations, respectively.

As the conflict in Tamaulipas rages on, state and private developments of infrastructure for the future extraction of oil and shale gas reserves continue to expand and private investment has flourished. Several reasons can be given for this. Firstly, the federal government has placed armed federal forces to guard such investments and has facilitated the presence of private security in areas of high criminality with the aim of providing security to gas and oil installations. Moreover, the recent structural reforms of Mexico's energy sector have attracted (and will potentially continue to attract) substantial private investment to the region and have, in turn, not prevented the decline of Pemex, a state company continuously mired in controversy. This has created a situation in which the weakening of Pemex and its loss of the monopoly of oil production has predictably attracted the presence of powerful oil and gas transnational corporations.

LAND AND ENERGY IN TAMAULIPAS

The war on drugs in Mexico has demonstrated remarkable similarities to what has occurred in other countries such as Colombia (Paley 2014). For instance, the population of Tamaulipas has experienced forced displacements that have produced dozens of ghost towns along the resource-rich border and coastal areas. Local economies of entire towns have deteriorated and inhabitants of key cities have witnessed heavy battles between organized crime groups or between organized crime groups and government authorities. This is the case in cities such as El Mante, Tampico, Ciudad Victoria, Ciudad Mier, Matamoros, Altamira, Madero, Valle Hermoso, Nuevo Laredo, and Reynosa. The turf wars that broke out between the Zetas and the Gulf Cartel reached all municipalities in the

Illustration 7.5: Violence in Tamaulipas
The darker municipalities have experienced more violence connected to the war in Mexico.

Source: Correa-Cabrera (2014).

state of Tamaulipas, but those located at the border with Texas, some along the Gulf Coast, and those along the trafficking routes were hit especially hard. The domination of key territories—mainly in the border region, the capital city (Ciudad Victoria), and the lands bordering the Gulf of Mexico (see Illustration 7.5)—was a defining aspect of this bloody armed conflict.

Organized crime syndicates have forced local ranchers to grant them access to and through their lands in order to transport any type of merchandise, and the control of trafficking routes has been focal in the clash between organized crime groups. In many cases, landowners simply leave their property, either by choice or by force (Martínez 2011). Paley reports that, by the end of 2010, approximately five thousand farmers had been displaced from Tamaulipas (2014, 215).[12] Here again, displacements have been more common in the municipalities that share a border with Texas. The coastal region of the state has also observed this phenomenon and has been at the centre of violence, as it provides adequate smuggling routes towards the northern part of the state. Members of organized crime groups used abandoned and stolen ranches for many purposes. A recurrent use of these ranches was as training camps for the hit men of both the Zetas and the Gulf Cartel (Paley 2014, 215).

Many of the lands that were stolen by organized crime groups were rich in oil and gas, and, thus, it is necessary to question who could benefit from these thefts and whether the land theft was carried out with the purpose of controlling the natural resources underground. As ranch owners left their properties, these lands were cleared for oil and gas exploration, which might enable the extraction of these hydrocarbons in the near future. A case in point is San Fernando, where one of the most important gas reservoirs in the country can be found, and where many families have fled due to violence; their abandoned ranches have since been stolen or occupied.

As established in this chapter, parts of the Tamaulipas northern border region and those municipalities located along the Gulf Coast have important hydrocarbon reserves. Many of the forced displacements from hydrocarbon-rich territories have taken place in *ejido* (communally owned) lands. According to INEGI's (2007) VIII *Agricultural, Livestock and Forestry Census*, approximately 32 percent of land in Tamaulipas is social—that is, *ejido* land (2007). This percentage is different in northern

---

12 This figure was found in a report prepared by Mexico's intelligence agency, CISEN (Centro de Investigación y Seguridad Nacional).

Tamaulipas, where the portion of social property land is substantially higher than the state's average. In northern Tamaulipas, *ejido* land represents 41 percent of the total area (Andrade, Espinoza, and Belmonte 2010, 73). It is more difficult to rent or purchase *ejidos* as compared to private lands. Due to forced displacement stemming from the war in Tamaulipas, some of these lands may be available and could be sold or leased at lower prices. Thus, violence along the Tamaulipas border and forced displacement in this region could have a positive effect for private investment in the framework of Mexico's energy sector reform.

TOWARDS A CONCLUSION

Although recent extreme violence in Tamaulipas was apparently generated by a turf war between factions of the Zetas and factions of the Gulf Cartel, it is important to mention that the spike in violence is, in fact, closely related to the deployment of the more than fourteen thousand state security force personnel engaged in the conflict over the past decade. What is more, the fear created by organized violence has negatively affected the ability of the populace to protest or gather peacefully. In fact, the authorities, far from providing security and well-being, have themselves participated in atrocious abuses and human rights violations. In San Fernando, for example, local police officers assisted armed cartel assailants and contributed to the killing of dozens of civilians. According to anonymous accounts, in this municipality local police detained and transported innocent civilians (many of them bus passengers) to locations controlled by the Zetas and allegedly assisted the group with mass executions. Corruption has worsened the already difficult security situation in border cities; often, local politicians operate in collusion with organized crime leaders.

Organized violence is prevalent in the state of Tamaulipas, and the local, state, and federal forces have been unable to provide stability and security to its inhabitants. The sheer scale and brutality of the violence have evidenced not only the collusion between government authorities and criminal organizations but also the inability of the federal government to communicate with other levels of government and to enforce the law. Amidst this violence, however, the federal government has been unwilling to open a working dialogue with the population in order to facilitate a de-escalation of violence. Far from ensuring freedom of the press and freedom of speech, the government has continuously engaged in acts of state terror and repression that have further censored the media (Correa-Cabrera 2015). The federal, state, and local authorities have done next to nothing to ensure that local nongovernmental associations can survive in a climate of extreme violence. This is true as the context becomes increasingly militarized, and it has situated the civilian population and migrants who cross through the Tamaulipas territory in a vulnerable situation.

Nonetheless, while much of the violence has been produced by the ongoing conflict between the Zetas and the Gulf Cartel, it has also become evident that the militarized approach towards the "drug problem" has failed. This unconventional (and unconstitutional) approach of the Mexican federal government has effectively made the civilian population a valid target. By militarizing local and state police agencies, the state has become unable to combat criminality and the alleged "drug problem" without using violence. This is especially important if one considers that most of the dead in the so-called war on drugs are civilians and not members of the Zetas or other cartels.

While violence in Tamaulipas has dropped in recent years, it is still well above the registered average for the years before the war on drugs. It is difficult to explain what exactly produced this de-escalation in violence, but it is worth noting that the leadership of both criminal organizations has been completely disarticulated. The main leaders of the Zetas were either killed or arrested by 2013; this severely affected the group's ability to manage large-scale criminal business operations. This is mostly due to a continuous onslaught enacted by the federal government that left many civilians dead and wounded. Hence, in the present era, the remaining factions (or so-called cells) of both groups have allegedly produced much of the violence. Moreover, violence in Tamaulipas, as illustrated by the events in the city of San Fernando, has in many cases been allowed, organized, assisted, or orchestrated by government actors, including local police organizations. It is not clear today who is fighting with whom in the different regions of this border state, but the violence is concentrated in zones rich in hydrocarbons or where strategic energy infrastructure is being built or will be constructed. In such a context, the state in itself still poses a threat to the security of the citizenry. This continues to be the context in which the battle for land and resources is taking place in Tamaulipas.

REFERENCES

Alvarado, Ignacio. 2012. "Una historia de narco-política." *El Universal*, June 17. http://www.eluniversal.com.mx/notas/853903.html.

Andrade, Elizabeth del Carmen, Martín Espinoza, and Francisco Belmonte. 2010. *La región agrícola del norte de Tamaulipas (México): Recursos naturales, agricultura y procesos de erosión*. Murcia, Spain: Ediciones de la Universidad de Murcia (Editum).

Cartocritica. 2014. *Hidrocarburos: Ronda uno y ronda cero*. http://www.cartocritica.org.mx/2014/hidrocarburos-ronda-cero-y-ronda-uno/.

Casey, Nicholas, and José de Córdoba. 2010. "Northern Mexico's State of Anarchy. Residents Abandon a Border Town as Vicious Drug Cartels Go to War." *Wall Street Journal*, November 20. http://online.wsj.com/article/SB1000142405274870410410457562284025688122.html.

Cedillo, Juan A. 2017. "Ejecutan en su casa a buscadora de desaparecidos en Tamaulipas." *Proceso*, May 11. http://www.proceso.com.mx/486005/ejecutan-en-casa-a-buscadora-desaparecidos-en-tamaulipas.

Correa-Cabrera, Guadalupe. 2014. "Violence on the 'Forgotten' Border: Mexico's Drug War, the State, and the Paramilitarization of Organized Crime in Tamaulipas in a 'New Democratic Era.'" *Journal of Borderlands Studies* 29 (4): 419–33.

———. 2015. "La guerra contra las drogas en redes sociales: El ciberespacio, el nuevo campo de batalla." Paper presented at the annual meeting for the Latin American Studies Association, San Juan, Puerto Rico, May 27–30.

Correa-Cabrera, Guadalupe, Michelle Keck, and Jose Nava. 2015. "Losing the Monopoly of Violence: The State, a Drug War, and the Paramilitarization of Organized Crime in Mexico (2007–2010)." *State Crime Journal* 4 (1): 77–95.

Daugherty, Arron. 2015. "Why Success of Mexico's Oil Security Plan May Not Matter." *InSight Crime*, February 3. http://www.insightcrime.com/newsanalysis/why-success-of-mexico-oil-security-plan-may-not-matter.

De la O, Ricardo. 2011. *Genealogía del narcotráfico (Part 4)*. Tijuana, Mexico: Peninsular Digital.

Dorantes, David. 2014. "Oil Sir, Welcome to Tamaulipas." *El Financiero*, April 8. http://www.elfinanciero.com.mx/monterrey/oil-sir-welcome-totamaulipas.html.

Escalante, Fernando. 2009. "Homicidios 1990–2007." *Nexos*, September 1. http://www.nexos.com.mx/?p=13270.

FBI (Federal Bureau of Investigation). 2005. "Intelligence Assessment. (U) Los Zetas: An Emerging Threat to the United States." http://nsarchive.gwu.edu/NSAEBB/NSAEBB499/DOCUMENTO2-20050715.pdf.

Gil Zuarth, Roberto. 2015. *Proposición de punto de acuerdo por el que el senado de la república exhorta respetuosamente al titular de petróleos mexicanos (PEMEX) a tomar medidas necesarias para resolver el problema de robo de combustible.* Senate of the Mexican Republic, September 22. http://sil.gobernacion.gob.mx/Archivos/Documentos/2015/11/asun_3295826_20151104_1446672442.pdf.

Government of Tamaulipas. 2014. *Agenda energética de Tamaulipas.* Ciudad Victoria, Mexico: Government of Tamaulipas.

Guerrero, Eduardo. 2010. "La guerra por Tamaulipas." *Nexos,* August 1. http://www.nexos.com.mx/?p=13889.

———. 2014. "El dominio del miedo." *Nexos,* July 1. http://www.nexos.com.mx/?p=21671.

Gurney, Kyra. 2014. "Mexico Criminal Groups Running Sophisticated Distribution Networks for Stolen Oil." *InSight Crime,* June 18. http://www.insightcrime.org/news-briefs/mexico-criminal-groups-running-sophisticateddistribution-networks-for-stolen-oil.

Haahr, Kathryn. 2015. "Addressing the Concerns of the Oil Industry: Security Challenges in Northeastern Mexico and Government Responses." *Mexico Institute,* Working Paper. https://www.wilsoncenter.org/publication/addressing-the-concerns-the-oil-industry-security-challenges-northeastern-mexico-and.

"Hallan yacimientos frente a la playa." 2011. *El Bravo,* August 11. http://www.skyscrapercity.com/showthread.php?t=804136&page=78.

INEGI (National Institute of Statistics and Geography). 2007. *Censo agropecuario 2007: VIII censo agrícola, ganadero y forestal 2007.* Aguascalientes, Mexico: INEGI.

———. 2018. "Mortalidad. Conjunto de datos: Defunciones por homicidios." http://www.inegi.org.mx/sistemas/olap/proyectos/bd/continuas/mortalidad/defuncioneshom.asp?s=est.

Klein, Naomi. 2007. *The Shock Doctrine: The Rise of Disaster Capitalism.* Toronto: Random House of Canada.

Macías, Teresa. 2013. "Invertirán 3mmdd en nuevo gaseoducto." *Conexión Total,* February 5. http://conexiontotal.mx/2013/02/05/invertiran-3-mmdd-ennuevo-gasoducto/.

Manilla, Enrique. 2012. "Es municipio líder de hidrocarburos." *El Mañana,* August 16. http://www.elmanana.com/diario/noticia/san_fernando/tamauipas/es_municipio_lider_de_hidrocarburos/1727453.

Martínez, Sanjuana. 2011. "En la ruta de la muerte." *La Jornada,* April 17. http://www.jornada.unam.mx/2011/04/17/politica/006n1pol.

Melander, Erik. 2015. *Organized Violence in the World 2015: An Assessment by the Uppsala Conflict Data Program.* Uppsala, Sweden: Uppsala Conflict Data Program.

Mejía, Camilo. 2014. "Rise in Tamaulipas Kidnappings Points to Lack of Mexico Govt Control." *InSight Crime,* August 21. http://insightcrime.com/news-briefs/rise-tamaulipas-kidnappings-lack-mexico-govt-control.

Mendieta, Eduardo. 2014. "Violencia en Tamaulipas es como un parte de guerra: Investigador." *Milenio,* August 12. http://www.milenio.com/

monterrey/inseguridad_Tamaulipas-violencia_Tamaulipasguerra_narco_
Tamaulipas_0_352764740.html.

Mexican Geological Survey. 2011. *Panorama minero del estado de Tamaulipas.*
Mexico City: Secretary of Energy, Government of Mexico.

———. 2017. *Petróleo en México.* Mexico City: Secretary of Energy, Government
of Mexico. https://www.sgm.gob.mx/Web/MuseoVirtual/Aplicaciones_
geologicas/Petroleo-en-Mexico.html.

RNPED (National Registry of Data of Missing or Disappeared Persons). 2018.
Database of Missing or Disappeared Persons, 2006–2017. Mexico City: RNPED,
SESNSP, SEGOB. https://www.gob.mx/sesnsp/acciones-y-programas/
registro-nacional-de-datos-de-personas-extraviadas-o-desaparecidas-rnped.

Paley, Dawn. 2011. "Off the Map in Mexico." *The Nation* 292 (21): 20–24.

———. 2014. *Drug War Capitalism.* Oakland, CA: AK Press.

Pemex (Mexican Petroleum). 2014. *Presente y futuro del Proyecto Burgos.*
Exploracion y produccion. Binational Center Library/Texas A&M
International University. https://www.tamiu.edu/binationalcenter/
documents/TexasEnergySummitPresenteyFuturodelProyectoBurgos
PEMEXBINCLIBRARY.pdf.

Pérez, Ana Lilia. 2011. *El cartel negro: Cómo el crimen organizada se ha apoderado de
Pemex.* Mexico City: Grijalbo Mondadori.

———. 2012. "Ordeña de gas condensado en la Cuenca de Burgos." *Contralínea,*
May 8. http://contralinea.info/archivo-revista/index.php/2012/05/08/
ordena-de-gas-condensado-en-la-cuenca-de-burgos/.

Pineda, Manuel. 2003. "La hidra del narco ajusta cuentas." *Contralínea,* July 14.
http://www.contralinea.com.mx/c14/html/sociedad/la_hidra.html.

SESNSP (Executive Secretariat of the National System of Public Security). 2018.
Informe de víctimas de homicidio, secuestro y extorsión 2017. Mexico City: SEGOB.

SHCP (Secretary of Finance). 2014. *Programa Nacional de Infraestructura
2014–2018.* https://www.ferroistmo.com.mx/Programa-Nacional-de-
Infraestructura-2014-2018.pdf.

Young, Shannon. 2013. "US-Supported Surveillance and Mexico's Energy
Sector." *South Notes* (blog), July 10.

CHAPTER 8

LEGAL AND ILLEGAL VIOLENCE IN MEXICO

ORGANIZED CRIME, POLITICS, AND MINING IN MICHOACÁN

Ana Del Conde and Heriberto Paredes Coronel

Four and a half hours' drive from Apatzingán, across the mountain range of Michoacán, is State Route 200—the road that ribbons up Mexico's entire coastal Pacific stretch. A steady stream of trucks passes through this area daily, carrying iron that is legally and illegally extracted and taken to the most important ports of the region: Lázaro Cárdenas and Manzanillo. It is also possible to see pickup trucks with armed passengers whose job is to ensure the trucks of iron arrive at their destination.

Since 2013, a navy post has stood on State Route 200, next to a small town known as La Placita. It does not seem to be a coincidence that it is also within this region that Mario Álvarez, the local cartel leader, and Felipe González, the *sicario* (hit man) commander, have their mansions—the former was also the mayor of Aquila, while the latter remains an important businessperson and landowner. In 2013, no one dared to go out at night; people walked with their heads lowered and one could feel a tense environment of fear. All the while, the navy remained at its post, with armoured cars and weapons, stopping and questioning people arbitrarily. Members of the criminal group Los Caballeros Templarios (the Knights Templar) were never stopped; on the contrary, they seemed to be shielded by the navy, receiving protection and a wave through whenever they passed. This opening sketch, written based on our experiences in the field, provides us with a window through which we believe it is most productive to approach the overlapping kinds of violence experienced in the Mexican state of Michoacán.

But any analysis that only describes experiences in the field falls short, because as we zoom out from lived experiences in this part of Michoacán, it is clear we need to take into account territory and natural resources if we are to understand the flows of violence in the region. In Mexico, 52 percent of national territory is classified as social property (CEDRSSA 2015)—that is, *ejidos*, and communal land. Over half of Mexico's natural resources, and 62 percent of nature reserves are located within these territories (Bunge Vivier 2012). In the state of Michoacán, there are a total of 2,835,652 hectares certified under the category of social property, equivalent to 49 percent of the state (Bunge Vivier 2012). It is key to consider these numbers when analyzing the challenges the communities that own these lands and natural resources confront.

Since the 1980s, neoliberal policies in Mexico, as in the rest of Latin America, have promoted the privatization of this land regime through the concession and sale of the land. This has led to a process of what Harvey calls "accumulation through dispossession"—that is, regulated practices that have facilitated the exploitation of natural resources by stripping away the land from communities (2004, 74).

However, more recently, these policies seem also to be facilitating a link between legal and illegal economies. These novel forms of il/legal economies are sustained through the terrorization of the population through killings, disappearances, and extortions. A practice we could name "accumulation through terror" (inspired by Harvey), and as a process that forms part of what Navarro Trujillo has labelled as dispossession in multiple dimensions (*despojo múltiple*) (Navarro Trujillo 2012). In this sense, our main hypothesis is that the social and political destabilization that has been generated in Mexico through the so-called war on drugs has opened economic opportunities where the line between the legal and the illegal is frequently blurry and inevitably depends on violent and oppressive practices against local communities (Paley 2014).

Pansters invites us to rethink public violence through three categories: institutional violence, counter-institutional violence, and para-institutional violence (2012, 87). The first is led by state forces, the second
is organized to replace or seize power from the state, and the last is carried out by agents that work for the state in a parallel, nonofficial manner. These distinctions are relevant to understanding the structures
of power that dictate the current experiences of violence in Mexico.
Instead of thinking of violence only as a series of isolated events, it is
important to analyze violence as acts carried out by networks of diverse
actors who respond to different interests, and thus are commonly in
conflict with each other (see the Introduction to this volume). This
analysis is useful to give a specific place to civil resistance as an organized and political force that at times resorts to violence as a strategy to confront and give solution to those situations where there are
oppressive structures present and a lack of protection from the state.
However, we believe it is important to rethink Pansters's classifications
through an additional lens, one that will seek to provide an understanding of the motivations of each of the actors that belong to these three
categories of public violence. This is especially important when trying
to understand the participation these groups have in the formation of
il/legal economies.

Koonings's (2012) category of new violence is useful to understand
the economic motivations that lie behind the violence that is being experienced in Mexico today. That is, the violence is not exclusively political.
When we focus on the production and distribution chain of narcotics in
particular, we see that the violent actions involved in the process create
an alternative economy. This economy not only sustains the production and distribution of narcotics but also maintains other businesses
operated by organized crime that run parallel to drug manufacturing
and transportation. This alternative economy appears to be equally or
even more powerful than the legal order and seems to also be regulating
a political order based on a system of fear and death (see Chapter 9 for
a discussion of this in another region of Michoacán, and Chapter 7 for a
discussion of similar patterns in Tamaulipas).

Our research makes use of these theoretical notions to focus on mining
extraction on the coast and in the highlands in the state of Michoacán—
specifically, in the municipalities of Aquila and Chinicuila. We seek to
explore the connections that exist between the current militarization of

the country and the proliferation of il/legal extractive projects in rural areas. Our analysis begins with ethnographic research conducted in Michoacán, and focuses on two mining zones: Las Encinas, a legal mine run by the Italian-Argentinian firm Ternium in Aquila, and La Nuez, an illegal mine exploited by the Knights Templar in Chinicuila.

PERSPECTIVES ON VIOLENCE, FROM THE COAST AND HIGHLANDS OF MICHOACÁN

With a large presence of four Indigenous groups and varying ecosystems, Michoacán is one of the states with the highest level of diversity in Mexico (INEGI 2016). Within its territory there are large areas of wooded lands, lakeside areas, mountain ranges, semi-arid terrains, wide valleys, and an expansive coast along the Pacific Ocean. The natural resources are many and include precious woods and minerals such as iron and gold. Corn, avocado, and lime are cultivated in these fertile lands, and there are also vast cattle ranges. Another important pillar of the local economy consists of: (1) planting, commercializing, and distributing marijuana; (2) producing methamphetamines and other synthetic drugs; (3) loading and unloading thousands of tons of cocaine year-round that come by sea from Colombia and have as their final destination the local market in the United States; and (4) an illicit trade in arms, which has increased significantly in the past four years (LopCam 2014).

In the 1990s, growing and selling marijuana became a profitable business, organized by small local groups led by the Milenio or Valencia cartel, which would later transform Michoacán's coast into a place for loading and unloading cocaine (Gil Olmos 2015, 73). In early 2002, under Governor Lázaro Cárdenas Batel,[1] a group led by Los Zetas (the Zetas) arrived to the state, unleashing a reign of terror while seizing

---

1   Lázaro Cárdenas Batel, Michoacán's governor from 2002 to 2008, is the grandson of Lázaro Cárdenas del Río, Mexico's president from 1934 to 1940. Lázaro Cárdenas del Río likely enjoys the highest historical acceptance rates by the population at large. Cárdenas Batel was governor as a member of the Partido de la Revolución Democrática (Party of the Democratic Revolution—PRD). Cárdenas Batel's father, Cuauhtémoc Cárdenas, and a small dissident group that came from the Partido de la Revolución Institucional (Institutional Revolutionary Party) founded the PRD.

this important connection to the Pacific Ocean (Moreno 2010, 71). These events triggered an unprecedented escalation of violence, leading to the formation of a group known as La Familia Michoacana (the Michoacán Family), who physically confronted Los Zetas. In this way, La Familia Michoacana managed to gain control over the territory, driving out this invasive cartel while deploying a discourse of an apparent reconstitution of the social fabric and support for the people of Michoacán (Morales 2012). From 2007 to 2009, under the state administrations of Cárdenas Batel and Leonel Godoy, La Familia Michoacana took control over all illegal commerce (including marijuana, cocaine, methamphetamines, kidnappings, and extortions) in Michoacán (Grillo 2011).

In 2006, Felipe Calderón deployed state and military troops through the military strategy known as Operation Conjunta Michoacán (Joint Operation Michoacán). This strategy was established as the first set of actions under the US-led Merida Initiative, often known as the war on drugs (see Chapter 9). Only three years later, it became clear the strategy had failed: the large number of military forces and Federal Police did not bring the criminal organization under control (Hernández Navarro 2014, 53). By 2009, the economy in Michoacán went into free fall, and violence increased dramatically in the form of kidnappings, extortions, and the confrontations between La Familia Michoacana and other criminal organizations that were trying to take over the state's economic power (Maldonado Aranda 2010).

A new rupture within La Familia Michoacana occured in 2010, leading to the creation of a new organization, the Knights Templar. This new cartel pushed La Familia Michoacana to the northern region of Michoacán, resulting in a larger presence of this group in the nearby states of Guerrero and Mexico state (Redacción La Jornada Michoacán 2010). The Knights Templar gained strength, increasing its presence in economic spheres that used to be controlled by the government as legal economies. Even though previously illegal activities conducted by criminal organizations remained possible, thanks to agreements that were established with municipal police or civil servants, since the founding of the Knights Templar, the functions criminal groups perform within the government have become more apparent. From late 2010 until 2013, the Knights Templar controlled: (1) part of the avocado and lime trade (especially distribution); (2) part of the state's budget; (3) clandestine laboratories; (4) sex trafficking; (5) local media; (6) the elections of 2011, through vote buying and the imposition of specific candidates—including the governor, Fausto Vallejo; (7) the legal and illegal extraction and export of iron and rare wood; and, finally, (8) extortions against businesspeople, ranchers, producers, and entire families (Martínez, Castillo, and Román 2010). This situation would create the conditions that eventually led to popular upheaval in different regions of the state (see Chapter 9).

LEGALIZED VIOLENCE: LAS ENCINAS

The coast and highlands region of Michoacán is widely recognized for its rich metal deposits (including iron, gold, and copper). The municipality of Aquila, located within this region, is the largest (by geographical size) in Michoacán, and is divided into four Indigenous communities: San Miguel Aquila, Coire, Pómaro, and Ostula.

The iron mine Las Encinas, currently owned by the international firm Ternium, has a long history of conflicts and confrontations with the Nahua community of San Miguel Aquila since the 1980s. In 1982, the people of San Miguel Aquila, backed by the communal landowner organization Unión de Comuneros Emiliano Zapata (Emiliano Zapata Co-Owners' Union—UCEZ), denounced the extraction of natural resources by Ternium's predecessor, HYLSA. Up to that point, the firm had only paid the community "a total of $4,000 pesos [approximately US$70 at that time] for the rights of land rent, two typewriters, ten high school scholarships, and small volumes of construction materials" for the exploitation of the iron from their land (Correa 1982, para. 7). This is how the movement against the mining company began, led by José Ramírez Verduzco and Efrén Capiz Villegas, both UCEZ members.

Ramírez Verduzco was killed in Aquila on April 29, 1989, an event that changed the course of struggles for the defence of the land. On December 15, 1990, HYLSA signed a transfer of rights with the communal landowners (*comuneros*) from Aquila, obtaining a temporary use contract for 383 hectares (Santos Cordero and Martínez Silva 2015; Las Encinas S.A. de C.V. 2007). In 2005, the Italian-Argentinian company Technit bought HYLSA, transforming it into Ternium Mexico, which today owns Las Encinas mine in Aquila (among other properties). It is with this transaction that the tensions between the community and the mining corporation arose again. The key conflicts revolve around two main issues: (1) the socio-environmental effects related to the iron extraction and the disposal of contaminants; and (2) Ternium's failure to pay royalties to the community for using its land (Rojas 2005; Méndez 2009).

It was not until 2010 that violence again began to directly impact the community via the presence of organized crime, triggering increased social and political instability. In December 2011, local people erected a blockade at the mine as an act of protest against the company's failure to pay royalties, which had not been paid that year, as well as a renegotiation of the payment terms, including an increase of payment for land use. These demands were not met, pushing the community to keep the blockade going until February 6, 2012, when approximately three hundred members of state security forces (including Federal Police, marines, and soldiers) tried to evict the protesters through violence and arbitrary detentions (Martínez Elorriaga 2012).

These detentions led to a repressive process, encouraged by the government of Michoacán, which resulted in the community being forced to sign an agreement with the company on March 18, 2012. This agreement stated that each *comunero* would receive an individual monthly payment of $18,000 pesos (approximately US$1,420). It is important to highlight that Aquila's main economic activities are agriculture and farming, despite the presence of the mine in the region. In this sense, as Santos Cordero and Martínez Silva (2015) argue, the community as a whole works as an advocacy institution. This socio-political constitution protects *comuneros* from changing capital cycles in the region. This configuration allowed the community to maintain its agrarian tradition within a context where mining became a predominant activity. The capital flows generated by the mining company did little to kick off economic development, as promised by the government. Instead, it facilitated a series of acts of corruption, which reached their highest levels with the presence of the Knights Templar.

On April 12, 2012, Ternium disclosed to the local press that an agreement had been signed with the community, claiming it was paying $12,000 pesos (US$914) to each one of the 464 *comuneros* on a monthly basis. The publication of this information was the act that would, in turn, condemn the people of Aquila, making them targets of the Knights Templar, who started to extort the local people by charging a percentage of the money they received in royalties.

On May 3, 2013, the community of Aquila rose up in arms against this extortion and finally managed to take over the local municipal offices on July 4. However, on August 14 of that same year, the state government, led by Jesús Reyna García[2] and Federal Security Commissioner Alfredo Castillo Cervantes, decided to disarticulate the movement using violence (see Chapter 10 for more discussion on Castillo, also known as the "Viceroy"). Two hundred *comuneros* were disarmed and over forty were arrested through arbitrary and nontransparent processes. Once more, a raid led by state forces that involved Federal Police, army, and navy targeted the people of Aquila. Instead of targeting criminal groups and the local extortionists, the state attack led to the detention of members of civil groups that had developed collective, alternative processes for their own protection.

ARMED MOBILIZATIONS AGAINST ORGANIZED CRIME IN MICHOACÁN: A SKETCH

Santa María Ostula, a Nahua community in the municipality of Aquila near the Las Encinas mine, was the first group to rise up in arms in 2009 against *caciques* (local powerbrokers), in order to repel those illegally occupying its territory. Later on, in 2011, the P'urhépecha community of Cherán created a community police force as a way of protecting its forests from illegal plundering and its territory from the presence of La Familia Michoacana. This project would eventually evolve into a political project of self-government for Cherán. Other communities across the Meseta P'urhépecha had similar projects of resistance and territory protection. However, many of them were eventually demobilized by organized crime (Paredes Coronel 2013b). This was the general panorama until February 2013, when some ranching groups and peasants decided to rise against the Knights Templar in the town of Felipe Carrillo Puerto, commonly known as La Ruana, in Buenavista, and in Tepalcatepec. The main distinction between the Indigenous mobilizations, known as

---

2 Reyna García was secretary of state in Michoacán from 2012 to 2014. He was named interim governor from April to October 2013, due to health issues forcing then Governor Fausto Vallejo to step down. In April 2014, Reyna García was arrested for having links with the Knights Templar and, as of mid-2017, remains in prison.

policías comunitarias (community police forces), and the upheavals by ranching groups, known as *autodefensas* (self-defence groups), is that the former responds to Indigenous customs and traditions and responds to a communal assembly, whereas the latter is formed by armed civil groups with no particular identity other than to protect their territory (see Chapter 9 in this volume).

Thanks to the different armed uprisings that took place in Michoacán in 2011 and 2014, first by community police forces and then by self-defence groups, things started to change in the state. Firstly, local quasi-militias managed to confront organized crime, disarticulating the Knights Templar almost entirely. The remaining Templars had to flee to a different state or hide to escape from the self-defence groups (Sergio Báez, interview, 2013). Secondly, thanks to the work of one of the self-defence coordinators, Dr. José Manuel Mireles Valverde, it was possible to make evident and question the link between organized crime and different sectors of political and economic power, at both state and federal levels (Paredes Coronel 2013a). The *autodefensas* opened up two fronts: one in the northeast reaching Apatzingán and Uruapan, and covering the region of avocado and lime production; and the other to the south towards the coast, in the municipalities of Aquila and Coahuayana, towards the port of Lázaro Cárdenas.

This organized and incipient operation reversed, to a certain extent, the logics of the necro-economy that was being exerted in Michoacán both by criminal organizations and state proxies. What the *autodefensa* movement is trying to accomplish today, along with the participation of diverse sectors of the population, are day-to-day actions that centre on the construction of projects of life and not death.

After the legalization of over half of the self-defence groups and an apparent pact with the federal government, both carried out by the federal security commissioner, Alfredo Castillo, old criminal groups re-emerged with different faces, recycling members of the Knights Templar. Groups such as Los Viagras, H3, Cartel de Michoacán, and Nueva Familia Michoacana (the New Michoacán Family) are all examples of cartel fragmentation. But, most importantly, these fragmented cartels represent a new series of interests and groups of power that remains intrinsically linked to Michoacán's most recent political structures after the collapse of Vallejo's government.

ILLEGAL VIOLENCE: "LA NUEZ"

Located in the centre of a deep gorge within the mountain range that divides the coast from Tierra Caliente, and edging the limits of Aquila, is the Nahua community of San Juan Huitzontla, in the municipality of Chinicuila. It only has two planned streets and a few loose trails. None of the streets are paved; the only construction that resembles urban planning is its tiny central plaza, with a kiosk and a church. The rest of the village consists of wooden houses with sheet metal roofs and porches full of flowerpots and chickens. The *jefatura de tenencia* (an office that represents the municipal government) is at the town's entrance. It consists of an abandoned building staffed by members of the community police, who also all participated in the *autodefensa* movement and who are today responsible for local security.

These men, who are between fifty and sixty years old, managed to expel organized crime with guns and security patrols operating twenty-four hours a day, seven days a week. During our visit, they welcomed us warmly, and, sitting in a sort of semicircle, they told the story of how things were before the *autodefensa* movement began. As community police member, Leónides Zambrano, describes:

> Here the Templars got in because someone within the community brought them. They weren't many, but they were heavily armed, and they began to threaten everyone. They had their parties in that store over there; they would play loud music, and they started recruiting some people from the community. If someone said something they would threaten to disappear or kill them, and they would always have their weapons hanging out. They would charge us quotas as they pleased, and those who couldn't or wouldn't pay decided to leave the community. This was mid-2011. (Interview, 2016)

Even though Huitzontla seems small and remote in comparison to other towns like Aquila or the coast of Michoacán, it is economically relevant because of the known existence of as yet untapped iron reserves. In fact, decades ago, the community resisted the arrival of Ternium (then HYLSA) and some illegal exploration that the firm decided to carry out in the 1980s (Correa 1982).

The mine the Knights Templar decided to illegally exploit is located just off the freeway that connects Tierra Caliente with the coast—located thirty-five minutes from Military Zone 65, within the Coalcomán municipality, and less than an hour from the navy post at Aquila. Here, vehicle traffic is constant, making it difficult to believe that no state or federal authority ever noticed thirty workers transporting heavy machinery and the presence of larger vehicles used to carry what, according to local calculations, could be around three hundred tons of iron daily.[3]

Since 2012, and until the self-defence group consolidated in Chinicuila in mid-2013, the Knights Templar transported the iron they were extracting directly to the state of Colima. "They were taking [the stolen iron] to Manzanillo. There, at the port of Manzanillo, they were taking it there," said Eustaquio Altanar Díaz, one of the key members of Chinicuila's communitarian police force (interview, 2016). Once there, the iron was stored in large containers used to illegally export the material to China, one of the principal countries with interest in this mineral (Hernández Navarro 2014; Redacción Sinembargo 2014). In fact, on May 1, 2014, a shipment was interdicted in Manzanillo containing 68,750 tons of illegally extracted iron (Jane's Information Group 2014). Commissioner Alfredo Castillo published a report incriminating the Knights Templar as the group responsible for the cargo, which was valued at approximately US$720,000. What is interesting about this instance is that once more the report only pointed to one specific criminal group instead of focusing on all the agents responsible in the port and customs, as well as the people or company buying the illegal iron.

Back in Chinicuila, the environment of fear spread across the community and the region, preventing the illegal mining operation from being shut down. The collusion of federal security officers, who openly allowed for this and other businesses to operate, provoked a feeling of uncertainty and helplessness across the community. As Eustaquio Altanar Díaz put it, "Organized crime had the entire municipality subjugated. Nothing could be done. They were also exploiting another mine up there, and they would bring down the material through this way too. It was a very tough situation" (interview, 2016).

News of the daily horrors, such as the killing and disappearances of many local residents, came from other towns. The Knights Templar, using the language of a discourse of a supposed uprising rooted in religion and social struggle (Moreno 2010) had taken over all spheres of

---

3   This number is an estimate given by local agrarian authorities.

public life, and, at the slightest hint of resistance, it would apply terrifying punishments—from beatings to brutal executions. This violence appears to be the main reason why it took so long for people to resist and fight against the Knights Templar: it was necessary for a larger movement to gather these fears in an organized way and to turn them into a community-led security and oversight strategy.

In May 2013, as national and international media coverage spread the news regarding the situation with the self-defence groups, the movement began to spread to diverse fronts as the self-defence groups tried to put an end to organized crime from the southern region of Tierra Caliente all the way to the coast. In a similar way to what had happened across other municipalities, some local people in Chinicuila secretly organized themselves, consolidating a self-defence group that would later be supported by groups coming from Tepalcatepec and Coalcomán. When the *autodefensas* reached Villa Victoria—the municipal centre of Chinicuila—they activated surveillance and search operations seeking the Templars, detaining many of the criminal actors and breaking apart the criminal organization in the region.

Little by little, with the help of the *autodefensas*, the people in Chinicuila heard testimony on the effects of violence and the horror stories that nearby communities had to face, being threatened with guns, killings, disappearances, rapes, and exorbitant extortions. Furthermore, they began to figure out the Knights Templar's modus operandi in matters related to mining exploitation, commercialization, and exportation.

In addition to fear, people also worried for their territory and environmental impacts due to contamination. The pollution of the natural environment, the illegal exploitation of their iron mines, and the collaboration of civil servants and security officers with organized crime are some of the key elements of the *accumulation through terror* that prevails in the region. It works as an organized system that operates both with and through the state—via institutional and para-institutional violence—exploiting and managing local communities, while exposing them to killings, disappearances, and complete land degradation.

NECROPOLITICS IN MICHOACÁN: TOWARDS A CONCLUSION

The activities of the Knights Templar in both case studies display how economic and political power no longer establishes simple alliances or strategic agreements with criminal power. The proximity and frequency of their associations have allowed both criminal power and the state to progress and consolidate into an amalgam that no longer allows us to distinguish the legal from the illegal—between who is governor, secretary of state, or local mayor, and who is cartel leader in a specific region within the state. Furthermore, the establishment of extractive projects, both in their legal and illegal forms, have constituted themselves through the imposition of fear and an active decision about who controls the land and who does not, who deserves security and protection, and who lives and who is killed—something that resembles Mbembe's conception of necropolitics. That is, "the ultimate expression of sovereignty [that] resides, to a large degree, in the power and capacity to dictate who may live and who must die" (2003, 11). The economic structures allowed a series of legal and illegal powers to constitute and maintain themselves through the decision to kill: a decision that became operative.

Subsequent to the formation of community police forces and self-defence groups in Michoacán, many of the points of protest that had previously existed in the state were channelled to a social renovation. Of course, this is not a simple task, and is even less so when these self-defence groups are unevenly armed and have been fragmented and divided by the federal government (see Chapter 9). Returning to Pansters's (2012) classification, community police forces in both Aquila and Chinicuila seem to represent a counter-institutional form of violence. And, through this organization, they have been able to generate safe spaces and recuperate their resources and goods. Furthermore, they created and practised social policy that worked from below as a way of thwarting processes of dispossession.

Following two years of open, violent confrontation between different organized criminal groups, state forces, community police, and self-defence groups, the people in several municipalities managed to foster increased political participation. Communities carried out local assemblies, where they discuss both the municipality's course of action and the decisions for the construction of a new political order. This new political order seeks to give more voice to both the local general assembly and a council of Elders, to monitor political parties and encourage local decision making as a way of strengthening local autonomy. In terms of security, the federal government has tried to impose a unified command as a way of eliminating existing police forces. The unified police command was a security strategy that sought to merge all police forces into one, managed from Mexico City. This strategy had two main elements: (1) to train all police forces to the same level; and (2) to establish a chain of command that responds all the way up to the National Security Council, passing through the governors instead of having local police forces controlled by local mayors. Citizen councils, community police, and the remaining self-defence groups have opposed this initiative, manifesting that it is they who can and should be responsible for security. Citizen councils have emerged at the local level (both in Indigenous and mestizo communities) as a way of creating alternative forms of local political organization through communal organization in order to avoid political parties.

Another relevant fact that is important to highlight in relation to the wave of violence and crime that affected Michoacán and to the case studies we have analyzed is the capacity that organized crime and political elites have to desacralize life, turning it into something that appears to have no value. Once rendered valueless, life can be taken away with no complications (Butler 2009). This is what has sustained a structure of biopower in Mexico during the second decade of the twenty-first century. The wave of violence and the alliances between governors, officials, and different criminal groups have allowed for their enrichment. More importantly, it has generated a fusion that will not be broken through palliative measures like welfare policies or symbolic political ceremonies. At the same time, market demand for legal and illegal commodities (such as iron or narcotics) seems to have a complete disregard for the lives that are being impacted by this violence—a violence that, as both case studies demonstrate, exploits and manages the population, exposing it to all sorts of dangers and risks (see Mbembe et al. 2016). Thus, it is only through an attempt to construct social, political, cultural, and economic alternatives from below that there will be space for another path in the future.

REFERENCES

Bunge Vivier, Verónica. 2012. "Los núcleos agrarios y su relación con la conservación de los recursos naturales." Instituto Nacional de Ecología y Cambio Climático, SEMARNAT. http://ine.gob.mx/descargas/cuencas/doc_trabajo_nucleos_agrarios_conservacion.pdf.
Butler, Judith. 2009. *Frames of War: When Is Life Grievable?* London: Verso.

CEDRSSA (Centro de Estudios para el Desarrollo Rural y Sustentable y la Soberanía Alimentaria). 2015. "La propiedad social rural y su perfil productivo." Mexico City: CEDRSSA.

Correa, Guillermo. 1982. "200 comunidades de Michoacán exigen a alfa 5,000 millones por saqueo." *Proceso*, June 5. http://www.proceso.com.mx/133611/200-comunidades-de-michoacan-exigen-a-alfa-5000-millones-por-saqueo.

Gil Olmos, José. 2015. *Batallas de Michoacán: Autodefensas, el proyecto colombiano de Peña Nieto*. Mexico City: Editorial Proceso.

Grillo, Ioan. 2011. *El Narco: Inside Mexico's Criminal Insurgency*. First American edition. New York: Bloomsbury Press.

Harvey, David. 2004. "The 'New' Imperialism: Accumulation by Dispossession." *Socialist Register* 40: 63–87.

Hernández Navarro, Luis. 2014. *Hermanos en armas: Policías comunitarias y autodefensas*. Texcoco, Mexico: Editorial Brigada Cultural.

INEGI (National Institute of Statistics and Geography). 2016. "Michoacán de Ocampo." México En Cifras. Aguascalientes, Mexico: Instituto Nacional de Estadística y Geografía.

Jane's Information Group. 2014. "Smuggling Operation Means Legitimate Mining Faces Delay to Iron Ore Exported through Mexico's Lázaro Cárdenas Port." Crimininology and Law Enforcement 86. The Americas. London: Jane's Country Risk Daily Report. http://silk.library.umass.edu/login?url=http://search.proquest.com/docview/1520547825?accountid=14572.

Koonings, Kees. 2012. "New Violence, Insecurity, and the State: Comparative Reflections on Latin America and Mexico." In *Violence, Coercion, and State-Making in Twentieth-Century Mexico: The Other Half of the Centaur*, edited by Wil G. Pansters, 255–78. Stanford, CA: Stanford University Press.

Las Encinas S.A. de C.V. 2007. "Proyecto de ampliación de la superficie de explotación de la 'Mina Aquila,' Aquila, Michoacán." SEMARNAT. http://sinat.semarnat.gob.mx/dgiraDocs/documentos/mich/estudios/2007/16MI2007M0010.pdf.

LopCam, Romeo. 2014. "Brevísima historia del crimen organizado en Michoacán (2 de 2)." *Agencia Autónoma de Comunicación Subversiones*, March 13. http://subversiones.org/archivos/21132.

Maldonado Aranda, Salvador. 2010. *Los márgenes del estado mexicano: Territorios ilegales, desarrollo y violencia en Michoacán*. Zamora, Mexico: El Colegio de Michoacán.

Martínez Elorriaga, Ernesto. 2012. "Policías y militares intentan desalojar bloqueo en Aquila." *La Jornada*, February 8. http://www.jornada.unam.mx/2012/02/08/estados/035n1est.

Martínez, Ernesto, Gustavo Castillo, and José Antonio Román. 2010. "De 1985 a 2009 el jefe del cártel la familia estuvo en la nómina del gobierno michoacano." *La Jornada*, December 9. http://www.jornada.unam.mx/2010/12/09/politica/015n1pol.

Mbembe, Achille. 2003. "Necropolitics." Translated by Libby Meintjes. *Public Culture* 15 (1): 11–40.

Mbembe, Achille, Amador Fernández-Savater, Pablo Lapuente Tiana, and Amarela Varela. 2016. "Achille Mbembe: 'Cuando el poder brutaliza el cuerpo, la resistencia asume una forma visceral.'" *Eldiario*, June 17. http://www.eldiario.es/interferencias/Achille-Mbembe-brutaliza-resistencia-visceral_6_527807255.html.

Méndez, Ángel. 2009. "Minera Ternium contrata empresa de relaciones públicas especialista en crisis." *Coahuayana: Visiones Urgentes*, November 27. http://coahuayanavisionesurgentes.blogspot.mx/2009/11/minera-ternium-contrata-empresa-de.html.

Morales, Edgardo. 2012. "Palabra de Caballero: Los Caballeros Templarios, un movimiento insurgente." Michoacán, Mexico: self-published.

Moreno, Nazario. 2010. "Me Dicen: 'El Más Loco.'" Michoacán, Mexico: self-published.

Navarro Trujillo, Mina Lorena. 2012. "Las luchas socioambientales en México como una expresión del antagonismo entre lo común y el despojo múltiple." *Observatorio Social en América Latina* XIII (32): 149–72.

Paley, Dawn. 2014. *Drug War Capitalism*. Oakland, CA: AK Press.

Pansters, Wil G. 2012. *Violence, Coercion, and State-Making in Twentieth-Century Mexico: The Other Half of the Centaur*. Stanford, CA: Stanford University Press. http://public.eblib.com/choice/publicfullrecord.aspx?p=881951.

Paredes Coronel, Heriberto. 2013a. "Autodefensa ciudadana en Tepacaltepec, Michoacán." *Agencia Autónoma de Comunicación Subversiones*, June 17. http://subversiones.org/archivos/8526.

———. 2013b. "Las rondas comunitarias P'urhépechas defienden el derecho a la vida." *Agencia Autónoma de Comunicación Subversiones*, July 16. http://subversiones.org/archivos/10604.

Redacción La Jornada Michoacán. 2010. "Nazario Moreno, dirigente del cártel y guía espiritual." *La Jornada Michoacán*, December 11. http://www.jornada.unam.mx/2010/12/11/politica/006n1pol.

Redacción Sinembargo. 2014. "Templarios envían hierro a China y les mandan químicos: WSJ; 'Cárteles compiten ya con empresas legítimas,' Dice." *SinEmbargo*, January 15. http://www.sinembargo.mx/15-01-2014/873559.

Rojas, Rosa. 2005. "Causa una minera daños a la salud y el ambiente en aquila, acusan representantes." *La Jornada*, December 2. http://www.jornada.unam.mx/2005/12/02/index.php?section=sociedad&article=053n1soc.

Santos Cordero, Blanca Ruth, and Eleocadio Martínez Silva. 2015. "El 'consentimiento' negociado entre dos comunidades mineras mexicanas y las trasnacionales Goldcorp y Ternium." *Región Y Sociedad* 27 (64): 285–311.

CHAPTER 9

CRIMINAL VIOLENCE AND ARMED COMMUNITY DEFENCE IN MEXICO

Antonio Fuentes Díaz

Translated from Spanish by Elisa Díaz

n February of 2013, media outlets in Michoacán and throughout the country reported that, in the community of La Ruana, a district of Buenavista located in the Tierra Caliente region, a group of people had seized weapons and two trucks from the municipal police to create their own security force after years of extortion and threats from criminal groups. Similar acts had also taken place simultaneously in the nearby district of Tepalcatepec; both began at noon on the last Sunday in February in the main plaza of each town.

The beginning of the community self-defence groups, made visible in La Ruana and Tepalcatepec during the first months of 2013, became widely known following the proliferation of these groups in the region, which totalled at least twenty-four. These self-defence events against organized crime in the country were neither isolated nor recent; seventeen years earlier, in the mountain and coastal regions of the state of

Guerrero, a security network had been assembled to protect the communities, leading to the creation of their own security force, known as the *policía comunitaria* (community police).

It was the violence experienced in different regions of Mexico—which has been felt with particular intensity in the state of Michoacán—that triggered the formation of the so-called self-defence groups. While greater visibility was given to community self-defence groups towards the end of 2013 in the region of Tierra Caliente, there were previous instances of similar groups in other regions of the state, such as in the case of Cherán, which began in 2011 in the Meseta P'urhépecha.

This chapter explores how community defence was organized in Michoacán, in the regions known as Tierra Caliente and the Meseta P'urhépecha.[1] It aims to identify some of the procedures and general characteristics that allow us to understand its development. In light of these examples, we will reflect on the establishment of social order by non-state armed actors, how organized violence operates through criminal rent, processes of appropriation of violence, self-determination and confrontation with the state that is showcased by the phenomenon of community self-defence, as well as the establishment of a grey area between legal and illegal actors.

SELF-DEFENCE GROUPS IN LATIN AMERICA AND MEXICO

Over the past decades, in a context including new forms of warfare, insecurity, and the erosion of the legitimate monopoly of violence in various parts of the world, a diversity of non-state armed actors has emerged (see Introduction). These groups have been brought together for a variety of objectives, ranging from the imposition of social order based on a religious, political, or ethnic orientation to the search for economic resources. Among some of these groups are guerrillas, militias, private

---

1   Michoacán is divided into 113 districts and ten regions according to their geographic and productive characteristics. Tierra Caliente and Meseta P'urhépecha are two of these regions. It is worth noticing that other self-defence groups exist in Michoacán, including in the coastal region, a strategic commercial area close to the port of Lázaro Cárdenas. See Chapter 10 on violence in Lázaro Cárdenas and Chapter 8 on community self-defence in Aquila, in the coastal region.

armies, drug trafficking groups, youth gangs, paramilitaries, and informal vigilantes (Schuberth 2015).

One particular formation, within the various non-state armed actors, are the community self-defence groups, which are created primarily against conditions of insecurity and risk for collectives and communities in order to organize structures to regulate security in their territories. In this chapter, we affirm that the containment of insecurity in the areas under study in Michoacán took place fundamentally as part of a confrontation between non-state armed groups: community self-defence groups against organized crime groups, in a dispute for the establishment of a new political order that would challenge the criminal order established through illegal activity.

Community self-defence groups were organized and became well known in rural areas of Colombia and Peru in the 1970s and 1980s. The emergence of these groups is directly related to the political and historical context from which they arose, each maintaining specific particularities.

In Colombia, the emergence of armed civilian groups happened in the context of the struggle against the communist threat, and this struggle was enshrined by the US-backed National Security doctrine. In 1968, after the Revolutionary Armed Forces of Colombia (the FARC) and the National Liberation Army (ELN) emerged,[2] the creation of private armies was promoted to restrain the armed insurgency from taking over property and assets of the Colombian oligarchy. The declaration of Law 48 regulated these paramilitary groups (Rivas Nieto and Rey Guerra 2008). In the 1990s, several of these armed civilian groups came together under the name of the Autodefensas Unidas de Colombia (United Self-Defence Forces of Colombia) and exercised political and commercial control in the territories they dominated, establishing cooperation and ties with the drug trade (Vargas Velázquez 2010; see also Chapter 6).

In Peru, towards the end of the 1970s, a series of communities in the provinces of Cajamarca and Piura founded a system of community defence. They formed Rondas Campesinas (Campesino Patrols), and their appearance had a measurable impact on the suppression of insecurity in rural regions practically outside state institutionality. The emergence of self-defence groups of armed civilians responds to particular historical contexts that give shape and sense to their formation.

---

2 The FARC emerged in 1964 and the ELN in 1965.

In Colombia, self-defence constituted a fundamental part of counter-insurgent strategy in a way that resembled the operation of the Patrullas de Autodefensa Civil (Civil Self-Defence Patrols—PACs) during the internal armed conflict in Guatemala. The PACs aimed to help the army's vigilance and control operations by patrolling villages and employing a network of informants to limit or prevent the infiltration of guerrillas in the communities (Snodgrass Godoy 2006).

In Peru, as Starn points out, "campesino patrols emerged in the context of a boom in criminal activity and of an utter distrust of official justice" (1991, 38). This experience, and its relationship to insecurity, is that which most corresponds to the appearance of self-defence groups that occurred in Mexico during the nineties, fundamentally structured against crimes of opportunity and in precarious contexts. A significant event that took place in Peru was that, when taking over security and surveillance functions, organized groups tended to provision themselves with other structures that surpassed the surveillance level. According to Starn, the groups that got together to make surveillance rounds led the government of Peru to establish an alternative system of justice that conducted open communal assemblies and solved an ample range of conflicts, from marital quarrels to disputes over land or cattle theft.

It is necessary to underscore the way in which grievances—and the lack of access to the justice system to resolve grievances—led to the instauration of security orders and justice structures parallel to the state justice system. In the Peruvian experience, Starn points out, "The peasants came to identify the patrols with a new spirit of local cooperation and autonomy...in some communities they made themselves responsible for small public works such as the construction of communal establishments, medical clinics, irrigation canals, and road maintenance" (1991, 44).

The rise of community defence groups in Mexico was first registered during the early 1990s. At that time, rising levels of criminal activity, the economic crisis, and the price liberalization of some agricultural products after the implementation of the North American Free Trade Agreement in 1994 created a perception of vulnerability on the part of various segments of the rural population and marginal urban sectors.

As a response, community defence groups were formed in different parts of the country. Such groups formed in Rincón de los Romos in Aguascalientes and in San Luis Potosí in 2001, the same year community-led justice brigades carried out operations against criminal activity in the state of Morelos and started to become well known. In 2006, two self-defence groups came together in Santa Cruz, Valle de Chalco-Solidaridad, and in Chimalhuacán, both in the state of Mexico (Ramón 2006). These early experiences were linked to conditions of insecurity and economic precarity connected to macro-structural transformations of neoliberal policies.

Communities that organized in self-defence in Guerrero created organizations that have supplanted the state functions of security. These groups have, through the exercise of self-government girded by customary laws, helped to form and strengthen locally organized governments, independent of the representational schemes on which state politics are based. These self-defence organizations formed the Coordinadora Regional de Autoridades Comunitarias—Policía Comunitaria (Regional Coordinator of Community Authorities—Community Police) in twenty villages of La Montaña and Costa Chica in the state of Guerrero.[3] There is also the example of Cherán, Michoacán, where the creation of the self-defence groups was part of a larger movement that, in the context of the 2011 state elections, established a communal council based on customary laws and practices. On August 26, 2011, the Indigenous community of Cherán sent a request to the Instituto Electoral de Michoacán (Electoral Institute of Michoacán), asking for its right to decide and choose the naming of community authorities as a historical prerogative. In this request, it noted that, as of April 15, 2011, the community would coordinate security and justice and recover community vigilance patrols (Instituto Electoral de Michoacán 2012).

Based on these experiences, it is possible to assert that the rise of community defence groups happens in accordance with the local political scenario and the historic context where they form, and that they can

---

3   The state of Guerrero is situated in southern Mexico, with Pacific coastline along a tropical region bordering Mexico state, Morelos, Puebla, Oaxaca, and Michoacán. The Costa Chica is one of the seven economic and cultural regions that make up the state of Guerrero. It begins to the southeast of Acapulco and extends through the central coast to the state of Oaxaca. This region is composed of fifteen municipalities, including San Luis Acatlán, Marquelia, and Ayutla de los Libres, with a total of 449,164 inhabitants (INEGI 2016).

take on a variety of social manifestations. The term *community defence* best encompasses the different particularities under which a defensive organization presents itself without skewing its interpretation towards a historically situated notion.

The qualitative change in security conditions in Michoacán over the past few years is the result of two factors. On the one hand, it is connected to the conflict between drug cartels and the public policy to confront them. This was the case with the war on drugs embodied by Operación Conjunta Michoacán (Joint Operation Michoacán) during the presidency of Felipe Calderón (2006–2012). On the other, it relates to the way in which drug-trafficking operations upset the communitarian basis of society, breaking equilibrium in the local environment between illegality and communities, and rising as a parallel power that infiltrated government state structures. Increases in insecurity are relevant in understanding the rise of community defence groups.

This new type of insecurity was ushered in by the neoliberalization of drug-trafficking organizations, which transformed into structures akin to transnational corporations dedicated to organized crime through a diversification of their revenues beyond the harvesting and trafficking of prohibited substances.

ORGANIZED CRIME AND LOCAL ORDER

During the last four decades of the twentieth century, the Dirección Federal de Seguridad (Federal Security Directorate—DFS), an intelligence organ of the federal government, regulated drug trafficking in Mexico. This regulation rested on the subordination of criminal organizations to the DFS through reciprocal benefit sharing, such as the handing over of the *plaza*,[4] and the distribution of profits. This regulation was part of a balanced order between drug traffickers, the communities where they operated, and the state at a regional level. In the 1990s, after the elimination of the DFS and a series of structural transformations in politics and the economy, this model of regulation was destroyed and decentralized towards local governments. This led to a transformation

---

4   We understand *plaza* as the exercise of territorial control by one group; generally, it is used to refer to the dominance over trafficking routes and markets by criminal organizations.

in how drug trafficking operated, including a diversification by criminal groups towards other profit-making activities (for a discussion of similar phenomena in Tamaulipas, see Chapter 7).

Drug-trafficking organizations have been present in Michoacán since the 1940s, but in the last few years the control of the illegal substance market and the diversification of criminal activities on the part of organized crime groups directly began to harm the communities where they operated and recruited members. Different groups have been present in Michoacán in recent years: Los Zetas (the Zetas), La Familia Michoacana (the Michoacán Family), and Los Caballeros Templarios (the Knights Templar). During the latter half of the 2000s, involvement of drug cartels in diverse activities was noteworthy: the Knights Templar employed a series of methods through which they maintained their high profit margin, which had been undermined by the state policy of military action against drug traffickers. These alternative methods included extortion, mineral trafficking (see Chapter 8), and the illegal importation of luxury items from China. Extortion was the most harmful of these new methods, as it broke the balance of local power between drug-dealing groups and communities that had been established over the years through relationships of collusion and mutual interest. It is in the context of the rupture of this equilibrium of local power that the emergence of community defence groups makes sense in both its regional manifestations: as community police and as self-defence groups.

The organization of community defence groups differs from that of community police in a number of ways: in the profiles of their members and the form in which community response is articulated through ethnicity; resources; commercial exchange; geographic location; the level of state participation in the public sphere; and the establishment of local political equilibrium under the context of illegality. The community defence groups that have risen up in Mexico are not homogeneous in their principles, internal organization, structures of responsibility, or political aspirations. One of the main challenges the federal government faced during the first months after the community defence groups appeared in 2013 was understanding the scope, dimensions, and the heterogeneous nature of the community defence groups in order to generate a relevant political response. "One of the federal government's mistakes in Michoacán has been that it superficially understands this situation as a confrontation between two or more self-defense groups, leading them to reach the conclusion that it was enough to choose and support one and supplant the other," according to Mexican organization México Evalúa (2014). The heterogeneous conformation of the self-defence groups explains the different denominations they have given themselves (community patrols, community police, or self-defence groups) and the differences in the way they negotiate with the government, which, in turn, should determine a distinct political and legal approach towards each group.

Francisco López Bárcenas (2014) proposes we understand the difference between community police and self-defence groups through the importance given to regulation and organization. Community police are organized around structures of control and accountability embedded in the use of customary law; based on community assemblies and charging schemes, as well as having their own detention and trial procedures as regulated by customary uses and practices with legal state recognition under the Second Article of the Mexican Political Constitution and the International Labour Organization's Convention 169 (Castellanos 2013).

On the other hand, community defence groups are not always subordinate to the control of a higher command structure, nor are they legally backed by recognized customary law. Community defence groups generally occur in mestizo populations that do not necessarily have a unified Indigenous identity. These differences, without a doubt, have led them to develop particular political strategies with regards to their forms of expression and confrontations with the state.

NEOLIBERAL RESTRUCTURING AND INSECURITY

The state of Michoacán is ranked as one of Mexico's leading producers of avocado, lime, guava, melon, mango, and papaya for national and international markets. The Meseta P'urhépecha possesses considerable expanses of temperate forests and precious wood, particularly in Cherán and in the Valle de los Reyes, where blackberries are produced for the international market, especially for Europe, Japan, and the United States. The Meseta P'urhépecha region is in the north-central area of Michoacán and is composed of thirteen districts. The region is characterized by expanses of temperate woods, a substantial Indigenous population, high indexes of poverty, marginalization, and unequal access to potable water.

Despite being home to important farming activities, Michoacán has the eighth-highest index of marginalization in Mexico and the third-highest rate of outwards migration to the United States.

Drug trafficking in Michoacán grew alongside the modernization of infrastructure and investment in development projects from the 1940s to the 1960s. Over several decades, the business of drug trafficking was intertwined with the regional economy, as legal and illegal activities constituted important circuits of value in the regions they operated. Drug trafficking acted as a catalyst for regional development, based primarily on the high revenues that resulted due to its illegality. Thus, drug trafficking in Michoacán's Tierra Caliente, the inland region bordering the Meseta, emerged in parallel to the modernization and capital investment that began in the 1960s (Malkin 2001). The agricultural transnationalization of the region mirrored the transnationalization of criminal activity and drug trafficking, which has since become an important part of day-to-day activities on the community level (Malkin 2001).

The transnationalization of criminal activity and the decentralized regulation on the part of the Mexican state after 1990 forced those involved in drug trafficking to diversify their activities to maintain high profit rates by means other than the cultivation and transportation of illegal substances to the United States. This criminal economic diversification manifested itself primarily in the extortion of people and institutions, kidnapping, control of iron mines, commercialization of harvests, trading in Chinese clothing, the theft of vehicles, and the clandestine logging of communal forests. In November 2013, the fact that most municipalities in Michoacán paid a fee or quota to criminal organizations was first made public ("Cien de 113 alcaldes michoacanos" 2013). This meant the illegal profile of drug-trafficking organizations had been transformed into a criminal business of organized crime.

In 2009, the Knights Templar appeared in Michoacán. This criminal group is recognized as a splinter of a previous group that called itself La Familia Michoacana. A feud ensued between different criminal groups for control of the state, which is valued due to its strategic importance in the production and transportation of illegal substances, as well as for its general economic relevance and natural resources. The Knights Templar controlled the exportation of iron to China by the ton, which was exchanged for the chemical precursors used in the elaboration of synthetic drugs (González 2014; see also Chapter 10 of this volume).

The diversification of criminal activities is part of what Luis Hernández Navarro describes as "the Templar enterprise," a corporation led by businessmen where illegal substances are but one of its business areas (2014). Hernández Navarro points out that this group is dedicated to administering violence, justice, and tax collection; its businesses, he contends, have woven an entrepreneurial network that controls the main productive trades of Michoacán (2014). In light of this situation, organized crime groups are capable of sustaining the relationship between diverse regions with agro-industrial production and violence within a framework that operates in complementarity with the legal economy.

It was predictable that the Templars' control would become an example of how the abuse of power by criminal groups harmed the inhabitants in their areas of influence. During fieldwork in Tierra Caliente, I could see that, beyond extortion, an overpowering grievance was sexual violence against women in various communities of the region. It is possible to understand that both the new extortion regimes and the sexual violence of the transformed criminal order were established as direct affronts against communities, which broke with the previously existing reciprocity between drug traffickers and local residents. In an interview, Hipólito Mora, spokesman for the self-defence group of La Ruana, commented, "If the Templars wouldn't have crossed the line with regards to extortion and abuses against our families, the self-defence groups would not have formed" (Interview, February 23, 2014).

COMMUNITY DEFENCE GROUPS IN TIERRA CALIENTE

On February 24, 2013, the first self-defence group started in Michoacán, in the community of Felipe Carrillo Puerto, locally known as La Ruana, in the municipality of Buenavista. La Ruana possesses large expanses of land used in the cultivation of agricultural exports, mainly limes. The Knights Templar gradually took over the commercial network of limes and began charging the producers extortion quotas. It is estimated that the amount of extortion collected by the Knights Templar in 2012 was US$176 million (Macias and Rosales 2013). This group, having positioned itself as an intermediary between producers and large-scale buyers, decided which producers to buy from and which to exclude, negatively affecting both day labourers and farm owners. These are the situations that led to the establishment of community defence groups in La Ruana, as it was one of the communities where agricultural production was most affected by extortion. Later, La Ruana would become the leader of the regional community defence movement. In Tepalcatepec, a neighbouring district to La Ruana, the community defence organization formed almost simultaneously and for the same reason: in response to the violations and extortion effected upon local livestock owners and upon nearly all of the formal economy. The "Templar Tax" was obtained by force and paid for through an increase in the price of basic consumer goods.

COMMUNITY POLICE IN CHERÁN

In the communities of the Meseta P'urhépecha, significant production of avocado and blackberries points to a dynamic market with high economic revenues, which also proved attractive for the diversification of organized crime activities. In this region, two significant organizations arose to defend the community: the community police in the district of Cherán, founded in 2011, and the community police in the municipality of Los Reyes, founded in July 2013.

On April 15, 2011, communal land owners of the district of Cherán, in the Meseta P'urhépecha, organized themselves to defend their territory in response to clandestine logging carried out by the Knights Templar. Through a system of complicity with district authorities, the Knights Templar had established territorial control in Cherán. The advantage of this association with the authorities allowed for the undue use of communal goods, such as the forest and water, as well as the extortion of regional merchants. By 2011, shops in Cherán had to pay as much as MX$10,000 pesos per month (roughly US$500) in extortion (Torres 2011).

The reaction against clandestine logging of the communal forests, as well as kidnappings and extortion of residents of Cherán, crystallized as a movement of self-defence initially led by women, which, months later, resulted in the creation of a permanent structure of security and oversight against the offensive actions of organized crime and its participation in clandestine logging and extortion. After confirming that members of the Ministerial Police (a police force with jurisdiction at the municipal level) had colluded with criminal groups in the area during a community assembly, a decision was made to dissolve the police in August of the same year. It was decided that local inhabitants would assume the safety functions.

With the goal of making these defence and security actions permanent, two distinct security structures were formed: community police were put in charge of civil security and patrolling the four neighbourhoods in the community, and a group of forest rangers was tasked with watching over communal woodlands. Notably, both security forces are articulated to other structures of command and representation in the community.

The indifference of state and district authorities in the face of the demands for security led the people of Cherán to leverage their activities towards territorial defence to take advantage of the midterm elections of 2011. Community members decided to transition towards a local government, independent of political parties. In this way, a communal government was established for the period from 2012 to 2015.[5] The communal government is structured through a series of councils, with territorial representation in each of the four neighbourhoods of the community. The highest authority is the full assembly, followed by a series of councils and assemblies from the four neighbourhoods. Within the autonomous government there is also a prosecutorial council and a council of oversight, the former coordinates the community police and the latter the forest rangers.

COMMUNITY POLICE IN LOS REYES

The district of Los Reyes is located in Tierra Caliente, in the northwest of Michoacán, bordering to the north with Tingüindin, to the west with Tocumbo, to the east with Charapan and Uruapan, and to the south with Periban and the state of Jalisco. In 2009, the district of Los Reyes had 64,164 inhabitants who lived in thirty-five rural communities. In this same year it had P'urhépecha inhabitants in nineteen communities, mainly in the mountains. Until recently, the economy of Los Reyes was based on the production of sugar in two refineries: San Sebastián and Santa Clara. However, during the worldwide sugar crisis

---

5   The Electoral Tribunal of the Federal Judiciary recognized the communal government in 2015 as a legal body that can present itself as a political option during electoral periods. Through this process, a new communal council was elected during interim elections in 2015 for the period 2015–2018, and the communal council will run in Cherán in the federal elections in 2018.

in the 1990s, the San Sebastián refinery closed, with the expectation that Santa Clara would process all the cane in the valley and, thus, the state would save on the production expenses incurred by the second refinery. This situation accelerated the productive reconversion of the region, as local landowners began to search for alternative harvests to sugar cane. This is how the cultivation of nontraditional berries for export (blackberries, strawberries, cranberries, raspberries, and blueberries) began in the area. Berry harvests have become so important in the district that within a few years Los Reyes ranked as the foremost blackberry producer in the world. Despite the growing number of hectares dedicated to berry plantations (approximately four thousand), there remains an even larger land base used for the sugar cane plantation (approximately five thousand hectares). The coexistence of both of these agricultural products in the area, together with other crops such as avocado, is evident to any visitor to the region. Mexico is the largest avocado producer in the world, and Michoacán the largest in the country.

For the last ten years, the Knights Templar has controlled the productive circuits in the blackberry and avocado sectors (Hernández Navarro 2014). Because Los Reyes is a region where commercial activity and exportation agriculture are so important, there was also a strong presence, according to residents, of organized crime. The collection of extortion fees did not happen in person. On the contrary, the Knights Templar charged transnational commercial enterprises one peso per blueberry box.[6] Its modus operandi in Tierra Caliente is similar to that used with the avocado production in the Meseta P'urhépecha.[7]

The villages of Cherato, Cheratillo, 18 de Marzo, and Oruscato, which are located in the mountainous area of Los Reyes, and which had previously been untouched by the criminal presence in the city centre located in the valley, began to experience the presence of organized crime and were forced to pay extortion quotas: producers paid two thousand pesos (just over US$100) for each hectare of avocado, and the small-scale sellers paid three pesos (about sixteen US cents) per kilogram. The

6 Fieldwork notes from Los Reyes, Michoacán, February 22, 2014.

7 The quota can be as high as ten US cents for each kilo produced, US$115 per hectare, and US$250 per hectare that produced exportation materials (Hottsen 2014).

communities asked the district of Los Reyes for protection in order to stop this extortion and received no response.

In March 2013, criminal groups kidnapped the "Person Responsible for Order"[8] in Cherato as retaliation for his not having paid the extortion fee. This event spurred the formation of a community defence group against organized crime in Cherato under the figure of the community police. One of its first actions was to establish roadblocks on the highway connecting the valley with the mountain range, which allowed it to control who accessed the communities.

On July 22, 2013, the murder of five members of the community defence group in Cherato was broadcast on national television. The five were killed during a march in front of the city hall of Los Reyes to demand the intervention of the local government to stop the extortions carried out by the Knights Templar. Following the massacre, on September 15, 2013, locals gathered in an assembly to discuss how they would form the community self-defence group, which they decided to base on their shared heritage as Indigenous peoples through the creation of the Community Police of Cherato.

EXTORTION SYSTEMS AND CRIMINAL ORDER

In Michoacán, as in other parts of Mexico, criminal groups sought legitimacy by presenting themselves as guarantors of security in the villages where they operated in exchange for *cuotas* (regular payments) that are a kind of extortion rent. Payment for security is a strategy used by criminal organizations around the world as a way to compensate for or increase their criminal earnings. Charging regular payments indicates there is a territorial control being created, as well as the instauration of a political-criminal system that requires the forced, permanent acquisition of resources for its subsistence, creating a system of extraction. We understand the extortion system imposed by these non-state armed groups (organized crime) as a form of organized violence (see the Introduction to this volume), given that it requires a kind

---

8 The "Person Responsible for Order" is a figure in the municipal government structure in the state of Michoacán who is the representative of the government and public administration in settlements located outside the municipal centre. It is an elected position with a three-year term.

of systematization so as to reach its economic and political objectives, generating a criminal regulatory order.

In my fieldwork in Tepalcatepec and La Ruana, I observed that all commercial activity was regulated by the Knights Templar, which charged a tax on basic goods, including meat, milk, and tortillas. It also charged a *cuota* of five pesos per child that attended the local schools, a *cuota* measured by the width of the front of houses, by kilogram of harvested product, as well as by charging in-kind. An anecdote I was told during an interview with a primary school teacher gives a notion of the criminal extortion system: an iguana seller was subject to extortion; for every eight iguanas he caught weekly to sell, the local capo, nicknamed El Toro, required him to hand over five or face death. On numerous occasions, once the capo had the iguanas, he forced the local primary school teacher, who had learned to cook in a restaurant in the United States, to cook them.[9] This anecdote allows us to understand the construction of a criminal order based on extortion. We can thus understand extortion as an extensive chain of profit extraction in a circuit of value that includes legal and illegal commodities, in which the use of force becomes a central element of production. This system of rent extraction generates a regulating force on the part of criminal actors, establishing a kind of criminal order with penalties and rewards, which disputes and complements state sovereignty, leading to a local rearrangement of power through the coordination of political and economic activities, carrying out security functions, killing or letting live, which is to say, carrying out the functions of the government (Fuentes Díaz 2018).

Extortion has become a central component of non-state armed groups, and constitutes a part of a value chain that links criminal activities with the accumulation of capital (see the Introduction to this volume), in a relationship that some have denominated criminal capitalism (Pegoraro 2015; Estrada 2008). In this part of Michoacán, as well as in other parts of the country, criminal groups are not directly dependent on a rational state command. Rather, they operate through mechanisms of extraction and regulation of surplus, in which private, public, legal, and illegal actors are present, all of them seeking to increase their rent. The relation between these groups and the state takes place in a zone of indistinct relations between criminals and the state, fundamentally at

9 Fieldwork notes from Tepalcatepec, Michoacán, August 18, 2016.

the municipal level (though, in Michoacán, this zone was active all the way to the state governor). This is a grey zone in which there is no distinction between the state and crime (Fuentes Díaz 2018).

IMAGINARIES OF LOCAL SOCIAL ORDER AND ADVERSARIAL PROCESSES

In the examples described in this chapter, we can begin to understand the differences in the formation of community defence groups in Tierra Caliente and community police in the Meseta P'urhépecha and the mountainous region of Los Reyes. Both defensive forms exhibit an attempt to reorganize the local environment in the midst of a disruption generated by the neoliberal diversification of drug cartel activities. In this attempt to reorganize local power structures, communities or parts of communities display strategies of force, appropriating security and justice and generating new *imaginaries of local social order*, which oppose criminal order and structure themselves around active conflict areas where the social composition of groups is important, as is the availability of material and symbolic resources (Escalona Victoria 2011). The trajectories of these groups allow for contentious resistance against the state while simultaneously confronting the parallel power of organized crime groups in various ways.

In the case of the community police of the Meseta P'urhépecha and the mountainous regions (*sierra*), their ethnic identification and their vindication of customary practices allow for their defensive organization experiences to converge as government structures (this happened in a concrete way in the case of Cherán). These particularities allow said communities to negotiate with the state through the use of juridical elements, such as the appeal of the Second Article of the Constitution, which delineates the right to self-determination of Indigenous villages, in order to back up their right to maintain their security forces while also ensuring a certain independence in their planning and organization.

Following federal intervention in the region during the first months of 2014, carried out through public policy meant to interrupt and control community self-defence groups, called Plan Michoacán,[10] the

---

10 Announced on February 5, 2014, the plan consisted of 250 actions towards the social reconstruction of Michoacán, structured around five pillars,...

proposal to legalize defensive groups emerged as a hegemonic process (Roseberry 2012); negotiation and contentious language were used to structure dialogue between rebel communities and the federal government. During the years before the community defences arose, members of settlements in the mountains of Los Reyes had spoken out about a drinking water shortage problem and had repeatedly put forth petitions for the perforation of a well that would supply communities with water. Similar requests had been put forth to create a health clinic and a middle school, which currently shares classrooms with the elementary school.

In February 2014, after a meeting of community police with representatives of the federal government under the framework of Plan Michoacán, community cafeterias sponsored by the program Sin Hambre (End Hunger)[11] were established in Cherato and Pamatácuaro, and an agreement was reached regarding the drilling of a well and the construction of a building that would become the middle school and the health clinic. A member of the Cherato Council who is the parent of a middle school student commented in an interview that if the community police had not been created and the highway accesses not closed, the assistance of the state and federal government would not have arrived. We see that non-institutional and non-legal pressure is the most efficient way for communities to elicit a response from the government. The use of legal and procedural channels had been repeatedly attempted; the institutional inefficiency and the incapability of the state to respond promptly are well known. Perhaps this is the way the state operates in some rural sectors of Michoacán and the rest of the country: it makes its form of domination felt through its own palpable intermittence, through long wait times in attending to the population. This confirms that resorting to the appropriation of force is both necessary and legitimate. Towards the end of 2014, once the health clinic had been built in Los Reyes, a new

---

...with an investment of 45.5 billion pesos, including an increase in social programs and in the budget of the federal Secretariat of Agriculture, Livestock, Rural Development, Fisheries and Food. This plan was initially designed for Tierra Caliente.

11 Sin Hambre is a government development program run by the current federal administration that strives to reduce hunger in marginal areas of the country through the creation of subsidized community cafeterias.

tempography of domination[12] arose: the administrative process of asking for a doctor and nurses (Auyero 2012).

Farmers and cattle ranchers convened the community defence groups that emerged in Tierra Caliente, where people identify with the figure of the rancher. Community defence groups in this area tended to come together under a model of vigilantism, operating with the dual purpose of opposing and weakening the Knights Templar, as well as preventing a new group from taking over criminal activities. Vigilantism here refers to a mode of crime suppression or to the instauration of a social order carried out by private individuals through extrajudicial means.

LEGALIZATION AND CRIMINALIZATION OF COMMUNITY DEFENCE GROUPS

At the outset of 2014, a new strategy of containment aimed at community defence groups in Michoacán was coordinated as part of state policy. The federal government named a Special Commission for the Comprehensive Development and Security of Michoacán, known colloquially as the "Viceroyalty," in which emphasis was placed on the legalization of community defence groups, be they self-defence groups or community police, through a process of incorporating them into state forces as Fuerza Rural (Rural Police Force) (Ramos Pérez 2014; see Chapter 8 and Chapter 10 for further discussion of the "Viceroyalty"). In this way, a fourth figure was created within police forces in Michoacán that previously did not exist: a state-level Rural Police Force that operates under the Secretary of Public Security of the State of Michoacán.[13]

In July of 2014, the first groups of the Rural Police Force were stood up and trained. Not all of those who participated in self-defence groups or community police were allowed to become Rural Police, as they failed aptitude tests, toxicology exams, or were below the legal age to enter into the formalized police force.

---

12 Auyero adds "tempography of domination" to the forms in which domination is experienced through time and waiting. "Waiting...is one of the key forms through which the effects of power are felt" (2012, 44); to make people wait, without destroying hope, works as a mechanism of control and demobilization.

13 Previously, there were three groups that constituted the police in Michoacán: Federal Police, state police, and municipal police.

196 | ORGANIZED VIOLENCE

Just as each community defence group had certain specific particularities, each group of Rural Police responded to particular contexts, which meant the process of implementation of the Rural Police was different from one place to another. During fieldwork, I was able to observe how, for example, in Tepalcatepec and La Ruana, the key demand of the community defence groups was the end of extortion and sexual violence, and when they could not become community police under Article 2 of the Constitution (which provides for the right to self-determination of Indigenous peoples), their strategy was incorporation and legalization through the figure of the Rural Police. In this way, members of these groups avoided the punishment that was forthcoming for members of the soon-to-be-illegal self-defence groups. In Cherato, the adoption of this strategy meant that its community police, formed in 2013 in adherence to Article 2 of the Constitution, would become part of the Rural Police. The negotiations to this end with the federal government resulted in agreements to comply with previous commitments, like the construction of a high school, the drilling of a well, and the building of a health clinic. Various self-defence groups, especially in the coastal and Tierra Caliente regions, did not participate in the legalization process and were reticent to form part of the Rural Police. Various leaders of the groups that resisted incorporation were jailed or killed. In other areas, like Cherán and Nurio, community police organizations did not incorporate into Rural Police because they were already operating under a legally recognized framework.

During the creation of the Rural Police Force, many members of community defence organizations and community police questioned the process, claiming that former members of the Knights Templar had entered into the Rural Police Force. This distrust proved grounded in reason when the federal government, through Commissioner Alfredo Castillo, encouraged the creation of an elite group from the region of Apatzingán, which was legalized into the Rural Police Force, into a group called G-250. Said group was created to capture the leaders of the Templars, particularly its spokesman, Servando Gómez (also known as La Tuta). G-250 was formed from ex-self-defence members, many of whom had previously belonged to criminal organizations like Los Viagras, led by the Sierra Santana brothers, and the Third Brotherhood (Los H3), headed by José Antonio Torres (Simón El Americano), who had operated as sharpshooters and hit men for La Familia Michoacana and the Knights

Templar. In this way, the strategy of Commissioner Castillo was to use criminal groups—that were rivals to the Templars but had legalized into the Rural Police Force—to pursue the Templars during an eight-month campaign in the mountains and Tierra Caliente. Once La Tuta was located, the G-250 group was dissolved and the alliance between the government and members of the smaller criminal organizations was broken.

During the period that the G-250 was legalized, there was a four-to-six-month delay in the payments promised by the federal government to the new members of the Rural Police Force. This led to desertion by various members, while others organized protests to demand payment of their salaries.[14] One of the bloodiest protests took place on January 6, 2015, in Apatzingan: sixteen people were killed. Around one hundred former members of the G-250 occupied the offices of the mayor to protest against Commissioner Castillo's dissolution of the group twenty days earlier, without payment or indemnities paid to members. Members of the Federal Police and the Mexican Army broke up the occupation, detaining forty-four people, killing sixteen others, and wounding dozens more, among them family members of demonstrators (Castellanos 2015). These extrajudicial executions carried out by the Federal Police and the army were not isolated. Months earlier, in Tlatlaya, Mexico state, twenty-two young people were killed by soldiers in an operation directed against a drug-trafficking organization, and, months earlier, on May 22, 2015, forty-two people were killed in a similar operation in Tanhuato, Michoacán, without any legal consequences for the perpetrators.

In April of 2016, the government of the state of Michoacán declared the Rural Police extinct and its members were moved over to a new state police force, called the Policía Única Michoacán (Unified Police of Michoacán), made up of 561 officers from the Rural Police (Pacheco 2016). The legalization process was in effect a process of draining the community defence movement, which had exploded in the face of insecurity generated by state omission and criminality, into state police forces. The endgame was to reduce a disruptive, complex, and polyphonic movement into a homogenous, controlled, and state-sanctioned police force. However, the situation on the ground remains highly complex because, though a unified police force has been created in Michoacán, there remain community defence groups that have not accepted state

---

14 Fieldwork notes from Los Reyes, Michoacán, July 22, 2014.

legalization or that did not enter into legal structures due to their failure to pass entry requirements. For these reasons, there remains a plurality of armed actors in the state, with varying capacities to regulate local life through force.

CONCLUSIONS

The analysis of Michoacán evidences the complex juncture that allows for the uprising of community defence groups. Tierra Caliente and the Meseta P'urhépecha exemplify the construction of organizations that replace or challenge state functions, establishing alternative forms of security and justice through the appropriation or reduction of violence in situations marked by a dispute over the *imaginaries of local social order* in the face of criminal groups and the state.

Based on my research in these areas, I believe we can understand that the emergence of self-defence groups is the result of different experiences of violence and of a series of material and symbolic factors that allow community defence groups to negotiate with various levels of government, while also confronting criminal groups. Local experiences, resources, and community structures give community defence groups the possibility to shape varying, long-term, political goals. The disputes discussed above, as well as the implementation of security, justice, and order from within communities, allow for negotiation processes to occur at the margins of state power, where legitimacy and the function of state institutionality are questioned and surpassed in favour of the defence of life.

REFERENCES

Auyero, Javier. 2012. *Patients of the State: The Politics of Waiting in Argentina*. Durham, NC: Duke University Press.

Castellanos, Laura. 2013. "Justicia propia, bajo amparo legal." *El Universal*, February 23. http://archivo.eluniversal.com.mx/estados/89645.html.

———. 2015. "Las ejecuciones de Apatzingán: policías federales, los autores." *Proceso*, April 18. https://www.proceso.com.mx/401646/401646-apatzingan-6-de-enero-matenlos.

"Cien de 113 alcaldes michoacanos pagan cuotas a Caballeros Templarios." 2013. *La Jornada*, November 10. http://www.jornada.com.mx/2013/11/10/estados/024n1est.

Escalona Victoria, José Luis. 2011. "El incompleto imaginario del orden, la inacabada maquinaria burocrática y el espacio de lucha: Antropología del Estado desde el sureste de México." In *(Trans)formaciones del Estado en los Márgenes de Latinoamérica*, edited by Alejandro Agudo Sanchíz and Marco Estrada Saavedra, 45–86. Mexico City: El Colegio de México-Universidad Iberoamericana.

Estrada Álvarez, Jairo. 2008. "Capitalismo criminal: Tendencias de acumulación y estructuración del régimen político." In *Capitalismo criminal: Ensayos críticos*, edited by Jairo Estrada Álvarez, 63–78. Bogotá: Universidad Nacional de Colombia.

Fuentes Díaz, Antonio. 2018. "Community Defense and Criminal Order in Michoacán: Contention in the Grey Area." *Latin American Perspectives* 45 (6): 127–39. First published in 2017. https://journals.sagepub.com/doi/10.1177/0094582X17719066.

González, Sergio. 2014. *Campo de Guerra*. Colección Argumentos. Barcelona, Spain: Anagrama.

Hernández Navarro, Luis. 2014. "La empresa templaria." *La Jornada*, February 11. http://www.jornada.com.mx/2014/02/11/opinion/017a2pol.

Hottsen, Jan Albert. 2014. "Aguacates de sangre: el lado oscuro del guacamole." Radio Nederland Internacional, June 2.

INEGI (Instituto Nacional de Estadística, Geografía e Informática). 2016. *Población cubos dinámicos DGIS / últimas proyecciones CONAPO*. Aguascalientes, Mexico: INEGI.

Instituto Electoral de Michoacán. 2012. "Especial Cherán: Elecciones por usos y costumbre." *Expresiones: Órgano Oficial de Difusión del IEM*, n. 15, Segunda época.

López Bárcenas, Francisco. 2014. "Policías comunitarias y autodefensas: Una distinción necesaria." *La Jornada*, January 24. http://www.jornada.com.mx/2014/01/23/opinion/017a1pol.

Macías, V., and R. Rosales. 2013. "Extorsión a aguacateros da a Templarios 2000 millones de pesos al año." *El Economista*, November 2. http://m.eleconomista/seguridadpublica.

Malkin, Victoria. 2001. "Narcotráfico, migración y modernidad." In *La Tierra Caliente de Michoacán*, edited by Eduardo Zarate, 549–84. Michoacán, Mexico: El Colegio de Michoacán/Gobierno del Estado de Michoacán.

México Evalúa. 2014. *Entender para atender: por una estrategia de Estado en Michoacán*. Michoacán, Mexico: Centro de Análisis de Políticas Públicas, A.C.

Pacheco, Juan. 2016. "Dan de alta a 561 elementos de la extinta fuerza rural." *Quadratín*, April 12. https://www.quadratin.com.mx/justicia/Dan-alta-561-elementos-la-extinta-Fuerza-Rural/.

Pegoraro, Juan S. 2015. *Los lazos sociales del delito económico y el orden social*. Buenos Aires, Argentina: Eudeba.

Ramón, René. 2006. "Ante el azote de la delincuencia nacen brigadas de autodefensa." *La Jornada*, December 2. http://www.jornada.com.mx/2006/12/03/index.php?section=estados&article=034n1est.

Ramos Pérez, Jorge. 2014. "Pactan legalizar las autodefensas." *El Universal*, January 28. http://archivo.eluniversal.com.mx/nacion-mexico/2014/pactan-legalizar-las-autodefensas-982975.html.

Rivas Nieto, Pedro, and Pablo Rey Guerra. 2008. "Las autodefensas y el paramilitarismo en Colombia (1964–2006)." *Confines* (7): 43–52.

Roseberry, William. 2002. "Hegemonía y lenguaje contencioso." In *Aspectos cotidianos de la formación del Estado*, compiled by Gilbert Joseph and Daniel Nugent. Mexico City: Era.

Schuberth, Moritz. 2015. "The Challenge of Community-Based Armed Groups: Towards a Conceptualization of Militias, Gangs, and Vigilantes." *Contemporary Security Policy* 36 (2): 296–320.

Snodgrass Godoy, Angelina. 2006. *Popular Injustice: Violence, Community and Law in Latin America*. Stanford, CA: Stanford Press.

Starn, Orin. 1991. *Reflexiones sobre rondas campesinas, protesta rural y nuevos movimientos sociales*. Lima, Peru: Instituto de Estudios Peruanos.

Torres, Alberto. 2011. "Pueblo purépecha se levanta contra criminales en Cherán." *El Universal*, May 4. http://archivo.eluniversal.com.mx/estados/80308.html.

Vargas Velázquez, Alejo. 2010. "La influencia de los poderes ilegales en la política colombiana." *Nueva Sociedad* (225): 156–70.

CHAPTER 10

LÁZARO CÁRDENAS, MICHOACÁN

FROM MINING ENCLAVE TO GLOBAL HUB

Patricia Alvarado Portillo

Translated from Spanish by Dawn Paley

I t could be argued that the area that became the Mexican city of Lázaro Cárdenas has had an orientation towards international commerce since its very beginning. Archeological remains suggest this with South American traces discovered in the area (Labarthe 1969; Pulido Méndez 2012). Colonial records show Christopher Columbus gave orders for the installation of a shipyard in Zacatula that could be used to explore the Southern Ocean (Díaz del Castillo 1796). We could think of this as a kind of historical vocation that was revived by the mining port project known as Las Truchas or Siderúrgica Lázaro Cárdenas-Las Truchas (Lázaro Cárdenas-Las Truchas Metallurgy Plant—SICARTSA).

This area is located in the delta of the Balsas River in the state of Michoacán, Mexico. Since pre-Hispanic times, this region has been known as Zacatula; the villages of Las Guacamayas, La Orilla, and

Melchor Ocampo del Balsas (later Lázaro Cárdenas) developed independently before eventually growing into a single municipality. Because of how close they are to each other, and as population growth brought these villages—which share social, cultural, and economic dynamics—together, throughout this chapter we will use the name Lázaro Cárdenas to refer to the entire metropolitan area.

The planning and construction of the mining and port project took forty-four years, which is to say seven full presidential terms, beginning with the government of General Lázaro Cárdenas del Río (1934-1940) and finally ending during the period of José López Portillo y Pacheco (1976-1982) (Schucking 1982). The political and economic manoeuvring required to bring the port online was complex; the fact that the project could be consolidated at all was due in large part to the tenacious and constant participation of General Cárdenas himself. As a way of recognizing his contribution, following his death, Michoacán's state Congress renamed the municipality of Melchor Ocampo del Balsas after him.

Initially, a national policy of import substitution industrialization determined the institutional framework for the implementation of the project. The Tepalcatepec Commission, which operationalized the early stages of the Las Truchas project, had already overseen developments in the irrigation districts of Tierra Caliente, as well as the Villita Dam, and, eventually, evolved into the Balsas River Commission. The Balsas Commission was extremely important, as it was a federal body whose employees knew the terrain, and had the influence and the connections to begin the construction of a project that was considered to be spearheading national development. Former President Luis Echeverría declared, "In reality we were planning the iron and steel industry of the entire country with the Las Truchas project, and if that is included part of the planning of the oil industry, with petrochemicals and electricity as fundamental factors in the economic development that our Revolution has sought, I commit—as I am doing now—to ensuring the project is realized" (Orive Alba 1974).

Unfortunately, the festivities did not last long. As Hiernaux Nicolas points out, "By the time the first [planned] step was taken, the integral development project the General dreamed of was already forgotten" (2004, 85). Other authors like Maldonado Aranda (2010) add that the Cárdenist project had been openly criticized since the government of Manuel Ávila Camacho (1940-1946). Following Camacho, President

Miguel Alemán shifted orientation away from the internal market, and transnational capital began to flow into national development projects, including SICARTSA.

To this day, three different administrations have, in Marxist terms, taken control of the means of production at the port of Lázaro Cárdenas.[1] Each time, these efforts led to profound changes in the internal organization of SICARTSA and, given that in each presidential administration unique management patterns can be identified, it is possible to trace three phases in the process of globalization of the port complex, which led to international interest in the region and which also transformed the constellations of power that surround it.

The first drastic changes in Lázaro Cárdenas began with the arrival of large groups of migrants to the region. For example, in 1940 the total population of the region comprised only 392 people, by 1970 there were 4,766 residents, and, after only four years of port operations, there were 19,150 residents. These changes are part of the first phase of the globalization of the port, which I have called state industrial colonization, as the entire state apparatus and federal machinery were focused on the area. This phase began in the early 1970s and ended in 1991, when SICARTSA was sold to Villacero Group. There were important capital flows into the region over this first period, and thousands of labourers arrived to build the foundations of where SICARTSA would be built. This process included major landscape modifications ranging from the diversion of the Balsas River to the building of entire neighbourhoods to house migrant workers, half of whom came from the Tierra Caliente region of Michoacán and western Guerrero, and the other half from various states of the republic (Pietri 1978). During this phase, the state provided SICARTSA with all the necessary services; this commitment led to construction of a maritime port, the expansion of the railway and highway networks, and the construction of a city, which is to say, of Lázaro Cárdenas (Orive Alba 1974; Comisión del Río Balsas 1965).

The second phase in the globalization of the port is defined by the first privatization of the iron-processing complex. This coincided with, or rather was a consequence of, a re-engineering of the state to promote decentralization and privatization of state-owned companies. This

---

1   For a detailed history of SICARTSA, we recommend three essential texts: Zapata (1978), Minello (1982), and Schucking (1982).

process began in 1991 when SICARTSA was acquired by Villacero Group and ended in 2006 when the facility was sold again. Villacero Group is a relatively important corporation in the iron sector, founded in 1955. This second phase is characterized by the 1995 decision of the government of Ernesto Zedillo Ponce de León to allow the participation of foreign capital in the administration of the new Mexican port system; "in the case of Lázaro Cárdenas, there was a considerable investment by Hutchison Port Holdings of Hong Kong...which designed an investment program...over a 20 year period" (*Lázaro Cárdenas Port Handbook* 2010, 31). One of the results of this transformation, and the first concession of the port's infrastructure, was the creation of the Administración Portuaria Integral de Lázaro Cárdenas (Integrated Port Administration of Lázaro Cárdenas). The industrial port, which was originally designed to receive and ship out coal, minerals, fertilizers, and grain, underwent a massive redesign to become a commercial port with loading and unloading facilities, a storage area for automobile shipping, and the infamous TEU (twenty-foot equivalent unit) shipping containers.

The third phase of globalization of the port began in 2006 with the sale of the complex to ArcelorMittal, a transnational company based in Luxemburg. SICARTSA, as many of the residents of Lázaro Cárdenas still call it, was transformed into another link in a complex global network that includes mines, administrative offices, commercial installations, and research and development centres in sixty-five countries across four continents. The investment made by the state during the construction and implementation of the project ended up in the hands of transnational corporations, which capitalized on an institutional framework built using public money over a period of more than thirty years. In addition to physical and technical infrastructure, there were also political and social transformations in the region that favoured ArcelorMittal, including the creation of a specialized working class, the conformation of local supply networks and clients, as well as connectivity, branding, concessions, agreements with *ejidatarios* (communal land owners) for the extraction of minerals, and so on.

THE DERIVATIONS OF THE WAR ON DRUGS

As part of the policy of attack against drug trafficking during the second presidential term (2006–2012) of the Partido de Acción Nacional

(National Action Party, a conservative political party) in Mexico, the executive started a "war on drugs" that generated an increase in levels of violence in the country. Since 2007, more than 230,000 people have been murdered, as well as tens of thousands more disappeared and potentially hundreds of thousands forcibly displaced (Molloy 2018; "México" 2017). These are the most visible outcomes of the violence; however, there are other impacts on people ranging from sexual violations of women and children, an increase in orphans and widows, as well as psychological, social, and economic impacts at the individual and collective levels, among many other consequences that can only be measured qualitatively but that end up affecting material realities. The social externalities of the violence have been absorbed by families without there being any accurate instruments to arrange reparation for damages, for access to justice, or for a serious and effective follow-up in legal cases (Ballinas 2007; Redacción Proceso 2013; Comisión Interamericana de Derechos Humanos 2015; Internal Displacement Monitoring Centre 2016).

The presence of the state and the relations between the national political order and local crime operators are evident and confirm a foundational logic, as "historical research in the Mexican case does not support the assumption of two separate fields: drug trafficking and its agents, on one side and the State on the other. Moreover, since the beginning of prohibition [in the 1920s], the illegal trade appeared related to powerful political agents in the production and trafficking regions" (Astorga 1999, 35)—a situation that is apparent in Lázaro Cárdenas and elsewhere in the country. In addition, drug trafficking in Mexico has deep rural origins. In the case we are examining, "the southern territories of Michoacan developed complex spatial economic, political and familiar networks that shape this drug trafficking region" (Maldonado Aranda 2012, 13). Therefore, when the territorial organization of the "traditional" Mexican cartels was altered, new groups took over those areas and crime rates spiked. Between 2000 and 2005, the number of homicides registered in the state of Michoacán decreased from 1,248 to 945. In 2006, there were 1,349 homicides. Between 2006 and 2014, the number of homicides increased, spiking to 2,370 in 2016 and 2,257 in 2017 (Secretariado Ejecutivo del Sistema Nacional de Seguridad Pública 2018).

The new criminal group in the case of the state of Michoacán, whose origins can be traced back to 1980 according to the US Congressional Research Service (Beittel 2013, 17), came out publicly as La Familia

Michoacana (the Michoacán Family) in 2006. The group's hallmarks are its open opposition to Los Zetas and the Jalisco New Generation Cartel mixed with faith in the gospel, which appeared to allow it to keep the state under its control (Redacción de Proceso 2009; de la O Martínez 2015; InSight Crime 2016). There is not adequate space in this chapter to examine the growth, expansion, and transformations of La Familia Michoacana; however, I will mention that following the murder of one of its leaders, the cartel was reorganized to form Los Caballeros Templarios (the Knights Templar), led by former school teacher Servando Gómez, alias La Tuta, who was imprisoned in February of 2015 (for more on the formation of these groups, see Chapters 8 and 9).

In order to fight La Familia Michoacana, and later the Knights Templar, the number of federal forces (soldiers, marines, and Federal Police) deployed to the state increased substantially under the framework of a federal strategy laid out by Felipe Calderón. An important part of Calderón's strategy was Operación Conjunta Michoacán (Joint Operation Michoacán), which included the deployment, especially in the coastal and Tierra Caliente regions of Michoacán, of 4,260 soldiers from the Mexican Army (SEDENA), 1,054 marines from the Secretariat of the Marines, and 1,420 Federal Police from the then Secretariat of Public Security (Presidencia de la República 2006).

Under Peña Nieto, this police operation was institutionally consolidated through the creation, by presidential decree, of the "Commission for the Security and Holistic Development of the State of Michoacán" on January 14, 2014. It is important to note that this commission was the result of a cooperation agreement signed one day earlier between Michoacán's then Governor Fausto Vallejo and members of the federal executive, as well as a request from Vallejo that Michoacán receive "the support of the Federal Government in regards to public security, with the objective of confronting the situation of violence and insecurity" (Presidencia de la República 2016, 1).

Under the framework established by the commission, the deployment of new troops escalated. Three thousand more troops arrived to Michoacán in February of 2012, as well as armoured vehicles, communication units, airborne vehicles, and patrol cars, and in August of the same year another four hundred troops arrived and then a further six hundred (Ramos 2012a, 2012b; Redacción Proceso 2012; Redacción El Informador 2009). The mobilization of security forces in the state has been so intense that, for example, on March 12, 2014, SEDENA declared "an average of 5,907 troops [were] carrying out actions to reduce violence" in Michoacán (SEDENA 2014a). By the end of the same month, SEDENA declared that the average number of troops in the state had increased to 7,069. Joint Operation Michoacán had the second-largest troop deployment after the Northeast Operation, which took place in the frontier states of Nuevo León and Tamaulipas (SEDENA 2014b, 2014c; see Chapter 7).

In October of 2015, another five hundred troops arrived to Michoacán, and security meetings were being held in a coordinated manner, led by the Interior Ministry (Secretaría de Gobernación) with high-level participation of various military branches (Arrieta 2015; Martínez Elorriaga 2015; Secretaría de Gobernación 2016).

According to Maldonado Aranda (2012), the rise of drug trafficking is closely linked to neoliberal reforms and policies of structural adjustment, which affected social mobility and economic well-being in Mexico, allowing "a successful market of illegalities, with particular emphasis on drugs," to flower (Maldonado Aranda 2012, 7). It can be argued that illegal drug trafficking has been one of the most popular strategies that allow (and has allowed) peripheral rural societies to embed themselves within the global economic system. Ribeiro (2006) defines these strategies as a kind of "non-hegemonic economic globalization" that is pyramid-like, and includes activities from money laundering to organ trafficking, corruption, and the sale of pirated goods, among others. This non-hegemonic economic globalization has been the alternative through which large segments of marginalized people (the bottom of the pyramid) have been able to access some kind of social mobility under a neoliberal state. In the case of Lázaro Cárdenas, the process of decentralization of SICARTSA (the second and third phases described above) implied a lessening of the state presence, preparing fertile ground with enough infrastructure (port, railways, connection to global markets) to allow for the establishment and expansion of illegal drug markets, and, eventually, for iron trafficking, in a highly militarized context.

The increase in soldiers, marines, Federal Police, and other police in the streets of Michoacán forced the cartels to look for innovative ideas of an economic nature to make up for their losses and the new costs the military operations implied for their bottom lines, as well as looking for new commercial routes for the movement of their merchandise. Their solution was creative and comprehensive: new products and new routes.

SOWING DISARRAY

In this context of cartel innovation and militarization, Lázaro Cárdenas became an important node because of the following characteristics: (1) infrastructure (port, airport, rail terminal); (2) connectivity to the Pacific (especially with China) and with the east coast of the United States through the Kansas City Southern train that connects Nevada and Chicago to Nuevo Laredo; (3) articulation to international trade routes; (4) the presence of global shipping lines; (5) proximity to raw metals (iron ore); and (6) because it is a space where actors who move at different scales (global, national, statewide, and local) and in different spaces of power (governmental, corporate, and union) are in contact.[2]

This setting was an ideal one for the development of a "kind of narcotrafficking" that was able to "adapt itself to globalization more quickly and better than nation states" (Chabat 2010, 6). For Maldonado Aranda, "the rise of narcotrafficking is an indirect product of the opening of a regional economy to internal and external markets" (2010, 32), an opening accompanied by the infrastructure needed to make it possible. This is how the Knights Templar were able to diversify their economic activities—and maintain those they already had—importing precursor chemicals that were paid for through the export of illegally obtained iron ore. This dynamic was maintained even though authorities claim, "Maritime trafficking remains the least common mode of transportation in terms of individual seizure cases" (UNODC 2015, 39).

One of the first indicators of this new dynamic appeared in September of 2007, when a boat carrying 2,593 tons of cocaine was interdicted (Secretaría de Marina 2007; Notimex 2007). However, the height of this phenomenon took place between 2011 and 2014. Between 2011 and 2012, 41.23 tons of illegal substances were decommissioned every month. These substances were mainly chemical precursors for methamphetamines, like monomethylamine and ethyl phenylacetate. Other than a couple of shipments from Italy and India (Expansión 2011), all of the rest of the interdicted product came from China (Shanghai, in particular)

---

2   Currently, the metropolitan area of the municipality of Lázaro Cárdenas is the fourth most populous city in the state of Michoacán, with 178,817 residents, and the city of Lázaro Cárdenas itself is the seventh most populous at 79,200 (INEGI 2010).

(Agencia AP 2011; PGR 2011a, 2011b; Presidencia de la República, SEMAR, and PGR 2011; Expansión 2011; Carvallo 2012; Notimex 2012; PGR 2016a, 2016b; Redacción de Prensa Libre 2011). Over the same time period, the exploitation of iron ore also increased; 2014 was the peak year, with the extraction of 29,864 tons per month, making a total of 358,379.09 tons that year (BBC, Redacción 2014; Martínez Elorriaga 2014; Redacción AN 2014a, 2014b; Redacción Lo de Hoy 2014; Redacción Sin Embargo 2014). There is, thus, a strong connection between the increase in the extraction of minerals and the production of methamphetamines, as if the first had been paid for by the second.

As Chabat (2010) argues, it is increasingly difficult to separate legal trade from illegal trade, as the diversification of commercial activities has been part of the response to militarization by drug trafficking groups. In the case of Lázaro Cárdenas, the drastic increase in legal and illegal mineral extraction and in the importation of chemical precursors even impacted official statistics. For example, in the *World Drug Report 2016*, considering that the tendencies of the curves are positive (see Figure 10.1), we can observe abrupt changes in the angles of the graphs between 2011 and 2013 (UNODC 2016). In the case of iron mining, the numbers published by INEGI (National Institute of Statistics and Geography) show anomalous movements that reflect how macroeconomic indicators absorbed the effect of illegal extraction, which is to say, the peaks in the curves on Figure 10.1 represent all of the illegal mined minerals that could have been "legally" exported through incorporation into national balance sheets.

In addition to the interdictions between 2011 and 2014, other problems were developing in Lázaro Cárdenas that called for immediate state intervention; for example, the assassination of Virgilio Camacho, the director of institutional relations at ArcelorMittal, whose body was found in an area of Las Guacamayas days after he was disappeared in April of 2013. Camacho had worked for the company for more than thirty years and had been a director since 2008. Almost a year and a half after his death, his murderers were found, among them was one of the principal operators of La Tuta. According to declarations by the State Attorney General's Office, Camacho was killed because it appeared he had become an inconvenience for the "interests in the mining branch of the criminal cell," though it is also rumoured he was killed because of the complaints he made regarding mineral extraction carried out by the Knights Templar (Mora 2013; García Tinoco 2014; Univisión 2014). There were other incidents in which it was rumoured the Knights Templar ordered the closure of particular businesses, tortilla shops, for example, generating collective confusion among residents. One of these events took place in September 2013, around 10 p.m., when a rumour spread that the next day there would be no gasoline sold, under punishment of death. The lines of cars waiting to fill up with gas at local gas stations lasted through until the morning, and, in effect, some stations did not open the next day, as their supply of gasoline was used up because of the increased demand.

In early 2013, the army, the marines, and the Federal Police arrived to Lázaro Cárdenas. All municipal police officers were disarmed and sent to Morelia, the state capital, for a month of training, according to media reports (Redacción AN 2013b; CNN 2013). The functions that municipal police carried out were taken over by federal forces, including control of security at the port. In the words of Governor Vallejo, this was due to the *desaseo* (disarray) at customs, as with regard to illegally mined iron, "it was evident that minerals extracted from Michoacán were exported with impunity, they weren't snuck out in rafts or boats, rather they were loaded up in the port" (Rosiles 2013). Interim Governor Salvador Jara declared later that "the State was governed by organized crime...most of the municipalities were infiltrated and so were the police" (CNN 2015). The narrative that violence is exclusively associated with criminal activities was broken, because, as Jara's declarations evidenced, a de facto partnership between the state—among political elites on the municipal and state level—and the violent drug trafficking groups had long since operated in the state of Michoacán. In fact, in 1999, Astorga already wrote that in Mexico "drug trafficking was supported from within the power structure," which leads us back to the notion of organized violence proposed in the Introduction to this volume as "violence as organized not only due to the formal structure of armed groups but also organized in its relationship to capitalism."

Following the arrival of soldiers to Lázaro Cárdenas in 2013, and at least three military deployments in January, June, and November of 2014, the ambushes, kidnappings, and killings continued. Certain demographic patterns among victims indicate many were women involved in human trafficking or the sex trade, and many others were police and soldiers, especially those associated with corruption and drug trafficking (Bautista 2013; Espinosa 2016; García Tinoco 2016; Notimex 2016; Redacción AN 2013a; Redacción Excélsior 2016).

Figure 10.1: Methamphetamine Interdiction and Iron Mining Production, World and Michoacán, 2006–2014

Amphetamines-Group Substances Intercepted–World: 2006–2014

Amphetamines-Group Substances Intercepted–Americas: 2006–2014

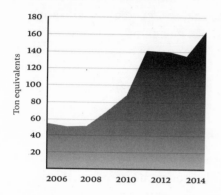
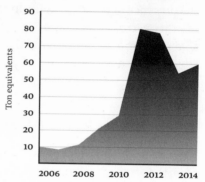

Iron Ore Production, Michoacán

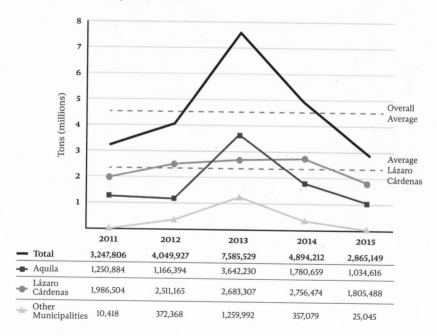

	2011	2012	2013	2014	2015
■ Total	3,247,806	4,049,927	7,585,529	4,894,212	2,865,149
▪ Aquila	1,250,884	1,166,394	3,642,230	1,780,659	1,034,616
Lázaro Cárdenas	1,986,504	2,511,165	2,683,307	2,756,474	1,805,488
Other Municipalities	10,418	372,368	1,259,992	357,079	25,045

Sources: Top images from UNODC *(2015, 2016); bottom image modified with data from* INEGI *(2016).*

The security of the port is considered a national priority. Inside the installations of the port there have been no reports of altercations or illegal activities other than the illegally exported mineral already mentioned. In addition to the massive human resources expended to ensure the takeover of port security, and the stress on infrastructure and resources, the presence of these elements in the field has repercussions on security in other sectors of society. For example, one month after the arrival of soldiers to the port of Lázaro Cárdenas in 2013, two women were threatened, tortured, and raped by soldiers who later blackmailed them so they would withdraw their complaints (Sin Embargo 2013).

THE VICEROYALTY

The federal government came up with a plan to "rescue" the municipality from the wave of violence and created, through the presidential decree of January 15, 2014, the Commission for the Security and Comprehensive Development of Michoacán. The commission worked as a decentralized administrative organization separate from the Interior Ministry; its objective was "to coordinate all of the federal authorities for the re-establishment of order and security in Michoacán and it's comprehensive development, under a wide ranging focus that includes the political, social, economic, and public security aspects of the state" (Presidencia de la República 2016, 2). Alfredo Castillo Cervantes was named commissioner. The commission was an entity with wide-ranging powers of decision that exercised influence in many affairs, to the point that it was able to remove representatives of the federal government in the state, as it was a direct representative of the Interior Ministry and the president (Presidencia de la República 2016, Art. 5. Fractions I and VIII). The symbolic and material power the nation conceded to the commissioner was so great that in local circles he became known as the "Viceroy," and his period of activity became known as the "Viceroyalty." The influence of Castillo was such that the local media published anecdotes about the ways he would impose himself upon local political elites in Michoacán (see, for example, Hernández Marín 2016).

Following the arrival of Castillo, actions to quiet the activities of drug traffickers were carried out, especially in Lázaro Cárdenas. One of the most extravagant took place on March 3, 2014, when the marines, the secretary of national defence, the secretary of environment and natural resources, as well as the Servicio de Administración Tributaria (Internal Revenue Service), the Federal Attorney's Office for Environmental Protection, and the Center for Research and National Security confiscated, in addition to machines and various vehicles, 119,000 tons of iron ore in various properties inside the port (Redacción AN 2014a, 2014b; Redacción Quadratín 2014).

In addition to taking down high-level members of criminal organizations, the commission also targeted active politicians. The former mayor of Lázaro Cárdenas, Arquímedes Oseguera, was charged and detained in April 2014 for having links with La Tuta, as was Secretary of Government and Interim Governor Jesús Reyna. Relationships between La Tuta and the legal political structure of the state were not unknown: even Rodrigo Vallejo Mora, son of the elected Governor Fausto Vallejo, was filmed in meetings with La Tuta, who also had relationships with various mayors in the Tierra Caliente area.

Also during the Viceroyalty, the population of Michoacán rose up against organized crime groups through self-defence movements (see Chapters 8 and 9). These were movements that came from the population, generating serious polemics but also counting on a certain amount of local loyalty. *Autodefensas* were de-articulated a short time later through an effort by the state to take advantage of their internal divisions and the lack of experienced leadership. Regardless of their popularity and support, many of the self-defence groups were disarmed and converted into Rural Police, and one of the leaders, medical doctor José Manuel Mireles, was imprisoned for almost three years until May 2017 (Hernández Navarro 2014a, 2014b; Le Cour Grandmaison 2014; Kadner López 2017).

THE STORY CONTINUES

Castillo ended his period as commissioner in January 2015, and La Tuta was captured a month later. Among the results of the commission were "the remanding of three former State Secretaries of Government, six mayors, one treasurer, two councillors, 11 municipal directors of public security, three sub-directors of public security, eight ministerial police, 29 state police and 150 municipal police" (Castillo Cervantes 2015). These numbers demonstrate the degree to which drug trafficking groups were able to penetrate state structures. This story has not ended; rather, it appears we are in a historical loop, in a kind of state amnesia, as President

Enrique Peña Nieto announced the construction of three new special economic zones to "create new development poles in [Lázaro Cárdenas], to create formal and well paying jobs" (Peña Nieto 2014). On the other hand, new banners have appeared announcing that the Nueva Familia Michoacana has been reorganized. What new institutional agreements may come out of this period are anybody's guess.

Lázaro Cárdenas is a complex space-time system, a hinge territory that has the particularity of articulating a *space of flows*, and another series of locations that have a special sensitivity to the local externalities created through the developmentalist neoliberal discourse, including drug trafficking. This activity occurs in a confusing political, economic, and cultural context in which the commodities in question (chemical precursors and iron ore) are in play globally as they enter and exit illegal and legal circuits of distribution and commercialization and mingle with complex interactions among old (state power) and new (*sicarios*, drug traffickers, narcos, *autodefensas*) forms of violence (Koonings and Kruijt 2004; Koonings 2012). Lázaro Cárdenas is best understood through a matrix of different perspectives. By focusing on global production networks or global value chains, for example, we can see how the "dynamic outcome of the complex interaction between territorialized relational networks and production networks within the context of changing regional governance structures" co-construct hegemonies in this system of power (Bridge 2008, 393).

Michoacán is in the middle of transnational economic interests because, as newspaper columnist Luis Hernández Navarro points out, it is a central location on the world map of new zones of influence that are being disputed on a global level by the United States, China, India, and Canada (2014b). The world borders that are being drawn appear to be fixed through the dispute for raw materials and commercial routes, and these disputes reinforce the relationship between violence and the economy that are at the heart of contemporary capitalism, which is the subject of this book.

For all these reasons, Lázaro Cárdenas is a clear example through which we can identify the rhythms, patterns, and temporal-spatial adjustments of capital, as well as the institutional arrangements that are created through the process of organized violence and territorialization generated through specific mechanisms of global capitalism's expansion.

REFERENCES

Agencia AP. 2011. "Incautan otras 120 toneladas de químico destinado a Guatemala." *Prensa Libre*, December 28. http://www.prensalibre.com/ noticias/Mexico-incauta-toneladas-destinado-Guatemala-0-617338451.

Arrieta, Carlos. 2015. "Desplazan a 500 militares en nuevo 'Operativo Michoacán.'" *Animal Político*, October 18. http://www.animalpolitico. com/2015/10/desplazan-a-500-militares-en-nuevo-operativo-michoacan/.

Astorga, Luis. 1999. "Drug Trafficking in Mexico: A First General Assessment." Discussion Paper 36. Management of Social Transformations. Paris: United Nations Educational, Scientific and Cultural Organization. http://unesdoc. unesco.org/images/0011/001176/117644eo.pdf.

Ballinas, Víctor. 2007. "CNDH: Graves abusos de militares en Michoacán–La Jornada." *La Jornada*, May 16. http://www.jornada.unam.mx/2007/05/16/ index.php?section=politica&article=003n1pol.

Bautista, Amanda. 2013. "Grupo armado mata a militar en Lázaro Cárdenas, Michoacán." *Excélsior*, July 10. http://www.excelsior.com.mx/nacional/2013/ 07/10/908225.

BBC, Redacción. 2014. "México: Decomisan buque con 68.000 toneladas de mineral de hierro del narco." *BBC Mundo*, May 1. http://www.bbc.com/ mundo/ultimas_noticias/2014/05/140430_ultnot_mexico_barco_decomiso_ hierro_en.

Beittel, June S. 2013. "Mexico's Drug Trafficking Organizations: Source and Scope of the Violence." Congressional Research Service, US Government. http://fpc.state.gov/documents/organization/208173.pdf.

Bridge, Gavin. 2008. "Global Production Networks and the Extractive Sector: Governing Resource-Based Development." *Journal of Economic Geography* 8 (3): 389–419. doi:10.1093/jeg/lbn009.

Carvallo, Manuel. 2012. "Lázaro Cárdenas, Michoacán, puerta de entrada de precursores químicos." *El Occidental*, January 4. http://www.oem.com.mx/ eloccidental/notas/n2371227.htm.

Castillo Cervantes, Alfredo. 2015. "Balance comisionado." Oficial. Comisión para la Seguridad y el Desarrollo Integral en el Estado de Michoacán. https:// www.gob.mx/cms/uploads/attachment/file/509/Balance_ComisionadoACC- Michoac_n_06012015.pdf.

Chabat, Jorge. 2010. "El estado y el crimen organizado trasnacional: Amenaza global, respuestas nacionales." *ISTOR: Revista de Historia Internacional* 11 (42): 3–14.

CNN. 2013. "Policías municipales regresan a Lázaro Cárdenas tras recibir capacitación." *Expansión*, December 3. http://expansion.mx/nacional/2013/ 12/03/policias-municipales-regresan-a-lazaro-cardenas-tras-recibir- capacitacion.

———. 2015. "La Policía Federal detiene a Servando Gómez 'La Tuta' En Michoacán." *Expansión*, February 27. http://expansion.mx/nacional/2015/02/27/detienen-a-servando-gomez-la-tuta.

Comisión del Río Balsas. 1965. *Planta siderúrgica de Las Truchas. Estudios y proyectos*. Ahuacatitlán, Morelos: Comisión del Río Balsas.

Comisión Interamericana de Derechos Humanos. 2015. *Situación de derechos humanos en México*. Organización de los Estados Americanos. http://www.oas.org/es/cidh/informes/pdfs/Mexico2016-es.pdf.

de la O Martínez, María Eugenia. 2015. "La violencia del narcotráfico en México y Centroamérica y las principales rutas del transporte de marihuana y cocaína hacia Estados Unidos." In *Subculturas del narcotráfico en América Latina: Realidades geoeconómicas y geopolíticas y la representación sociocultural de una nueva ética y estética en Colombia, México y Brasil*, edited by Nelson González-Ortega, 168–97. Mexico City: Universidad de los Andes, Universidad Nacional Autónoma de México, University of Oslo.

Díaz del Castillo, Bernal. 1796. *Historia verdadera de la conquista de la Nueva España*. Eleventh edition. Sepan cuántos 5. Mexico City: Editorial Porrúa, S.A.

Espinosa, Martín. 2016. "Emboscan a militares, ahora en Lázaro Cárdenas–Quadratín." *Quadratín Michoacán*, October 3. https://www.quadratin.com.mx/principal/emboscan-a-militares-ahora-en-lazaro-cardenas/.

Expansión. 2011. "Michoacán: Incautan 18 toneladas de precursores químicos para drogas." *Expansión*, August 28. http://expansion.mx/nacional/2011/08/28/michoacan-incautan-18-toneladas-de-precursores-quimicos-para-drogas.

García Tinoco, Miguel. 2014. "Capturan a presuntos asesinos de directivo de Arcelor Mittal." *Excélsior*, October 1. http://www.excelsior.com.mx/nacional/2014/10/01/984644.

———. 2016. "Ejecutan a tesorero municipal de Lázaro Cárdenas, Michoacán." *Excélsior*, October 8. http://www.excelsior.com.mx/nacional/2016/10/08/1121336.

Hernández Marín, Rebeca. 2016. "Comienzan a contar historias de miedo sobre actuar de Castillo." *Quadratín Michoacán*, August 31. https://www.quadratin.com.mx/politica/comienzan-a-contar-historias-miedo-actuar-castillo/.

Hernández Navarro, Luis. 2014a. *Hermanos en armas: Policías comunitarias y autodefensas*. Mexico City: Para Leer en Libertad A.C.

———. 2014b. "El salvaje oeste Michoacano." *La Jornada*, February 18. http://www.jornada.unam.mx/2014/02/18/index.php?section=opinion&article=017a2pol&partner=rss.

Hiernaux Nicolas, Daniel. 2004. "Del fordismo periférico al enclave mundial: Relatos de una investigación sobre las formas territoriales en ciudad Lázaro Cárdenas." In *El fin de toda la tierra: Historia, ecología y cultura en la costa de Michoacán*. Mexico City: El Colegio de México, Centro de Investigación Científica y de Educación Superior de Ensenada, El Colegio de Michoacán.

INEGI (National Institute of Statistics and Geography). 2010. *Censo nacional de población y vivienda 2010: Principales resultados por localidad.* Aguascalientes, Mexico: INEGI.

———. 2016. "Estadística mensual de la industria minero metalúrgica." *Instituto Naciona de Estadística y Geografía,* July 29. http://www.inegi.org.mx.

InSight Crime. 2016. "Familia Michoacana." *Insight Crime,* October 10. http://es.insightcrime.org/noticias-sobre-crimen-organizado-en-mexico/familia-michoacana-perfil.

Internal Displacement Monitoring Centre. 2016. *Global Report on Internal Displacement.* Norwegian Refugee Council. http://www.internal-displacement.org/assets/publications/2016/2016-global-report-internal-displacement-IDMC.pdf.

Kadner López, Marién. 2017. "José Manuel Mireles, líder de las autodefensas de Michoacán, sale de la cárcel." *El País,* May 12. https://elpais.com/internacional/2017/05/11/mexico/1494533441_851724.html.

Koonings, Kees. 2012. "New Violence, Insecurity, and the State: Comparative Reflections on Latin America and Mexico." In *Violence, Coercion, and State-Making in Twentieth-Century Mexico: The Other Half of the Centaur,* edited by Wil G. Pansters, 255–78. Stanford: Stanford University Press.

Koonings, Kees, and Dirk Kruijt, eds. 2004. *Armed Actors: Organized Violence and State Failure in Latin America.* London: Zed Books.

Labarthe, María de la Cruz. 1969. *Provincia de Zacatula: Historia social y económica.* Maestría, Mexico: Escuela Nacional de Antropología e Historia.

Lázaro Cárdenas Port Handbook. 2010. http://trumasa.com/documentos/lazaro_cardenas.pdf.

Le Cour Grandmaison, Romain. 2014. "Understanding in Order to Address: For a State Strategy in Michoacán." *Noria Research,* July. http://www.noria-research.com/understanding-in-order-to-address-for-a-state-strategy-in-michoacan/.

Maldonado Aranda, Salvador. 2010. *Los márgenes del estado mexicano: Territorios ilegales, desarrollo y violencia en Michoacán.* Zamora, Mexico: El Colegio de Michoacán A.C.

———. 2012. "Drogas, violencia y militarización en el México rural: El caso de Michoacán." *Revista Mexicana de Sociología* 74 (1): 5–39. http://www.revistas.unam.mx/index.php/rms/article/view/29532.

Martínez Elorriaga, Ernesto. 2014. "Decomisan autoridades 119 mil toneladas de hierro en Lázaro Cárdenas." *La Jornada,* March 3. http://www.jornada.unam.mx/ultimas/2014/03/03/embargan-119-toneladas-de-hierro-en-operativo-en-lazaro-cardenas-8996.html.

———. 2015. "Llegan 500 policías militares a Michoacán." *La Jornada,* October 18. http://www.jornada.unam.mx/ultimas/2015/10/18/llegan-500-policias-militares-a-michoacan-9338.html.

"México, el país donde hay más de 32.000 desaparecidos." 2017. CNN *Español*, September 13. http://cnnespanol.cnn.com/2017/09/13/mexico-el-pais-donde-hay-mas-de-32-000-desaparecidos/.

Minello, Nelson. 1982. *Siderúrgica Lázaro Cárdenas-Las Truchas: Historia de una empresa*. Mexico City: El Colegio de México.

Molloy, Molly. 2018. "More than 29,000 Homicide Victims in Mexico in 2017." *Frontera List*, January 24. https://fronteralist.org/2018/01/24/more-than-29000-homicide-victims-in-mexico-in-2017/.

Mora, Arnulfo. 2013. "Exige Mittal esclarecer crimen de funcionario." *Quadratín Michoacán*, April 9. https://www.quadratin.com.mx/regiones/Exige-Mittal-esclarecer-crimen-de-funcionario/.

Notimex. 2007. "Aseguran dos toneladas y media de cocaína en Michoacán." *Terra Noticias*, September 15. http://noticias.terra.com/noticias/aseguran_dos_toneladas_y_media_de_cocaina_en_michoacan/act966893.

———. 2012. "Aseguran Más de 194 Toneladas de Precursor Químico En Michoacán." *El Economista*, January 17. http://eleconomista.com.mx/seguridad-publica/2012/01/17/aseguran-mas-194-toneladas-precursor-quimico-michoacan.

———. 2016. "Alerta de género en 14 municipios de Michoacán." *La Jornada*, June 27. http://www.jornada.unam.mx/ultimas/2016/06/27/osorio-chong-emite-alerta-de-genero-en-14-municipios-de-michoacan.

Orive Alba, Adolfo. 1974. *SICARTSA: Siderúrgica Lázaro Cárdenas-Las Truchas S.A.* Mexico City: Secretaría de la Presidencia.

Peña Nieto, Enrique. 2014. "Mensaje a la nación del Presidente de Los Estados Unidos Mexicanos, Licenciado Enrique Peña Nieto: Por un México en paz con justicia y desarrollo." Mexico City: Palacio Nacional, Gobierno de la República.

PGR (Procuraduría General de la República). 2011a. "PGR aseguró en Michoacán más de 17 toneladas de psicotrópicos y precursores químicos." *Sala de Prensa, Procuraduría General de La República*, May 16. http://archivo.pgr.gob.mx/Prensa/2007/bol11/May/b50811.shtm.

———. 2011b. "El gobierno federal asegura aproximadamente 25 toneladas de precursores químicos, en Michoacán." *Procuraduría General de La República*, July 29. http://archivo.pgr.gob.mx/Prensa/2007/bol11/jul/b98111.shtm.

———. 2016a. "Inicia PGR carpeta de investigación por el aseguramiento de más de 22 toneladas de psicotrópico. Comunicado 760/16." *Procuraduría General de La República*, January 6. http://www.gob.mx/pgr/prensa/inicia-pgr-carpeta-de-investigacion-por-el-aseguramiento-de-mas-de-22-toneladas-de-psicotropico-comunicado-760-16?idiom=es-MX.

———. 2016b. "Asegura PGR en michoacán más de 14 tons de precursor químico, utilizado para la fabricación de drogas sintéticas. Comunicado Conjunto 786/16." *Gob.mx*, July 6. http://www.gob.mx/pgr/prensa/

asegura-pgr-en-michoacan-mas-de-14-tons-de-precursor-quimico-utilizado-para-la-fabricacion-de-drogas-sinteticas-comunicado-conjunto-786-16?idiom=es.

Pietri, René. 1978. "Los hombres y el espacio." In *Las Truchas: Acero y sociedad en México*, edited by Francisco Zapata, 121–78. Mexico City: Colegio de México.

Presidencia de la República. 2006. "Anuncio sobre la operación conjunta Michoacán." *Prensa, Presidencia de la República: Felipe Calderón Hinojosa*, December. http://calderon.presidencia.gob.mx/2006/12/anuncio-sobre-la-operacion-conjunta-michoacan/.

———. 2016. *Decreto por el que se crea La Comisión Para La Seguridad y El Desarrollo Integral en El Estado de Michoacán: Diario Oficial de La Federación*. http://www.dof.gob.mx/nota_detalle.php?codigo=5329743&fecha=15/01/2014.

Presidencia de la República, SEMAR (Secretaría de la Marina), and PGR. 2011. "Comunicado conjunto: El gobierno federal asegura más de 44 toneladas de precursores químicos en Lázaro Cárdenas." *Prensa, Presidencia de La República: Felipe Calderón Hinojosa*, July 13. http://calderon.presidencia.gob.mx/2011/07/el-gobierno-federal-asegura-mas-de-44-toneladas-de-precursores-quimicos-en-lazaro-cardenas/.

Pulido Méndez, Salvador. 2012. "Zacatula, un rincón del imperio. dinámica social en una periferia conquistada." PhD dissertation, Escuela Nacional de Antropología e Historia, Mexico City.

Ramos, Dulce. 2012a. "Refuerzan lucha anticrimen en Michoacán con 3 mil militares." *Animal Político*, February 3. http://www.animalpolitico.com/2012/02/refuerzan-lucha-anticrimen-con-3-mil-militares-en-michoacan/.

———. 2012b. "Envían 400 policías más a Michoacán." *Animal Político*, August 15. http://www.animalpolitico.com/2012/08/envian-400-policias-mas-a-michoacan/.

Redacción AN. 2013a. "Asesinan a jefe policíaco en Lázaro Cárdenas, Michoacán." *Aristegui Noticias*, July 29. http://aristeguinoticias.com/2907/lomasdestacado/hayan-muerto-a-jefe-policiaco-en-lazaro-cardenas-michoacan/.

———. 2013b. "Segob anuncia operativo federal de seguridad para el Puerto Lázaro Cárdenas, Michoacán." *Aristegui Noticias*, November 4. http://aristeguinoticias.com/0411/mexico/segob-anuncia-operativo-de-seguridad-para-el-puerto-lazaro-cardenas-michoacan/.

———. 2014a. "Decomiso de minerales en Michoacán desarticula finanzas del crimen organizado: Castillo." *Aristegui Noticias*, March 4. http://aristeguinoticias.com/0403/mexico/decomiso-de-minerales-en-michoacan-desarticula-finanzas-del-crimen-organizado-castillo/.

———. 2014b. "Gobierno embarga 119 mil toneladas de minerales en Lázaro Cárdenas." *Aristegui Noticias*, March 4. http://aristeguinoticias.com/0403/mexico/gobierno-embarga-119-mil-toneladas-de-minerales-en-lazaro-cardenas/.

Redacción de Prensa Libre. 2011. "Crece producción de droga en el país." *Prensa Libre*, December 28. http://www.prensalibre.com/noticias/Crece-produccion-droga-pais_0_617338278.html?commentsPage=1.

Redacción de Proceso. 2009. "'La Familia,' el cártel del sexenio." *Proceso*, July 21. http://www.proceso.com.mx/117163/117163-la-familia-el-cartel-del-sexenio.

Redacción El Informador. 2009. "El ejército 'sella' Michoacán." *El Informador*, July 21.http://www.informador.com.mx/mexico/2009/122468/6/el-ejercito-sella-michoacan.htm.

Redacción Excélsior. 2016. "Balean al hijo de exalcalde de Lázaro Cárdenas, Michoacán." *Excélsior*, July 4. http://www.excelsior.com.mx/nacional/2016/07/04/1102856.

Redacción Lo de Hoy. 2014. "Sigue decomiso de minas y mineral de hierro en Michoacán." *Lo de Hoy En El Puerto*, August 1. http://lodehoyenelpuerto.com/noticias/index.php?option=com_k2&view=item&id=8752:sigue-decomiso-de-minas-y-mineral-de-hierro-en-michoac%C3%A1n&Itemid=11.

Redacción Proceso. 2012. "Llegan a Michoacán cuatro mil soldados para reforzar combate al narco." *Proceso*, February 2. http://www.proceso.com.mx/297000/llegan-a-michoacan-cuatro-mil-soldados-para-reforzar-combate-al-narco.

———. 2013. "Michoacán: Toman calles y autopista en repudio a abusos de militares." *Proceso*, January 30. http://www.proceso.com.mx/332236/michoacan-toman-calles-y-autopista-en-repudio-a-abusos-de-militares.

Redacción Quadratín. 2014. "Once, las empresas porteñas intervenidas por la federación." *Quadratín Michoacán*, March 3. https://www.quadratin.com.mx/politica/Once-las-empresas-portenas-intervenidas-por-la-Federacion/.

Redacción Sin Embargo. 2014. "Gobierno federal realiza decomiso histórico de minerales en Lázaro Cárdenas; detiene a 6 chinos." *SinEmbargo MX*, March 3. http://www.sinembargo.mx/03-03-2014/921321.

Ribeiro, Gustavo Lins. 2006. "Economic Globalization from Below." *Etnográfica* x (2): 233–49.

Rosiles, Luis Felipe. 2013. "'Desaseo' en API, origen del operativo militar en LC: Fausto." *Quadratín Michoacán*, November 28. http://www.quadratin.com.mx/politica/%e2%80%9cDesaseo%e2%80%9d-en-API-origen-del-operativo-militar-en-LC-Fausto/.

Schucking, Rainer Godau. 1982. *Estado y acero: historia política de Las Truchas*. El Colegio de México, Centro de Estudios Sociológicos.

Secretaría de Gobernación. 2016. "Encabeza Secretario de Gobernación reunión de seguridad en Michoacán." *Gob.mx*, March 22. http://www.gob.mx/segob/prensa/encabeza-secretario-de-gobernacion-reunion-de-seguridad-en-michoacan.

Secretaría de Marina. 2007. "Incinera la armada de México más de dos y media toneladas de cocaína en el puerto de Lázaro Cárdenas, Michoacán." Comunicado de prensa 126/2007. Lázaro Cárdenas, Michoacán: Secretaría de Marina. http://2006-2012.semar.gob.mx/sala-prensa/prensa-2012/1076-comunicado-126-2007.html.

Secretariado Ejecutivo del Sistema Nacional de Seguridad Pública. 2018. *Datos abiertos de incidencia delictiva. Reportes de incidencia delictiva estatal al mes de enero 2018.* Mexico City: Secretaría de Gobernación. http://secretariadoejecutivo.gob.mx/incidencia-delictiva/incidencia-delictiva-datos-abiertos.php.

SEDENA (Secretary of National Defence). 2014a. "Respuesta a solicitud de información." Oficial Folio 0000700026214. Lomas de Sotelo, D.F.: Secretaría de la Defensa Nacional. https://www.infomex.org.mx/gobiernofederal/moduloPublico/rMedioElectP.action?idFolioSol=0000700026214&idTipoResp=6#.

———. 2014b. "Respuesta a solicitud de información." Oficial Folio 0000700042214. Lomas de Sotelo, D.F.: Secretaría de la Defensa Nacional. https://www.infomex.org.mx/gobiernofederal/moduloPublico/rMedioElectP.action?idFolioSol=0000700026214&idTipoResp=6#.

———. 2014c. "Respuesta a solicitud de información." Oficial Folio 0000700042614. Lomas de Sotelo, D.F.: Secretaría de la Defensa Nacional. https://www.infomex.org.mx/gobiernofederal/moduloPublico/rMedioElectP.action?idFolioSol=0000700026214&idTipoResp=6#.

Sin Embargo. 2013. "Mujeres de Lázaro Cárdenas, Michoacán, denuncian a policías militares, que vigilan el puerto, por violación." *Vanguardia*, November 27. http://www.vanguardia.com.mx/mujeresdelazarocardenasmichoacandenuncianapoliciasmilitaresquevigilanelpuertoporviolacion-1883999.html.

Univisión. 2014. "El minero que se opuso a los *Templarios*." *El Universal*, December. http://estados/2014/el-minero-que-se-opuso-a-los-templarios-1060173.html.

UNODC (United Nations Office on Drugs and Crime). 2015. *World Drug Report.* Executive Summary. http://www.unodc.org/documents/wdr2015/World_Drug_Report_2015.pdf.

———. 2016. *World Drug Report 2016.* "Global Seizures of Amphetamines-Group Substances: 2005–2013." http://www.unodc.org/wdr2016/field/9.3.1._Seizures_of_illicit_drugs_by_region_and_high_ranking_countries_2014_-_ATS.pdf.

Zapata, Francisco. 1978. *Las Truchas: acero y sociedad en México.* Mexico City: Colegio de México.

CHAPTER 11

ELITES, VIOLENCE, AND RESOURCES IN VERACRUZ, MEXICO

Michelle Arroyo Fonseca and Jorge Rebolledo Flores

Translated from Spanish by Dawn Paley

Evidence suggests that in Veracruz there is a direct link between violence and the availability of resources (Correa-Cabrera 2017), which allows for an explanation of the configuration of networks organized to extract resources in an illegal manner. Experience indicates that in dysfunctional spaces where institutions function without transparency, authorities can participate or collude with criminal groups. In effect, in states in transition and in those in which governments have low levels of legitimacy and social-political cohesion, governing elites make strategic and selective use of the application of laws, administering insecurity and violence according to their political and electoral objectives (Sørensen 2001). The elites who are in power thus become active agents in violence, inverting the Weberian principle that the state maintains a monopoly of violence to preserve the rule of law (Trejo and Ley 2016).

In Mexico, there is no re-election, and the absence of effective accountability mechanisms means that bureaucracy is carried out with a short-term vision. Politicians concentrate on the extraction of material benefits of public goods, which in turn generates a vicious cycle that makes the construction of legitimacy and the consolidation of institutions difficult. According to this logic, elites perceive any criticism of their activities as a threat, which leads them to use violence to quiet opposition and continue pillaging. Scholars of the Mexican elite emphasize the importance of family and personal ties in Mexican politics (Ai Camp 1982). In Veracruz, we see that a handful of families make the fundamental decisions that impact the rest of the state's population. These families own the most important businesses in the state, and hold positions as civil servants within local governments, which they have used for their personal gain, authorizing the issuing of multimillion-dollar government contracts to "ghost" companies in their own networks.

The state of Veracruz is located along the Gulf of Mexico, along a 720 km strip of coastal land. Statistical data from January 2016 indicates that Veracruz is the third-largest Mexican state by population, with 5,699,727 eligible voters. According to findings of the Consejo Nacional de Población (National Population Council), Veracruz has a high level of social marginalization, even while it is one of the richest states in Mexico and is home to the most important commercial maritime port in the country. According to the Instituto Nacional de Estadística y Geografía (National Institute for Statistics and Geography—INEGI), the main economic activities in the state are linked to agriculture, forestry, and fishing. Veracruz also has important industrial infrastructure for petrochemical activities and electricity generation. Though Veracruz has the sixth-largest economy in the country, it is the fourth most marginalized state in the country.

Because of its geographic location, Veracruz is an entry and exit port to the world, as well as a key access route to the centre of Mexico. It is the only state in the country that is connected both to states along the south border (Chiapas and Tabasco) as well as along the north border (Tamaulipas), which explains its role as a natural corridor for trade flows and people (including migrants), as well as drugs and weapons.

In the 1980s, the traditional elites of Veracruz began to understand the logic within which compensation and extra comforts derived from neoliberalism are distributed. Faced with a reduction in the activities of the state, private entities became the primary beneficiaries of contracts designed to carry out public services previously covered by the government. In the absence of mechanisms to ensure transparency, government contracts were awarded via an illicit system of cash payments of a percentage of said contracts to government workers, which increased corruption.

The flows obtained by public servants through these methods were split between them and their political bosses. They were also used to fund political campaigns and to reinforce the corporatism that has always been operated by the Institutional Revolutionary Party (PRI), which is a manner of explaining the survival and continuity of governing elites and the enrichment of their highest ranks. This practice began to generate criticism, which political elites quelled through censorship and, in many cases, through violence.

The rotation of political parties on a national level in Mexico since the year 2000 reconfigured the dynamics and the relations between political elites from Veracruz and the federal government. Given that between the year 2000 and 2012 the presidency of Mexico was not held by the PRI, a competitive electoral authoritarianism developed, through which a proliferation of governments, which in the interests of ensuring the continuity in power of their party—ensuring their own impunity into the future—control the short-term uncertainty created through the results of competitive elections (Schedler 2013). This leads to a constant drive to finance the corporatization and the cooptation of political will, which increases systemic corruption.

In 2004, Fidel Herrera Beltrán became governor, and, without pushback from the federal government, he exercised power in a self-serving manner. Herrera was accused of having received financing for his gubernatorial campaign from Francisco "Pancho" Colorado, who, since June 2012, has been a prisoner in a federal prison in Houston, Texas, accused of money laundering for Los Zetas (the Zetas) (Gagne 2016). During the Herrera administration, the state debt grew exorbitantly and government spending was especially difficult to track. By February 2012, Fidel Herrera and Javier Duarte de Ochoa (Herrera's former finance secretary) were responsible for a 67,000 percent increase in the accumulated debt of Veracruz, according to the Taxation and Public Credit Secretariat (Martínez 2012). Although, officially, Veracruz had only formally registered its debt with banks ($21.874 billion pesos), members of the opposition said the real amount was over sixty billion pesos, if debt across other institutions was counted.

During the governorship of Javier Duarte (2010–2016), the theft of state resources continued and violence increased to levels never previously experienced. For many years levels of insecurity and violence in Veracruz were above the national average and, from 2011 onwards, both increased drastically. Until 2011, the most violent municipalities in the state were those with a presence of drug traffickers neighbouring the state border with Tamaulipas; however, after September 2011, acts of violence carried out by organized crime, as well as state police, began to take place in Veracruz-Boca del Río and Xalapa. The remaining years under Governor Javier Duarte saw acts of violence spread to the rest of the state. In July 2016, homicides in the state hit a new monthly record: 132 murders, the highest total since 1997. It is worth noting that, with a few honourable exceptions, the majority of the media did not cover what was taking place in the state, or they did so in a partial manner because of the disarray of the government, official censorship, or intimidation by criminal groups.

This chapter recognizes the centrality of Marxist approaches to understand exploitation, reproduction of capital, and how elite politics are subsumed to the dictates of transnational capital in a host of states in Latin America. It also maintains, as established in the volume's Introduction, "economic transformation under neoliberalism alongside violence not as separate phenomena, but as generative and mutually reinforcing elements that buttress capitalism in its current stage." This chapter also draws upon critical Weberian state theory to explain how state organizations can be subverted by informal and illegitimate patterns of authority and decision making, which undermine their legitimacy (Hinings and Greenwood 2002, 412). In this view, according to Charles Fombrun (1986, 404), actors manipulate systems to perpetuate their ability to achieve parochial ends. Accordingly, the analysis highlights the role of local elites to intentionally undermine the state's monopoly of violence in order to hang onto the use of violence in support of their own power (Pearce 2010).

In the view of Méndez, O'Donnell, and Pinheiro, who discuss the problem of "lawless violence" in *The (Un)Rule of Law and the Underprivileged in Latin America* (1999), incomplete democratic transitions encourage a weakening of the state's monopoly of violence. This approach adds to our understanding of the relationship between state institutions and non-state armed groups, as well as the operation of the latter within state institutions (see also Arias and Goldstein 2010).

Taking into account the interaction of governing elites and organized crime, neoliberalism not only reduces the state but serves to collapse "the notion of freedom into freedom for economic elites" (Harvey 2005, 48). Neoliberalism thus becomes a mechanism for the upward redistribution of wealth while criminalizing opposition to it (Wilson Gilmore 2007). Thus, official discourse tries to construct an image of neoliberalism as a way towards development.

DRUG TRAFFICKING IN VERACRUZ: THE ROOT OF THE PROBLEM

Evidence of drug trafficking through Veracruz, carried out by large trafficking organizations, began to emerge at the end of the 1980s. However, these activities did not cause significant increases in violence in the state. By 1993, investigations by the Mexican Attorney General's Office had found that the Gulf Cartel had a safe house in the Port of Veracruz. Over time, the Gulf Cartel gained influence in Mexico's northeast (Beittel 2015). Regardless of the key strategic value of Veracruz, there was no dispute between the most powerful trafficking organizations for control of the state. This suggests the distribution of the routes and territories used by diverse trafficking organizations during the 1980s was carried out under governmental supervision.

It was in this context that the Gulf Cartel positioned itself in Veracruz and was able to co-exist peacefully with local authorities and regional strongmen. In this period, the group known as Los Zetas formed, initially from ex-members of special forces of the Mexican Army who deserted to join the Gulf Cartel and became its hired guns at the end of the 1990s (see Chapter 7). The strength the Gulf Cartel gained with the incorporation of Los Zetas allowed control of routes from Guatemala to the Texas-Tamaulipas border, and its power allowed it to dominate local gangs dedicated to car theft, trafficking in migrants, extortion, tapping oil pipelines, cattle theft, break and enters, and small-scale drug dealing.

Upon arrival to a city or a region, Gulf Cartel members identified the leaders of local criminal groups and began to charge them a tax or quota so they could continue to operate. Those who refused to pay were brutally assassinated and their bodies exhibited, so as to gain control over petty criminals from whom they collected profits while also opening new criminal activity (Valdés 2013). This scheme was completed with the expansion of this operational logic to nearby villages, where small groups of Zetas were sent to operate under the command of a local boss. These groups would also pay off local police, which would begin to operate under their command. In this way, they secured not only police protection but also information about the activities of the army, the marines, and federal and state police.

The new modus operandi of Los Zetas, in which the group began to prey on society, began because Osiel Cárdenas, its creator, cut off the resources available to Los Zetas to purchase weapons. Though Los Zetas were initially part of the Gulf Cartel, they separated in 2010 (Valdés 2013; Beittel 2015). The expansion of the Gulf Cartel required Los Zetas, and its inclusion in activities related not only to defence but also to attack. Given the relevance Los Zetas came to achieve within the Gulf Cartel, they quickly transformed from a salaried organization into a group that demanded to be treated as partners (Valdés 2013). This circumstance led to the break between Los Zetas and the Gulf Cartel. Having separated, the principal activity of Los Zetas was not narcotics trafficking but organized violence. Los Zetas has an "extractive model" based on theft of petroleum products, extortion, human trafficking, and kidnapping, all of which are widely regarded to inflict more suffering on the public than does transnational drug trafficking (Beittel 2015).

The war on drugs launched by President Felipe Calderón at the beginning of his mandate generated spirals of violence throughout the country. In Veracruz, the violence became marked beginning on September 20, 2011, when thirty-five bodies were displayed in the heart of the most important commercial area of Boca del Río, a municipality connected to the Port of Veracruz. In the following days, more corpses appeared in nearby locations. This took place amid the deployment of thousands of federal troops that were guarding the eleventh National Meeting of Presidents of Supreme Tribunals and Attorney Generals that was taking place in the Fiesta Americana Hotel in Boca del Río. The immediate reaction of authorities in Veracruz was to present those executed as members of Los Zetas (without any investigation) and blame the killing on Mata Zetas (Zeta Killers), the armed wing of another cartel active in Veracruz as of a few months earlier, the Cartel Jalisco Nueva Generación (New Generation Jalisco Cartel—CJNG).

Collective suspicions arose: Why was the CJNG going after Los Zetas in Veracruz if it was not within its natural corridor of operations? At the same time, it was argued that the Zeta Killers were (and are) a paramili-tary group formed or supported by the military and the marines. In this context, on October 4, 2011, Operation Secure Veracruz was launched, a federal strategy that deployed hundreds of marines, soldiers, and Federal Police, as well as surveillance and patrol flights and the establishment of military checkpoints throughout the state that were welcomed by a state government in over its head.

At the same time, there was an intervention in various municipal police departments that had been penetrated by organized crime (Ciudad Cardel, Veracruz, Boca del Río, Tierra Blanca, and Papantla). Initially, Operation Secure Veracruz was presented as a great success by federal and state governments, who claimed that thanks to the operation there had been a reduction of criminal activity and that calm and order had been restored; over the medium term, insecurity and violence continued.

Later, high-calibre shootouts between federal armed forces and crim-inal groups, as well as kidnappings and disappearances, began to sug-gest the presence of drug-trafficking organizations throughout the state (Zavaleta 2016). The government of Javier Duarte began to attack critical voices to the point of trying to control the use of social networks by those who were expressing concern in the state through the promulgation of a law known as the "Twitter Law," which criminalized criticism of the government via the online platform. In June of 2013, the Suprema Corte de Justicia de la Nación (National Supreme Court of Justice) determined that said law was unconstitutional. During Duarte's period as governor, seventeen journalists were assassinated in Veracruz, transforming the state into one of the most dangerous places in the world to work as a journalist. In every case, the victims of these crimes were criminalized. Over the same period, intimidation and censorship of academics and activists were carried out according to a similar government logic.

The staunch refusal to acknowledge the presence of drug trafficking and the links between local politicians and organized crime, and its pen-etration of municipal police, generated a situation of ungovernability and extreme impunity that was taken advantage of by criminal groups in order to strengthen their organizations. Data from the Secretariado Ejecutivo del Sistema Nacional de Seguridad Pública (Executive Secretariat of the National System of Public Security—SESNSP) reveal that, during Duarte's term, the state registered its highest levels of homicides. The historical record of homicides dates back nineteen years, and the highest levels recorded include 101 investigations for homicide in September 2011, 97 in each of May and October 2012, and 132 in July of 2016 (SESNSP 2016). These statistics challenged the government's version that everything was calm. It was not until April of 2014 that it was discovered that the government's numbers had been manipulated to hide the actual situation in Veracruz.

The statistics reported by SESNSP in Veracruz in 2013 showed initially that there were forty-eight thousand preliminary investigations, but in April 2014 SESNSP clarified that, in fact, there were seventy-two thousand, which meant there were twenty-four thousand crimes that were reported in the state that were hidden from the public and not reported to federal authorities. The 2014 SESNSP report stated that kidnappings in Veracruz increased 51.81 percent compared to the first six months of 2013. As we have seen, official numbers cannot be trusted. INEGI estimated that in 2014 in the state of Veracruz 13.7 percent of all crimes were reported (in 2013 it was 10.8 percent), of which 61.2 percent led to preliminary investigations, meaning a preliminary investigation was only carried out for 8.4 percent of crimes (5.1 percent in 2013) (SESNSP 2016).

One final reference can help understand the climate of insecurity and violence in Veracruz. The 2015 National Survey of Victimization and the Perception of Violence found that 80.5 percent of people over the age of eighteen in Veracruz felt unsafe. That number has evolved since 2011, when 64.8 percent of citizens felt unsafe, rising to 70 percent by 2012, 75.4 percent in 2013, and 80.7 percent in 2014. The perception of Veracruzanos with regard to local authorities shows they most trust the marines (81.6 percent), followed by the army (76.6 percent), and lagging well behind are public prosecutors and state attorneys general (35.9 percent), municipal police (29.5 percent), and, in last place, transit police (22.6 percent) (INEGI 2015).

The increase in crime rates occurred simultaneously with the increase in awareness of the corruption committed by Governor Javier Duarte and his closest collaborators. This has allowed civil society to become more aware of what took place during his administration, as well as precipitating his fall from power. By 2016, brigades organized by families of disappeared people had carried out ground searches in the state. In April 2016, the National Searchers Brigade reported it had found fifteen clandestine graves containing an unknown number of bodies, while another group of family members of those disappeared found twenty-eight graves with more than forty bodies. Colectivo Solecito (Little Sun Collective), consisting of fifty mothers of disappeared people, revealed that in October of 2016 they found 105 clandestine graves in an area known as Colinas de Santa Fe, in the Port of Veracruz. These graves must be added to those uncovered in Rancho El Limón (in Tlalixcoyan), Rancho El Diamante (between Tres Valles and Cosamaloapan), Rancho El Lagostillo (in Puente Nacional), Rancho San Pedro (in Acuitzingo), and in two ranches in the municipality of Acayucan (Animal Político 2016).

As a product of ungovernability in the state, a new cartel was detected in 2016: the United Cartels (made up of cells of the Gulf Cartel and the Sinaloa Cartel), which, through social networks, announced its arrival to fight the Zetas in the Papaloapan Basin. Given this situation, self-defence groups have formed in many parts of the state—notoriously in the Zongolica mountains, the poorest region of Veracruz—in order for locals to defend themselves. The defeat of the PRI in state elections in 2016 produced an absence of authority; in state and local governments the logic of every man for himself reigns. The vacuum created by the state government through its refusal to provide services serves as a warning of the next great security crisis in Mexico.

THE NEXUS OF ORGANIZED VIOLENCE AND LOCAL ELITES IN AREAS OF RESOURCE EXTRACTION

It is possible to identify three rationales in the exercise of power, the violence, and the extraction of resources by political elites from Veracruz. First, that of post-revolutionary Mexico, in which the development of Veracruz is kick-started in the context of strong political leaderships that combined co-optation and repression; in this manner resources are extracted that benefit a minority of people who are always linked to the state government. Second, with the implementation of neoliberalism in Mexico, beginning at the end of the 1980s, this post-revolutionary dynamic was changed for one in which resources are extracted and political favours are doled out. The reduction of the state restricted the availability of those favours, and the availability of privileges. Benefits are channelled to the group in power through rigged tenders, which are won by companies created ad hoc by governing elites. The neoliberal model requires new infrastructure projects to be built in regions in which there is resistance by social groups who would be displaced by modernization. For many years, the "legitimate" violence of the state allowed the continuity of these projects and the flow of resources to governing elites. Finally, a third scenario emerges out of increasing political competition, and from the uncertainty generated by this opening. The extraction of resources in this scenario becomes the formula through which to ensure political survival. Regardless, the distribution of the benefits of resource extraction is increasingly restricted, which intensifies the embezzlement of public funds and the use of violence to quell abuses of public power.

The oil industry has long been an important sector in the Mexican economy, and many of the activities in this sector are concentrated in Veracruz. According to the *White Book*, published by Pemex, there were 14,182 kilometres of pipeline in Mexico in 2011 (Pemex 2012), which includes 5,198.7 kilometres of oil pipelines and 8,992.7 kilometres of pipelines carrying multiple hydrocarbons. Regardless, it has been impossible to confirm that Veracruz is the state with the most oil pipelines in its territory, because neither Pemex nor the Secretary of Energy have made information about new pipeline construction public, even though the Instituto Nacional de Transparencia, Acceso a la Información y Protección de Datos Personales (Federal Institute for Access to Information) specifically requested this information in March of 2015. In addition, Veracruz is home to petrochemical complexes Cangrejera, Cosoleacaque, Morelos, and Pajaritos, as well as the General Lázaro Cárdenas refinery, meaning this is the most important petrochemical area in the country. Though Pemex has been the primary engine of economic growth in the area, the consequences of its extractive activity have included health issues and severe environmental problems.

Mining is also important in Veracruz, and there are parallels with the oil sector. The Caballo Blanco open-pit mine, which is operated by Goldgroup Mining Inc. (through its subsidiary Minera Cardel), in a priority conservation area, provides a key example of how mining companies in this region operate. In 1998, Goldgroup carried out the first exploration perforations without the proper permission, and it was not until 2010 that it presented its environmental impact statement, following a complaint by people in the region. In February of 2012, permission to carry on the project was denied due to ambiguities and omissions regarding the amount of water to be used, the distance to the nuclear plant at Laguna Verde, and the irreversible loss of 472 hectares of fertile land.

In terms of hydroelectric power plants, months after the energy reform was approved in December 2013, the Comisión Federal de Electricidad (Federal Electricity Commission) released the measures planned to strengthen a productive activity that is outside what the reform calls "strategic areas in electricity" and which profoundly transforms the hydrocarbon and electric industries so as to allow private investment in nearly all of the phases of the productive processes of both (Secretaría de Energía 2014). Hydroelectric power plants are the main source of renewable electric energy that Mexico has; there are sixty-four hydroelectric power plants that represent 22.3 percent of the installed capacity of the public service of electric energy (Llaven 2015). In 2012, it was reported that, in Mexico, there are 510 sites selected for small and miniature dams, of which 112 will be developed on 7 waterways in Veracruz (of note are 56 projects planned for the Bobos-Nautla River and 29 for the Actopan River). With the arrival of megaprojects in dams and hydroelectric power plants, communities in Veracruz have stood up and held off the installation of twenty-four dams.

The natural wealth that characterizes the state of Veracruz has long been taken advantage of by members of the state's elite. In 2010, without permission to mine gold from Caballo Blanco, the directors of Goldgroup Mining Inc. gave assurances they were continuing with the project, with which they "maintain a close relationship" (Ruiz 2012), a statement that leaves the door open for suspicion regarding the declaration by the Secretariat of the Environment and Natural Resources of a "suspension" of the paperwork (not rejection), which still appears as an "exploration project." In 2015, Pemex reported having given Javier Duarte, the governor of Veracruz, just over 2.160 billion pesos in cash and coupons that can be used for purchasing asphalt and gasoline, which were resold by colleagues of the governor, brothers Francisco García González and Mariano García González, the latter being the representative of the state government to Pemex (Guerrero 2016).

Robbery is not only the domain of the political sphere. Gasoline robbery has also been adopted by Los Zetas, converting organized crime into a major challenge for Pemex. According to Lohmuller (2015), Pemex lost more than $1.5 billion dollars due to fuel theft in the first nine months of 2014. Los Zetas has demonstrated its capacity to develop sophisticated networks for the distribution of stolen oil and gas (see Chapter 7). In Mexico, the quantity of clandestine, illegal taps into Pemex pipelines grew from 155 in 2000 to 5,252 in 2015 (Gallegos 2016). Given the complexity of these activities, it is clear that the inability to stop hydrocarbon theft is the result of collusion between organized crime, security forces, and public servants at all levels (Beittel 2015).

Since 2011, there has been a drastic increase in violence in Veracruz linked to the territorial disputes of groups of organized crime seeking to control the theft of oil and gas. The violence in these regions spread to new segments of the population: students, public servants, journalists, and environmental defenders. In January of 2016, five students were disappeared from the region of Tierra Blanca—where clandestine activities linked to the difficulty of accessing the area flourish— from which natural gas is obtained and hydrocarbons are processed. The participation of Police Chief Mario Conde in the disappearance of the students showed a clear link between local authorities and organized crime (Rojas 2016). The latest report on the situation of environmental defenders in Mexico (Presbítero, Cerami, and Romero 2015) affirms there were 109 attacks against environmental defenders between May 2014 and June 2015. The attacks happened in twenty states, and Veracruz was the site of attacks against four defenders who were fighting a dam in the Zongolica region. The aggressors were identified as local authorities and people related to the extractive industries.

CONCLUSIONS

To better explain and understand the critical process in which violence is generated in connection to natural resources requires an analysis of political *habitus* (Bourdieu 2007) in the country, which began to change in the year 2000. The habitus does not imply social practices due to mechanical imposition of the structures, but these dispositions are shaped by past events and structures and shape current practices and structures and condition our perception. The habitus is not fixed and can be changed under certain conditions or over a period of time. The habitus with which internal structures are arranged guides the actions of the political system, through mechanisms built from customary practices. In theory, the concept of customary practices emanates from studies of Indigenous political systems in election practices, and has been used to claim Indigenous rights as customary rights. However, the customary practices transcend wider social levels, such as the system of social actions and practices, a system of collective norms that have been internalized by people throughout history. In this sense, the legitimization of facts, acts, and social processes comes from the collective consensus in accordance with its own moral principles and justice derived from tradition.

Currently, we have data, numbers, and analysis showing Mexican elites and multinational corporations behave as governing bodies in the lives of citizens. This makes it impossible to avoid a discussion regarding the regulations these elites impose through low-intensity democracy, as state institutions promote profit and create ideal conditions for the juridical structures of dispossession. As mentioned by Granovsky-Larsen and Paley in the Introduction to this book, "States and the elite interests they represent continue to shape the national contexts within which organized violence operates, and they participate in violence either openly or from behind the plausible deniability facilitated through the formal and informal subcontracting of violence to non-state armed actors."

The many cases of corruption and criminality involving members of the governing class (politicians at all levels, including Mexico's president, dozens of governors, a countless number of mayors, as well as numerous business people) are expanding to levels that are becoming unsustainable. This time, the "rotten apple" theory does not apply. These criminal acts involve the entire political and business class, which maintains close links with leaders of organized crime groups. The case of Veracruz shows how power and public budgets can be misused to promote clientelism and to buy political loyalty, which assures the survival of elites and the persistence of institutions that favour the particular interests of the governing class.

Given this, it is necessary to promote a new cycle that leads to a critical opening that changes the direction of Veracruz and the whole country. Citizen mobilization and the appearance of new political and social protagonists are obvious responses, as it is they who have the most motivation to encourage the punishment of acts of corruption carried out by officials. Regardless, the socialization of fear has made it very difficult to start a movement of this kind.

REFERENCES

Ai Camp, Roderic. 1982. *Mexican Political Biographies, 1935–1981*. Tucson: University of Arizona Press.

Animal Político. 2016. "Colectivo encuentra en 3 meses 105 fosas clandestinas en colinas de Santa Fe, Veracruz." *Animal Político*, October 20. http://www.animalpolitico.com/2016/10/fosas-clandestinas-veracruz.

Arias, Enrique Desmond, and Daniel M. Goldstein, eds. 2010. *Violent Democracies in Latin America*. Durham, NC: Duke University Press.

Beittel, June S. 2015. *Mexico: Organized Crime and Drug Trafficking Organizations*. Congressional Research Service.

Bourdieu, Pierre. 2007. *Pensamiento y acción*. Buenos Aires, Argentina: Libros del Zorzal.

Correa-Cabrera, Guadalupe. 2017. *Los Zetas Inc.: Criminal Corporations, Energy, and Civil War in Mexico*. Austin: University of Texas Press.

Fombrun, Charles J. 1986. "Structural Dynamics within and between Organizations." *Administrative Science Quarterly* 31: 403–21.

Gagne, David. 2016. "US Sentences Mexico Businessman in Zetas Money Laundering Case." *Insight Crime*, March 25. http://www.insightcrime.org/news-briefs/us-sentences-mexico-businessman-in-zetas-money-laundering-case.

Gallegos, Zoraida. 2016. "El robo de combustible se dispara en México." *El País*, June 7. http://internacional.elpais.com/internacional/2016/06/04/mexico/1464993349_247192.html.

Guerrero, Claudia. 2016. "Duarte desaparece recursos de Pemex." *Noreste*, March 21. http://www.noreste.net/noticia/duarte-desaparece-recursos-de-pemex/.

Harvey, David. 2005. *A Brief History of Neoliberalism*. Oxford: Oxford University Press.

Hinings, C. R., and Royston Greenwood. 2002. "Disconnects and Consequences in Organization Theory?" *Administrative Science Quarterly* 47: 411–21.

INEGI (Instituto Nacional de Estadística y Geografía). 2015. *México en cifras*. http://www3.inegi.org.mx/sistemas/mexicocifras/default.aspx?e=30.

Llaven Anzures, Yadira. 2015. "Confirma gobierno federal instalación de nueve hidroeléctricas para Puebla." *La Jornada*, January 2. http://www.lajornadadeoriente.com.mx/2015/01/02/confirma-gobierno-federal-instalacion-de-nueve-hidroelectricas-para-puebla/.

Lohmuller, Michael. 2015. "Will Pemex's Plan to Fight Mexico Oil Thieves Work?" *Insight Crime*, February 18. http://www.insightcrime.org/news-briefs/pemex-oil-pipelines-theft-mexico.

Martínez, Regina. 2012. "Veracruz: otra deuda exorbitante." *Proceso*, February 2. http://www.proceso.com.mx/296926/veracruz-otra-deuda-exorbitante.

Méndez, Juan E., Guillermo O'Donnell, and Paulo Sérgio Pinheiro, eds. 1999. *The (Un)Rule of Law and the Underprivileged in Latin America*. Notre Dame, IN: Notre Dame University Press.

Pearce, Jenny. 2010. "Perverse State Formation and Securitized Democracy in Latin America." *Democratization* 17 (2): 286–306.

Pemex. 2012. *Infraestructura de plantas de proceso, sistema de ductos y terminales de almacenamiento y reparto 2006–2012 (Libro Blanco Pemex Refinación)*. http://www.ref.pemex.com/files/content/03transparencia/RC/REF05.pdf.

Presbítero, Analuz, Andrea Cerami, and Felipe Romero. 2015. "Informe sobre la situación de los defensores ambientales en México 2015." Centro Mexicano de Derecho Ambiental A.C. http://www.cemda.org.mx/wp-content/uploads/2011/12/Informe-defensores-2014-2015_final2.pdf.

Rojas, Laura. 2016. "El otro botín de los carteles." *Blog.expediente. mx*, February 2. http://www.blog.expediente.mx/nota/17853/periodico-de-veracruz-portal-de-noticias-veracruz/el-otro-botin-de-los-carteles-.

Ruiz, Juan Carlos. 2012. "Caballo Blanco, ¿nueva vergüenza nacional?" *La Jornada*, April 5. http://www.jornada.unam.mx/2012/04/05/opinion/017a1pol.

Schedler, Andreas. 2013. *The Politics of Uncertainty: Sustaining and Subverting Electoral Authoritarianism*. Oxford: Oxford University Press.

Secretaría de Energía. 2014. "Estrategia nacional de energía 2014–2028." https://www.gob.mx/cms/uploads/attachment/file/214/ENE.pdf.

SESNSP (Secretariado Ejecutivo del Sistema Nacional de Seguridad Pública). 2016. "Reporte de incidencia delictiva del fuero común por año." https://www.gob.mx/sesnsp/acciones-y-programas/incidencia-delictiva-del-fuero-comun?idiom=es.

Sørensen, Georg. 2001. *Changes in Statehood: The Transformation of International Relations*. London: Palgrave Macmillan.

Trejo, G., and S. Ley. 2016. "Federalismo, drogas y violencia por qué el conflicto partidista intergubernamental estimuló la violencia del narcotráfico en México." *Política y gobierno* XXIII (1): 11–56. http://www.politicaygobierno.cide.edu/index.php/pyg/article/view/741/598.

Valdés Castellanos, Guillermo. 2013. *Historia del narcotráfico en México*. Mexico City: Ediciones Aguilar.

Wilson Gilmore, R. 2007. *Golden Gulag: Prisons, Surplus, Crisis, and Opposition in Globalizing California*. Berkeley: University of California Press.

Zavaleta, Noé. 2016. *El infierno de Duarte: Crónicas de un sexenio en picada*. Mexico City: Ediciones Proceso.

CHAPTER 12

PUNITIVE DISPOSSESSION
AUTHORITARIAN NEOLIBERALISM AND THE ROAD TO MASS INCARCERATION

Elva F. Orozco Mendoza

On July 13, 2015, a group of approximately forty people, most of them women, gathered in the city of Guanajuato, Mexico, to block access to the city's highway toll booth. Their goal was to denounce the inhumane treatment of detainees in the Valle de Santiago's prison: CERESO Mil. The group gathered under the banner, Todos Unidos por los Presos (All United for Prisoners—TUP). They began to organize in 2014 to protest torture and dehumanization inside CERESO Mil. "Prisoners suffer repeated beatings and humiliations; they have little to no contact with family members," Ramona Chávez Campos, spokesperson of the group and sister of a male inmate, explained to local media that covered the event (Castro 2015). The group demanded dignified treatment for detainees, as the level of punishment is particularly severe and fully authorized by the prison's warden (Miranda 2014). As Chávez Campos maintained, guards keep prisoners locked in their cells twenty-three hours a day, significantly limiting their recreation time (Castro 2015; Due Process of Law Foundation 2016; Weinstein 2016).

Health and sanitary conditions are extremely poor. Prisoners lack access to medical attention, clean food, and safe water. As a result, they are constantly ill and poorly nourished. Food is contaminated with flies, cockroaches, and other insects (Castro 2015; Miranda 2014). Families have to purchase uniforms, shoes, tissue, shampoo, soap, and all manner of personal items to bring to their relatives.

Chávez Campos's words above illustrate two contradictory aspects of punishment. On the one hand, they reflect the excessive violence used against prisoners. On the other, they reveal the state's politics of neglect that denies inmates basic human services, furthering a greater dependency on friends and relatives. This twofold form of punishment, I argue, is paradigmatic of neoliberal governments and destroys prisoners' bodies, as well as those of their families, through a combination of extreme violence and neglect as a neoliberal logic prevails today "in statecraft and the workplace, education, culture, and a vast range of quotidian activity" (Brown 2015, 17). Since 2008, elites, technocrats, and legislators in Mexico have promoted state of exception laws to address organized crime (Calveiro 2010; Cannon 2016; Pérez Correa 2015a). These laws permit military intervention in civilian affairs, resulting in a greater number of arrests and extrajudicial killings (Pérez Correa 2015a, 21). Regarding carceral policy, state of exception laws furthered prisons as a primary solution to delinquency (Pérez Correa 2017; Calveiro 2010).

This hard line approach was justified by the alleged need to reinforce the criminal justice system amidst a pandemic escalation of violence resulting from organized crime, including drug cartels' diversification of operations to areas like car theft, kidnappings, human trafficking, extortion, and more (Calveiro 2010; Martin 2007; Schedler 2014; see also Chapters 7 and 9 in this volume). In Mexico, no other president showed such concern with the strengthening of the state's security apparatus in recent years as did Felipe Calderón, who launched a war on drugs a few days after his inauguration as president (Correa-Cabrera 2014; Pérez Correa 2015a). Mexico's entry into the war, however, was also driven by US interests, as indicated by the US$1.4 billion funds initially attached to Washington's regional anti-drug-trafficking policy known as the Merida Initiative (Cannon 2016). Prison reform, the militarization of law enforcement, and the rapid expansion of maximum-security facilities are direct outcomes of the Merida Initiative. Proponents of the program maintained that this initiative would eliminate corruption, anarchy, and the reproduction of criminality inside Mexican correctional facilities. As a result, the prison population rose from 210,140 in 2006, the year Calderón assumed the presidency, to nearly 260,000 in 2016 (World Prison Brief 2016). In 2016, Mexico was ranked seventh among countries with the highest number of prisoners worldwide, with nearly two hundred imprisoned individuals per one hundred thousand inhabitants (World Prison Brief 2016). This trend is likely to grow as five more federal prison facilities are under construction and measures are being taken to increase the warehousing capacity of existing ones (Pantaleón 2016; United States Embassy 2016).

In light of the above, this chapter asks the following questions: How is mass incarceration facilitating capitalist expansion in Mexico? In what concrete ways are thousands of people dispossessed through the carceral state? Which sectors of the population are targeted for dispossession? Finally, I interrogate the web of discourses, technologies, and procedures that are mobilized to legitimize dispossession. I argue that maximum-security prisons in Mexico reflect the two dimensions of punishment characteristic of neoliberal governments. On the one hand, they illustrate that the state's approach to organized crime rests on a disproportionate use of organized violence (see the Introduction to this volume; Pérez Correa 2015a). On the other, they illuminate a state politics of neglect, which profits from carceral expansion, lucrative public contracts granted to private service providers, and by directly extracting wealth from the poor, who pay for their own punishment. The result is a booming prison economy built on the criminalization, detention, and confinement of poor and marginalized people.

The chapter will proceed as follows: I first develop the concept of punitive dispossession, building on Judith Butler and Athena Athanasiou's overarching theory of dispossession. Next, I relate the notion of dispossession through incarceration, first, to the larger context of neoliberal governance in Mexico and, second, to Calderón's war on drugs. In the third part of the chapter, I will elaborate on the notion of punitive dispossession with reference to four themes: the criminalization of poor populations through a series of constitutional reforms and penal changes implemented in the aftermath of Calderón's war, which resulted in the multiplication of violent acts mainly directed against the civilian population; the expansion of maximum-security infrastructure, including maximum-security prisons and related security services; the transfer of the cost of captivity to prisoners' families, mainly wives, mothers, sisters, and grandmothers; and, finally, the creation of lasting barriers to economic freedom for prisoners and families alike. I conclude this chapter by briefly discussing the challenges faced by the nascent anti-prison movement in Mexico, including Todos Unidos por los Presos.

This chapter offers a new approach to the study of organized violence and the expansion of capital in Latin America through a contemporary analysis of the Mexican prison system. Doing so brings to the fore how recent legal reforms to the penal code and in-justice system unleashed disproportionate state violence, benefitting both political leaders as well as security and prison-related businesses, among others.

DISPOSSESSION: TWO DIMENSIONS OF PUNISHMENT

In *Dispossession: The Performative in the Political*, Butler and Athanasiou define the concept of dispossession in two distinct but complementary ways. First, dispossession entails "an induced form of suffering" (Butler and Athanasiou 2013, ix). As the authors note, dispossession happens when a large group of people—like women, trans, Indigenous, African Americans, the poor—are robbed of their land, citizenship, rights, way of life, or community, leaving them exposed to a differential distribution of precarity and violence. Examples of this form of dispossession include, but are not limited to, criminalization, forced migration, unemployment, homelessness, occupation, and conquest (Butler and Athanasiou 2013). Normative and normalizing powers that define cultural and political intelligibility force the dispossessed on a path to subjection, systemic violence, poverty, securitarian regimes, neoliberal governmentality, and precarization (Butler and Athanasiou 2013, 2). As such, dispossession imposes an abject position in society onto certain (undesirable) bodies, effectively instrumentalizing them and limiting their possibility of survival.

To this notion of dispossession Butler and Athanasiou add a second dimension, which is social. Understood in this way, dispossession signals "a limit to the autonomous and impermeable self-sufficiency of the liberal subject" (Butler and Athanasiou 2013, 2). In this more positive sense, dispossession stands for human interconnectedness, responsiveness, and interdependency that mark the formation of the human subject. Thus, a dispossessed subject is "one that avows the differentiated social bonds by which it is constituted and to which it is obligated" (Butler and Athanasiou 2013, ix). This conception of dispossession is central to any theorization of those elements of society that trigger political or economic responsiveness. This sense of dispossession, moreover, is attentive to losses experienced by others in such a way that "one is moved to the other and by the other—exposed to and affected by the other's vulnerability" (Butler and Athanasiou 2013, 1).

Butler and Athanasiou's theory of dispossession provides the conceptual framework for my own intervention. However, unlike them, who give social dispossession an empowering dimension, my use of the term "punitive dispossession" highlights the fact that both dimensions of the term can, in fact, be mobilized by sovereign power to multiply punishment. Stated differently, while Butler and Athanasiou contend that social dispossession—the fact that we are fundamentally constituted as relational beings—might create the necessary conditions to resist negative forms of dispossession—subjugation, privation, violent instrumentalization of bodies—I argue that punitive dispossession, as is currently enacted in Mexican prisons, expands the act of punishment as it reaches beyond prisoners themselves to their families. As such, punitive dispossession denotes the expulsion of entire groups of people from institutional systems of support that make a meaningful life possible so as to discipline them according to a neoliberal logic.

Understood in this way, punitive dispossession illuminates an excess of violence in the punishment of prisoners, as well as those processes that set prisoners and their families on a path of subjugation, poverty, and disposability. With this, I do not deny that solidarity, collective action, or prison activism are possible. My goal is rather to offer some reflections about the strategies used by the carceral state to dispossess a larger number of people, albeit in different ways. While punitive dispossession cannot be solely identified with a specific date or event, the process that I call by this name is concomitant with authoritarian neoliberalism: "a process of states reconfiguring themselves in nondemocratic ways in response to capitalist crisis" (Bruff 2012, 114). In this sense, Calderón's war on drugs—presumably launched in response to the crisis of insecurity—and ensuing constitutional reforms provided fertile ground for the criminalization of a greater number of people. As of January 2018, Mexico's war on drugs has generated extreme levels of violence: more than 230,000 homicides and 32,000 people have been officially recorded as disappeared (Molloy 2018; "México" 2017). As this chapter demonstrates, punitive dispossession through incarceration is an integral part of this war.

This chapter contributes a critical perspective to the growing scholarship on mass incarceration in Mexico. Most of existing literature on this topic focuses on individual forms of dispossession: costs to female relatives (Pérez Correa 2015b), expansion of capital through incarceration (Paz 2015), or prison labour (Alexander and West 2012; Davis 2005). This chapter takes a more comprehensive approach by examining maximum-security prisons as contemporary spaces impacted by the authoritarian logic of neoliberalism. Few studies exist that see the punitive turn in Mexico as a direct effect of the war on drugs first initiated by Calderón and fully embraced by Enrique Peña Nieto. Calveiro (2012) and Paley (2012, 2014) are important exceptions. My study both builds upon and departs from these works to theorize punitive dispossession, identifying mass incarceration as being part of modern techniques of capitalist expansion premised upon the violent ravaging of already vulnerable people. One of the contributions to be made to the critical literature on prison studies is how the imprisonment of the poor is lucrative, and who benefits. Moreover, this approach identifies some of the challenges ahead for those invested in prison reform and a more humane treatment of prisoners.

THE AUTHORITARIAN ROOTS OF NEOLIBERALISM

Evidence gathered from protests organized by members of Todos Unidos por los Presos suggests maximum-security prisons are more than mere spaces designed to control, neutralize, and discipline prisoners. In addition, they constitute an extractive system in their own right. Under PRI rule—Institutional Revolutionary Party—one of the defining features of the Mexican prison system was repression. In this respect, Markus-Michael Müller explains, "with the enacting of the Mexican Penal Code of 1931, [the prison] became fully incorporated into the repressive and frequently extralegal workings of power of the post-revolutionary Mexican state" (2016, 228). The repressive function of the prison remained intact through almost all of PRI's governments. However, after the 1980s, Mexican prisons began to assume a new role. As Pilar Calveiro explains, under neoliberalism, the prison system is "conceived as a national security issue where the main role of the state is to lock prisoners in and to neutralize them to guarantee the safety of producers and investors" (Calveiro 2010, 61). Calveiro's statement is true, but understanding Mexico's carceral turn solely through the lens of capital protection misses a crucial point. Incarceration is *profitable*, namely, it enables the accumulation of capital through a direct, and sometimes indirect, exploitation of imprisonment. Building on the Marxist theory of profit, which Marx attributed to "the power of capital to exploit labor" (Robinson 1971, 25), this chapter posits that prison profits are generated when the act of imprisonment enables the accumulation of capital for both political and economic entrepreneurs (Chaffee 1984). In what follows, I explore how Mexican prisons constitute an extractive system in their own right. But, first, I begin with a few remarks about neoliberalism.

Wendy Brown notes how neoliberalism is commonly perceived as "a loose and shifting signifier" (2015, 20), but there are several coordinates that can orient us in the scope and potency of this word. Neoliberalism has been theorized as (1) a political and philosophical project, (2) a set of economic policies, (3) a period covering the last decades of the twentieth century and those of the twenty-first, and (4) a mode of reasoning (Bernstein and Jakobsen 2012/2013; Brown 2015; Gonzales 2016, 83; Zilberg 2011, 4). Despite its polysemy, the dominant tradition of neoliberalism defines it "as a set of policy prescriptions...grouped around trade liberalisation, easier foreign direct investment (FDI), and the reduction of government and state intervention in the economy in favour of the private sector and the markets" (Cannon 2016, 29). Proponents of neoliberalism offered this particular definition as a prescription for increasing economic development, prosperity, and individual freedom (Brown 2015; Cheng 2012/2013, 3; Martin 2007).

In contrast, for Antonio Vázquez-Arroyo, neoliberalism is an economic and a political doctrine that finds its roots in the philosophy of liberal democracy, a kind of democracy that tends towards the destruction of democratic values for its liberal ethos (Vázquez-Arroyo 2008). Simply put, neoliberalism runs counter to substantial democracy. Ian Bruff offers the term authoritarian neoliberalism to designate a "process, of states reconfiguring themselves in increasingly non-democratic ways in response to profound capitalist crisis" (2012, 114). The two key ideas here are political reconfiguration and crisis. Authoritarian neoliberalism, therefore, signals the exercise of repressive power in response to an alleged emergency. These remarks beg the question of how authoritarian neoliberalism manifests in Mexican prisons, which I will return to shortly.

Chile provides a good example of the links between authoritarian rule and neoliberal economic policy. To be sure, without General Augusto Pinochet, it is unlikely that the implementation of monetarism, the early term for neoliberalism, would have succeeded in Chile (Gonzales 2016; Martin 2007; Vázquez-Arroyo 2008). Indeed, military power helped in the restoration of elite authority after a socialist government had been elected in 1970 (Martin 2007). Prisons were a fundamental part of this process. They were used as centres of detention, interrogation, torture, and murder of dissidents and civilians (Macias 2014; Timerman 1981). From then on, neoliberalism became the dominant economic model in most of Latin America. To accomplish this, military regimes cooperating with the United States were organized (Cannon 2016). Prisons continued to play a fundamental role in the destruction of the opposition.

While also central to its history, the link between authoritarianism and neoliberalism in Mexico seems less obvious, as the violence that accompanied early attempts to introduce neoliberal reform in the country appeared less extreme. Initially, economic adjustment was achieved mainly through the political system (Cannon 2016). Consequently, violence in Mexico remained "discrete, anonymous, prolonged and quotidian" (Martin 2007, 61). However, this changed over the years, as political leaders showed more willingness to deploy violence against civilians to impose economic reform. For the sake of periodization, I divide the trajectory of neoliberalism in Mexico into four stages. First, its prehistory, ranging from the late 1970s to the 1980s (Martin 2007). Second, the period formally known as the onset of neoliberalism introduced in Mexico by former President Miguel de la Madrid in 1982 (Martin 2007, 59; Rousseau 2010). Third, the early 1990s were a decisive period marked by the inauguration of NAFTA, the North American Free Trade Agreement proposed by Carlos Salinas de Gortari (Rousseau 2010). Fourth, the so-called war years, which began with Calderón's presidency in December 2006 (Cannon 2016; Müller 2016).

As I mentioned above, for most of the twentieth century, the Mexican prison system continued to function as an instrument of repression and punishment typical of authoritarian PRI governments (Gibler 2014). However, judging by the rise in incarceration rates, the Mexican prison system also began developing its own economy as the number of imprisoned people in the nearly four decades of neoliberalism in Mexico went from 42,943 in 1976 to 255,638 in 2014 (World Prison Brief 2016). Two decisive moments in the history of prison expansion are the years following the economic crisis of 1994, as well as the period that followed the initial declaration of war against drugs. Available data indicates that in 1995 there were 93,574 people in prison. However, by the year 2000, Mexico housed 154,765 prisoners (World Prison Brief 2016). In turn, during the war on drugs, Mexico's prison population rose from 210,140 in 2006 to 255,638 in 2014 (World Prison Brief 2016).

MEXICO'S WAR ON DRUGS AND CRIMINALITY

We can conclude from the above that the state's use of violence to further a more aggressive economic (neoliberal) reform is premised upon the language of crisis. Mexico's war on drugs is a case in point. The war was crucial to implement more radical economic reforms, as NAFTA proved insufficient to fully open Mexico to privatization (Paley 2014). Economic policies under NAFTA pushed for the sale of state-owned companies in most sectors except for oil and energy (Calveiro 2012; Paley 2012). As a result, a whole range of services was gradually cut, including health care, education, retirement, and more. But, as Paley notes, from a capitalist perspective, Mexico's economy seemed to require yet greater doses of reform at the turn of the twenty-first century, given the energy sector was not fully open to foreign investors (Paley 2014). Thus, technocrats pushed "a comprehensive strategy proven to increase foreign direct investment. This strategy had to ensure that the local police and army and eventually the entire legal system, would operate according to US standards. This approach is colloquially known as the war on drugs" (Paley 2012, 22).

Drug trafficking has had a long historical presence in the country; however, it was not until Calderón's administration that the issue began to be treated as a threat to national security (Müller 2016). Calderón's justification for this militarized approach towards fighting drug-related activities came via a media campaign that instilled fear of the violence unleashed by warring drug-trafficking organizations: "decapitations, dismemberment, car bombs, mass kidnappings, grenade attacks, blockades, and the widespread execution of public officials" (Correa-Cabrera 2014, 3).

As Calderón put it, "criminality is trying to terrorize and immobilize [our] society and government...I promise to fight to take back public security" (quoted in Parish Flannery 2013, 192). I don't mean to suggest criminality does not exist or that it lacks an empirical basis, violence perpetrated by criminal organizations does exist. My point is, rather, that we should critically interrogate the official discourses that determine a priori who the criminal is and how she should be eliminated in order to understand what other forms of violence are employed in the process.

The war on drugs in Mexico is a strategy to impose a more aggressive line of capitalist expansion (Paley 2014). The justification by the United States for outsourcing the war on drugs to Mexico is that it has been a victim, harmed by the drug economy occurring outside its borders (Gonzales 2014). This does not mean, however, that the war is a mere imposition, since the Mexican state profits politically, symbolically, and economically from the war. Politically, the war on drugs was used to legitimize Calderón's presidency amid widespread accusations of electoral fraud (Correa-Cabrera 2014). Symbolically, the war has been used to reaffirm the legitimacy of the state, in the face of persistent criticism, by portraying a deep concern with citizens' safety. Economic profit as explained above is a central aspect of this war. It is to this topic I turn next.

The US-led drug war brought to Mexico security programs previously applied in southern nations such as the Merida Initiative, the largest multi-year US foreign aid and security package for Latin America, modelled after Plan Colombia (Cannon 2016; Müller 2016; Paley 2014). The Merida Initiative was designed to provide security assistance to Mexico, with a particular emphasis on the military component. Tellingly, the Merida Initiative has been a "driving force behind the expansion of (federal) police and military powers related to the war on drugs in Mexico" (Müller 2016, 232). In addition, the Merida Initiative has sought to modernize the prison system, hitherto perceived as inoperable, corrupt, filthy, and easily fooled from an American vantage point (Hayner and Richter 1942). From a US perspective, Mexican prisons are closely linked to Mexican "traditions" and seen as rudimentary (Hayner and Richter 1942). The plan to reform Mexican prisons was explained in a press release issued in April 2016 in the city of Merida, announcing the collaboration between Mexico and the US Embassy "to improve the jails and prisons in the whole country" (United States Embassy 2016). The goal, the document notes, is to ensure that all Mexican prisons conduct their operations according to guidelines dictated by international organizations to prevent long-standing problems like corruption, escapes, insurrection, and the spread of criminality.

PUNITIVE DISPOSSESSION

In the remaining parts of this chapter, I turn to four main themes that I discuss under the notion of punitive dispossession in contemporary Mexico, as well as the larger effects for prisoners and their families. Overall, my goal is to demonstrate that one distinct feature of Mexican prisons under neoliberalism is profitability. Above, I established the association between totalitarian neoliberalism, the war on drugs, and prison reform. Together, these elements provide the historical and political context for what I call *punitive dispossession*: the sovereign expulsion of entire groups of people from those systems of support that make a meaningful life possible so as to discipline them under the logic of neoliberalism. The Mexican prison system facilitates punitive dispossession through (1) the criminalization of the poor; (2) the expansion of security infrastructure, including maximum-security prisons and related security services; (3) the extension of punishment from prisoners to their families, including wives, mothers, sisters, and grandmothers who pay for punishment; and (4) the creation of lasting barriers to economic freedom for prisoners and families alike.

While central to the logics of the drug war, mass incarceration has been less studied in Mexico, despite the fact that a plethora of scholars have shown that the prison crisis in the United States is the most visible outcome of this war there (Alexander and West 2012; Davis 2005; Reiman and Leighton 1979). Former President George H. W. Bush articulated this connection: "Using illegal drugs is against the law. Doing drugs, you risk everything, even your freedom. If you do drugs, you will be caught. And when you're caught, you will be punished. Some think there won't be room for them in jail. We'll make room" (Bush 2005, 1181). Bush's words materialized two and a half decades later in 2015 in an estimated five thousand US prisons: 1,800 state and federal facilities and 3,200 local and county jails (Ingram 2015). Today, the United States has 25 percent of the world's prison population while its share of the world's population is only 5 percent (Davis 2005). For abolition activist Susan Norton, these figures prove "the United States is a prison nation and the birthplace of the prison industrial complex" (Visions of Abolition 2012). Importantly, US wars against poverty and drugs have proved to be wars waged on poor people, particularly Black and Brown people, who make up "two out of three people who are locked up in prison" (Visions of Abolition 2012). Something similar can be said about Mexican prisons, which are rapidly becoming abodes for the poorest.

CRIMINALIZING THE POOR

Just as the war on drugs is not primarily about stopping the movement of drugs across national borders, mass incarceration has little to do with the reduction of criminality. In fact, the contrary is true, judging by the recent constitutional reforms that implemented a "tough on crime" approach in the country. Two main factors have triggered the criminalization of the poor in recent decades: first, the almost permanent context of economic crisis, and, second, the alleged crisis of insecurity that opened the door to the passage of constitutional reforms. With the inauguration of NAFTA and the ensuing economic crisis of 1994, Mexico saw an alarming loss of jobs, the rapid spread of poverty, migration, and a significant expansion of the informal economy (Müller 2013). The rates of street crime, assaults, robberies, kidnappings, and petty theft grew significantly, creating a climate of insecurity in major urban areas (Bergman 2013; Pérez Correa 2008). Mexico never fully recovered from the crisis, and the climate of insecurity continued to grow as more people dwelled on the streets or resorted to drugs to alleviate their suffering (Mercille 2011). As reported by the Índice Global de Impunidad (*Global Index of Impunity*), Mexico ranks fifty-eighth out of fifty-nine countries with the highest impunity rates (Le Clercq Ortega and Sanchez 2016). This means that even if more people are victims of crime in Mexico, their cases are rarely investigated. On the contrary, in many cases, these crimes are forgotten or lost in a sea of bureaucracy (Pérez Correa 2008). To be sure, the levels of impunity, defined as "[protection] actively provided to the gamut of armed groups who commit crimes and acts of terror against citizens, migrants, and the poor" surpass 95 percent (Paley 2014, 17; Gibler 2011).

The above suggests that incarceration rates are not directly correlated with more efficiency or expediency in the administration of justice. Rather, mass incarceration stems from greater powers that have been given to police forces, prosecutors, and the courts through recent reforms (Pérez Correa 2008). Several factors stand out. A widespread discontent with the Mexican justice system, commonly perceived as inefficient and corrupt (Pérez Correa 2008), led to the passage of constitutional reforms that sought to change this perception. As a result, reforms to Article 16 of the Mexican Constitution were approved in 1993, 1999, and again in 2006. Broadly speaking, these reforms brought about a politics of exception that resulted in greater discretionary powers granted to police forces and prosecutors to detain suspects, harsher criminal laws and sentences, the excessive use of preventive prison, and the authority to arrest people without warrants in "urgent cases" (Pérez Correa 2008; 2015a). Thus, the process of restructuring the criminal justice system itself provoked an expansion of the prison population. The constitutional reforms that modified existing precepts on penal justice, public safety, and organized crime are mainly used against petty criminals caught in the act or accused by police officers that use their power at will to detain them (Müller 2013; Pérez Correa 2008).

Perhaps the most important constitutional change was in the definition of organized crime, which, according to Article 16 of the Mexican Constitution, reads: "by organized crime we understand the association of three or more people to commit crimes in a permanent or repeated manner, in terms of the law of the matter" (Constitución Política de los Estados Unidos Mexicanos). As these words show, the definition of organized crime is so broad that almost any activity can be classified as organized crime if three or more people, including those who commit minor offences, plan it. Moreover, the mere intention of engaging in organized crime, without actually carrying out the deed, is susceptible to punishment. Thus, international drug trafficking, automobile theft, and the kids who sell copied CDs and DVDs can all be classified as organized crime. But, unlike the powerful drug lords or corrupt politicians, the Mexican poor do not have the means to avoid prison (Calveiro 2012, 169). Largely, the majority of individuals currently serving time in prison were petty criminals caught in the act or directly accused of engaging in criminal activity. But when confronted with a "thought crime" approach to fighting "delinquency," people with minor criminal charges find it difficult to avoid a de facto criminal system that profits from their detention.

These factors, in addition to the introduction of arrest quotas, police violence, and failing institutions, explain why imprisonment rates are on the rise (Müller 2013). It also shows why those serving time in Mexican prisons are not the most dangerous drug lords but, rather, the poor.

EXPANDING MAXIMUM-SECURITY INFRASTRUCTURE

Evidence that the Mexican prison system is profitable can be found in the plans to reform the prison system. Such reforms, pushed under the Merida Initiative, ordain the *adaptation* of special detention centres with heightened surveillance measures to handle individuals suspected or accused of committing organized crime. It is in the name of these reforms that a massive transfer of funds is taking place as prison construction and security services of all kinds are added to the structure of the Mexican prison system. Accordingly, federal money is being destined for the construction of additional federal prisons, or CEFERESOS, to house "high risk, dangerous criminals." Anthropologist Elena Azaola notes how, before Calderón's administration, there were only four federal prisons, housing more than three thousand inmates. By the end of Calderón's administration, Mexico had thirteen federal prisons, with nearly fifty thousand inmates (Paz 2015). Today, this figure continues to grow—the number of federal prisons has reached twenty-one and there are four more are under construction (Paz 2015). In addition, state prisons have also moved to adapt maximum-security modules inside their facilities (Calveiro 2012). CERESO Mil in Valle de Santiago is one of the 379 penitentiary centres currently undertaking these reforms (SEGOB 2015). It is no secret, then, that the beneficiaries of growing rates of incarceration are, among others, construction and security companies. Raúl Mijango, a key peace mediator between the gangs of El Salvador and the state, corroborated this in an interview with Guadalupe Correa-Cabrera in 2016. As he put it, "The beneficiaries of the violence [in El Salvador] are local and US businessmen who control private security and the arms trade" (Mijango as quoted in Correa-Cabrera 2016).

Another aspect of the Merida Initiative is the certification of Mexican prisons through the American Correctional Association (ACA) (United States Embassy 2016). This certification has the strategic objectives of "increasing bed space, updating architectural diagrams and security equipment, increasing personnel, standardizing current regulations in major areas such as classification of inmates and creating new treatment programs and controlling supplies" (Slack, Shelor, and Black-Dennis 2012).

Certification through ACA is purported to reduce widespread impunity, escapes, corruption, overcrowding, prisoner abuse, and loss of security. From this perspective, the problems with the Mexican prison system relate to security rather than to corruption or wealth extraction. Consequently, Merida Initiative funds are used to increase the security apparatus of the whole prison system through new metrics, practices, and logics of certification. However, as Chávez Campos from Todos Unidos por los Presos explained above, the level of punishment and control *is* indeed severe inside maximum-security facilities; prisoners who are labelled high-risk criminals are effectively isolated, chained, locked up, and kept incommunicado. To that extent, ACA's certification simply represents the standardization of punishment rather than its reduction or elimination.

Punitive dispossession, therefore, takes place through a massive transfer of funds from both the Mexican and US governments to construction companies, security providers, and private vendors. While it may be argued that the use of Merida Initiative money to institute prison reform in Mexico does not directly entail extracting money from the poor, it remains a form of dispossession since it is the Mexican poor who provide an endless pool of so-called high-risk individuals to be locked in maximum-security facilities, many times due to minor offences (Paz 2015). In 2016, the US Embassy announced that USAID (United States Agency for International Development) will assign US$25 million out of the 2.5 billion total allocated to the Merida Initiative to "reform all Mexican prisons in the whole country" (United States Embassy 2016). The money, however, is not delivered to the Mexican government or to Mexican prison administrators but to ACA's representatives. Tellingly, ACA assumes that corruption and inoperability of Mexican prisons is a problem of the failing system of security rather than a problem created by sovereign power. In this respect, ACA's certification has an ideological function: it is in place to suggest that the lawlessness of maximum-security prisons, largely a fiction, as explained by members of TUP, can be addressed through standardized metrics. In reality, however, Mexico is simply standardizing its punitive practices through ACA.

MAKING FAMILIES RESPONSIBLE

One of the strongest pieces of evidence that Mexican prisons constitute an extractive system in their own right can be found in the authorities' withholding of basic services to inmates, which sets in motion an aggressive form of dispossession that goes beyond prisoners themselves into their family networks (CNDH 2014). Prisoners' families, especially wives, mothers, sisters, or grandmothers, are also punished. This phenomenon occurs due to the state's abandonment of prisoners as it cuts its spending in services. While the majority of individuals imprisoned on charges of organized crime are poor, this has not been an impediment for the Mexican state to run prisons based on an extractive model. I explain the entanglement of the family in the act of punishment in what follows.

In a recent study, legal scholar Catalina Pérez Correa found that women usually take the responsibility of economically supporting their imprisoned relatives, often with permanent economic costs for the entire family (2015b; TUP 2014). In a context where sovereign states fail to meet their obligations of providing basic services to men and women behind bars, social dispossession, as explained by Butler and Athanasiou, makes sense. Recall that Butler and Athanasiou conceive social dispossession as the fundamental interconnectedness of human beings. In their view, we depend on one another and are obliged to one another since vulnerability, rather than self-sufficiency, marks the formation of human subjectivity. Seen in this way, social dispossession helps us appreciate the central role that wives, mothers, sisters, or grandmothers play when they support their imprisoned relatives. Yet, as judged by the logic of the prison system, social dispossession also facilitates the expansion of punishment from the prisoner to the family, as these women are made to pay for the punishment of their relative.

To be sure, the state's withholding of basic services to inmates translates in the hyper-disciplining of their wives, mothers, sisters, and grandmothers, who have to find multiple sources of employment to make ends meet for themselves, their relatives, and for other dependents. Nearly 65 percent of the women who participated in Pérez Correa's study said they work, in contrast to 37.4 percent of women who participate in the labour force nationwide, nearly twice the national average (Pérez Correa 2015b). Nearly 30 percent of these women work as maids. Merchants and private employees are the two other significant categories of employment (Pérez Correa 2015b). From this, it can be inferred that women with a relative in prison are overworked and exhausted, since many of them hold multiple jobs to afford the high cost of living inside Mexican prisons. In CERESO Mil, for example, families of prisoners are required to buy all the personal items utilized by inmates: sweaters, uniforms, shoes, socks, underwear, tissue, soap, sweaters, shampoo, sheets, blankets, pillows, sanitary pads for women, water, medicines, etc. (TUP 2014). Also, families are required to leave a monthly stipend for inmates. However, this money is never seen or touched by the prisoner. The prison administration keeps it and uses it for the inmate expenses inside the prison (TUP 2014).

In many cases, families travel long distances to visit their relatives in a maximum-security facility, usually found in areas that are difficult to access. In the case of CERESO Mil, the facility is officially registered in the city of Valle de Santiago. But the prison can only be reached via private transportation. Thus, to visit their relatives, families have to travel by car or pay a taxicab that charges on average nine dollars for a one-way trip. While this amount of money may seem insignificant for an American working person, many blue-collar workers in Mexico are paid less than US$9 for a whole day of work. Travelling expenses, however, do not end there, as some families begin their journey from different cities and states to see their relatives, resulting in greater costs for a visit. Families also have to pay for the food they bring to their relatives on visitation day, and for books, telephone cards, etc.

The bulk of expenses stem from the legal costs incurred even when families are assigned a public defender. In such cases, the lawyer might charge families all the administrative expenses associated with the specific case: psychological experts if needed, a day of work when witnesses are available to testify on behalf of the detainee, fuel, photocopies, food for the public lawyer when he or she goes to visit their client, etc. In contrast, families who can afford a private lawyer soon realize that legal expenses have to be paid on a continuous basis until the case is fully processed. In most cases, this may mean years of legal costs until their relative is released or sentenced (TUP 2014). In many cases, these legal expenses lead to the economic ruin of the family (Pérez Correa 2015b). This is because families need to sell their cars, houses, land, and other property in order to afford legal representation. In other cases, relatives take loans and incur serious debt, as they are responsible for the upkeep of their incarcerated relative. Others resort to criminal activity to be able to pay. Additionally, some guards may charge the families a fee to spare the prisoner from torture or beatings. While some prison facilities allow detainees to work, the profits companies may make out of prison labour are not as significant as the economy that develops around prison facilities. To these expenses, Pérez Correa adds the cost of supporting the children or any other dependents left behind (2015b).

ENDING ECONOMIC FREEDOM

Punitive dispossession also creates lasting barriers to economic freedoms for prisoners and families alike. This form of dispossession can affect generations to come as families forced to pay for the punishment of their relatives are overworked, which leaves little room for them to pursue education, specialization, or leisure that is fulfilling to them. The amount of debt acquired as a result of imprisonment condemns the family to a cycle of poverty in a way that makes incarceration seem almost like destiny. Under such conditions, families find it very difficult to break the cycle of poverty despite that all they do is work. They may also find it impossible to amass wealth or simply save for retirement.

Ironically, the neoliberal conception of citizenship is premised upon individual responsibility, even as punishment is collective. It is by taking responsibility for themselves that individuals are said to contribute to society. Former British Prime Minister Margaret Thatcher put it thus: "There's no such thing as society. There are individual men and women, and there are families. And no government can do anything except through people, and people must look after themselves first. It is our duty to look after ourselves and then, also, to look after our neighbours" (Thatcher and Keay 1987). As this quote suggests, advocates for neoliberalism urge citizens, regardless of race, class, gender, ability, or nationality, to take responsibility for themselves. However, this happens in a context where neoliberal governments create the legal conditions for failure.

When looked at through the lens of a neoliberal subjectivity, the relative of an imprisoned person is the prototype of the neoliberal subject, in the sense that she takes responsibility for herself, her relative, and dependents when these exist. This person may hold two or more jobs to make ends meet. And, yet, she finds it impossible to live up to the values of economic success dictated by those champions of neoliberalism, given the economic burdens on her shoulders. Alas, this paradigmatic neoliberal subject is totally disregarded by the carceral state. While profiting from women, incarceration causes substantial lifelong damage to the prospects of attaining economic freedom, precisely because the prison system reproduces the criminal subject it is meant to rehabilitate.

The claim here is not only that imprisoned people face greater obstacles to finding a job upon release, or that they may experience severe physical and psychological impediments as a result of incarceration by forcing them to take responsibility for their imprisoned folks. These effects are true and important, but they are not collateral damage. Rather, they are consciously induced on populations that are already vulnerable. Incarceration impacts both prisoners and families, locking them in a cycle of economic violence and subjugation.

CONCLUSION

The 2014 protests by members of Todos Unidos por los Presos were not successful in changing the harsh and inhumane conditions of imprisonment in Valle de Santiago. Indeed, conditions appear to have worsened, as authorities punished inmates whose relatives participated in the protests. This is because the Merida Initiative made it easier for Mexico to adopt state of exception laws that suspend all the rights of individuals accused of participating in organized crime. Likewise, these laws permit authoritarian treatment of detainees while increasing the ability of police and prosecutors to decide the fate of prisoners (Calveiro 2010, 59). Prison activism in Mexico, I would suggest, would do well to join the demand for prison abolition, given that prison reform is a key factor in the expansion of wealth extraction. As we saw, certification programs like ACA are used to legitimize and standardize punishment instead of eliminating it. Furthermore, demands to improve the living conditions of prisoners do not address the punishment that is extended to the families.

The abolition movement has a long trajectory in the United States, held up through figures such as Angela Davis, Michelle Alexander, Andrea Smith, and many others whose calls for abolition have resonated with a significant part of the working poor around the world. In Mexico, however, government propaganda has been successful in creating stigma against the prison population. As the rates of imprisonment in Mexico continue to grow, more individuals will be caught in the cycle of poverty, detention, and criminalization created by the very system that is supposed to end it. As this chapter has shown, reform creates more sophisticated and perverse forms of punishment, which incorporate a greater number of people. This is why the abolition of the prison system is the only logical response to punitive dispossession.

REFERENCES

Alexander, Michelle, and Cornel West. 2012. *The New Jim Crow: Mass Incarceration in the Age of Colorblindness*. New York: New Press.

Bergman, Marcelo. 2013. *El crecimiento del delito en Latinoamérica. Cuadernos del Consejo Mexicano de Asuntos Internationales*. http://www.academia.edu/3986889/Crecimiento_del_delito_cuaderno_9.

Bernstein, Elizabeth, and Janet R. Jakobsen. 2012/2013. Introduction to "Gender, Justice, and Neoliberal Transformations," edited by Elizabeth Bernstein and Janet R. Jakobsen. Special issue, *The Scholar & Feminist Online* 11.1–11.2 (Fall/Spring). http://sfonline.barnard.edu/gender-justice-and-neoliberal-transformations/introduction/.

Brown, Wendy. 2015. *Undoing the Demos: Neoliberalism's Stealth Revolution*. New York: Zone Books.

Bruff, Ian. 2012. "Authoritarian Neoliberalism, the Occupy Movements, and IPE." *Journal of Critical Globalization Studies* 5: 114–16.

Bush, George. 2005. *The Public Papers of the Presidents of the United States: George Bush, 1989: Book 1*. Ann Arbor: University of Michigan Library.

Butler, Judith, and Athena Athanasiou. 2013. *Dispossession: The Performative in the Political*. Oxford: Wiley. http://site.ebrary.com/id/10687857.

Calveiro, Pilar. 2010. "El tratamiento penitenciario de los cuerpos." *Cuaderno de Antropología Social* 32: 57–74.

———. 2012. *Violencias de estado: La guerra antiterrorista y la guerra contra el crimen como medios de control global*. Buenos Aires, Argentina: Siglo Veintiuno Editores.

Cannon, Barry. 2016. *The Right in Latin America: Elite Power, Hegemony and the Struggle for the State*. New York and London: Routledge.

Castro, Saul. 2015. "Con bloqueo demandan mejores tratos para reos." *Periódico Correo*, July 14. https://periodicocorreo.com.mx/reiteran-protestas-por-maltrato-a-reos-del-cereso-mil/.

Chaffee, Wilber A. 1984. "The Political Economy of Revolution and Democracy: Toward a Theory of Latin American Politics." *The American Journal of Economics and Sociology* 43 (4): 385–98.

Cheng, Sealing. 2012/2013. "Embodying the Sexual Limits of Neoliberalism." In "Gender, Justice, and Neoliberal Transformations," edited by Elizabeth Bernstein and Janet R. Jakobsen. Special issue, *The Scholar & Feminist Online* 11.1–11.2 (Fall/Spring). http://sfonline.barnard.edu/gender-justice-and-neoliberal-transformations/embodying-the-sexual-limits-of-neoliberalism/.

CNDH (Comision Nacional de los Derechos Humanos de México). 2014. *Diagnóstico nacional de supervisión penitenciaria 2014*. http://www.cndh.org.mx/sites/all/doc/sistemas/DNSP/DNSP_2014.pdf.

Constitución Política de los Estados Unidos Mexicanos (Mexican Constitution). https://www.juridicas.unam.mx/legislacion/ordenamiento/constitucion-politica-de-los-estados-unidos-mexicanos#10551.

Correa-Cabrera, Guadalupe. 2014. Foreword to *Drug War Capitalism*, by Dawn Paley. Oakland, CA: AK Press.

———. 2016. "La tregua con las maras que destruyó el estado." *Revista Noroeste*, June 7. http://www.noroeste.com.mx/publicaciones/view/la-tregua-con-las-maras-que-destruyo-el-estado-en-el-salvador-1030252.

Davis, Angela Y. 2005. *Abolition Democracy: Beyond Empire, Prisons, and Torture.* New York: Seven Stories Press.

Due Process of Law Foundation. 2016. "Organizations Explain to the Inter-American System How the Privatization of Mexican Prisons Threatens Human Rights." http://www.dplf.org/en/news/organizations-explain-inter-american-system-how-privatization-mexican-prisons-threatens-human.

Gibler, John. 2011. *To Die in Mexico: Dispatches from Inside the Drug War.* San Francisco, CA: Open Media Series City Lights Books.

———. 2014. *Tzompaxtle: La fuga de un guerrillero.* Mexico City: Tusquets Editores.

Gonzales, Alfonso. 2014. *Reform without Justice: Latino Migrant Politics and the Homeland Security State.* Oxford: Oxford University Press.

———. 2016. "Neoliberalism, the Homeland Security State, and the Authoritarian Turn." *Latino Studies* 14 (1): 80–98.

Hayner, Norman S., and Oscar T. Richter. 1942. "Recientes observaciones sobre las prisiones mexicanas." *Revista Mexicana de Sociología* 4.1: 73–83.

Ingram, Christopher. 2015. "The U.S. Has More Jails than Colleges. Here's a Map of Where Those Prisoners Live." *The Washington Post*, January 6. https://www.washingtonpost.com/news/wonk/wp/2015/01/06/the-u-s-has-more-jails-than-colleges-heres-a-map-of-where-those-prisoners-live/?noredirect=on&utm_term=.bffa980444ea.

Le Clercq Ortega, Juan Antonio, and Gerardo Rodriguez Sanchez. 2016. Índice global de impunidad México. Puebla, Mexico: Centro de Estudios sobre Impunidad y Justicia, CESIJ.

Macias, Teresa. 2014. "Tortured Bodies: The Biopolitics of Torture and Truth in Chile." In *At the Limits of Justice: Women of Colour on Terror*, edited by Suvendrini Perera and Sherene Razack, 309–30. Toronto: University of Toronto Press.

Martin, Patricia. 2007. "Mexico's Neoliberal Transition: Authoritarian Shadows in an Era of Neoliberalism." In *Contesting Neoliberalism: Urban Frontiers*, edited by Helga Leitner, Jamie Peck, and Eric S. Sheppard, 51–70. New York: Guilford Press.

Mercille, Julien. 2011. "Violent Narco-Cartels or US Hegemony? The Political Economy of the 'War on Drugs' in Mexico." *Third World Quarterly* 32 (9): 1637–53.

"México, el país donde hay más de 32.000 desaparecidos." 2017. CNN *Español*, September 13. http://cnnespanol.cnn.com/2017/09/13/mexico-el-pais-donde-hay-mas-de-32-000-desaparecidos/.

Miranda, Miguel Angel. 2014. "Denuncian maltratos a internos en el Cereso Mil." *Periodico Correo*, December 7. http://periodicocorreo.com.mx/denuncian-trato-inhumano-de-presos-en-valle-de-santiago/.

Molloy, Molly. 2018. "More than 29,000 Homicide Victims in Mexico in 2017." *Frontera List*, January 24. https://fronteralist.org/2018/01/24/more-than-29000-homicide-victims-in-mexico-in-2017/.

Müller, Markus-Michael. 2013. "Penal Statecraft in the Latin American City." *Social & Legal Studies* 22 (4): 441–63.

———. 2016. "Penalizing Democracy: Punitive Politics in Neoliberal Mexico." *Crime, Law, and Social Change* 65: 227–49.

Paley, Dawn. 2012. "Drug War Capitalism: Militarization and Economic Transformation in Colombia and Mexico." *Against the Current*, July/August. http://www.solidarity-us.org/pdfs/Dawn.pdf.

———. 2014. *Drug War Capitalism*. Oakland, CA: AK Press.

Pantaleón, Israel. 2016. "Quieren vender la technologia de las prisiones de EU para cárceles mexicanas." *Forbes*, April 8. https://www.forbes.com.mx/la-empresa-quiere-traer-ciberseguridad-las-carceles-mexicanas/.

Parish Flannery, Nathaniel. 2013. "Calderón's War." *Journal of International Affairs* 66 (2) (Spring/Summer): 181–96.

Paz, Susana. 2015. "Las cárceles en México y América Latina." Conacyt Agencia Informativa. http://www.conacytprensa.mx/index.php/ciencia/humanidades/1878-las-carceles-en-mexico-y-america-latina.

Pérez Correa, Catalina. 2008. "Front Desk Justice: Inside and Outside Criminal Procedure in Mexico City." *Mexican Law Review* 1 (1) (January). https://revistas.juridicas.unam.mx/index.php/mexican-law-review/article/view/7712/9674.

———. 2015a. *De la detención a la prisión: La justicia penal a examen*. Mexico City: Centro de Investigaciones Jurídicas, UNAM.

———. 2015b. "Mujeres invisibles: Los verdaderos costos de la prisión." *Nexos*, December 1. http://www.nexos.com.mx/?p=26995.

———. 2017. "The Foundations of Modern Criminal Law and Gender Inequality." *Seattle Journal for Social Justice* 16 (1) (Summer): 1–39.

Reiman, Jeffrey H., and Paul Leighton. 1979. *The Rich Get Richer and the Poor Get Prison: Ideology, Class, and Criminal Justice*. New York: Wiley.

Robinson, Joan. 1971. *Economic Heresies: Some Old-Fashioned Questions in Economic Theory*. New York: Palgrave Macmillan.

Rousseau, Isabelle. 2010. "Las nuevas élites y su proyecto modernizador." In *Del nacionalismo al neoliberalismo, 1940–1994*, edited by Elisa Servín, 242–94. Mexico City: Fondo De Cultura Económica.

Schedler, Andreas. 2014. "The Criminal Subversion of Mexican Democracy." *Journal of Democracy* 25 (1): 5–18.

SEGOB (Secretaria de Gobernación). 2015. "Cuaderno mensual de información estadística penitenciaria nacional." December. http://www.cns.gob.mx/portalWebApp/appmanager/portal/desk?_nfpb=true&_pageLabel=portals_portal_page_m2p1p2&content_id=810211&folderNode=810277&folderNode1=810281.

Slack, Cathy, Ben Shelor, and Kathy Black-Dennis. 2012. "Accreditation of the Mexico Federal Prison System: Utilizing Core International Standards." *Corrections Today*, February 1. https://www.thefreelibrary.com/Accreditation+of+the+Mexico+Federal+Prison+System%3A+utilizing+core...-a0287868394.

Thatcher, Margaret, and Douglas Keay. 1987. "Interview for Woman's Own," Margaret Thatcher Foundation. September 23. https://www.margaretthatcher.org/document/106689.

Timerman, Jacobo. 1981. *Prisoner without a Name, Cell without a Number*. New York: Knopf.

TUP (Todos Unidos por los Presos). 2014. WhatsApp Chat. Access granted by Ramona Chávez.

United States Embassy. 2016. *Estados Unidos apoya prisiones mexicanas mediante Iniciativa Mérida*. https://mx.usembassy.gov/es/estados-unidos-apoya-prisiones-mexicanas-mediante-iniciativa-merida/.

Vázquez-Arroyo, Antonio Y. 2008. "Liberal Democracy and Neoliberalism: A Critical Juxtaposition." *New Political Science* 30 (2): 127–59.

Visions of Abolition: From Critical Resistance to a New Way of Life. 2012. https://fod-infobase-com.ezproxy.tcu.edu/PortalPlaylists.aspx?wID=104549&xtid=50872.

Weinstein, David. 2016. "Privatization of Prisons in Mexico and the Right of Persons Deprived of Liberty." *Human Rights Brief*. http://hrbrief.org/hearings/privatization-of-prisons-in-mexico-and-the-rights-of-person-deprived-of-liberty/.

World Prison Brief. Consulted in 2016. http://www.prisonstudies.org.

Zilberg, Elana. 2011. *Space of Detention: The Making of a Transnational Gang Crisis between Los Angeles and San Salvador*. Durham, NC: Duke University Press.

VIOLENCE, EXPANSION, RESISTANCE

Simon Granovsky-Larsen and Dawn Paley

From Paraguay to Colombia, Panama to Guatemala, and across many Mexican states, organized violence rages alongside the neoliberal expansion of capital. As authoritarian transitions from the Cold War opened Latin America to neoliberalism, organized violence has been systematically downplayed, depoliticized, and recast as criminal activity. This book has explored cases from a cross-section of countries where state and parastate violence has been particularly bloody in the contemporary period: those most closely allied to the United States, including Mexico, Guatemala, Honduras, Colombia, and Paraguay. This responds to an explicit desire on our behalf to explore issues of violence in which the victims, as discussed in the opening chapter, are largely considered unworthy by the US government and media. As demonstrated across all of the book's chapters, those victims, rather than being bystanders of senseless violence or somehow complicit in their own deaths, were caught up in complex webs of organized violence and resistance, economic extraction and production, and blurred lines between states and their violent counterparts.

Books that use a particular lens to delve into contemporary issues across the combined region of Mexico, Central America, and South

America are rare, as areas and countries tend to be separated out and siloed off in published works. To bring together accounts of the paramilitarization of transnational mining in Colombia, the violent expansion of the agricultural frontier in Paraguay, and killings and disappearances over the last twelve years in Mexico is a task that is both difficult and urgent.

The chapters in this book do an excellent job of highlighting important national cases and international connections, but the volume cannot cover all possible cases or countries. For example, events in Brazil, the largest country and economy in South America, were not included, nor were experiences from non-Spanish speaking countries in South America, any countries of the Caribbean, or US-allied Peru and Chile. Also absent are examples from struggles in the United States or Canada, though it is clear that, in many Indigenous land defence efforts there, private security participates together with state forces in ways similar to the cases discussed in this book. This was clearly demonstrated at Standing Rock, where Indigenous people were targeted on their own lands as though they were insurgents (Brown, Parrish, and Speri 2017). Our focus on Latin America, and on the strongest US allies within that region, made the project more coherent, but further work on the links between the deployment of violence within and across the regions of the hemisphere would illuminate important trends.

This volume brings forward areas for future collaboration among scholars and journalists working on seemingly disparate regions. For example, comparisons between the violence related to palm oil production explored by Tyler Shipley (Chapter 2) connect to the expansion of soya farming in Paraguay and illuminate, in the words of Arturo Ezquerro-Cañete (Chapter 4), the "neoliberal militarization of the countryside and the associated criminalization of resistance." Both countries play host to US military installations, and, since the turn of the twenty-first century, both underwent coup d'états tolerated or supported by Washington. Ezquerro-Cañete also examines the notion of the militarization of Paraguay as "an extension of Plan Colombia."

Case studies directly connected to specific mining projects, like Tahoe Resources' Escobal mine in Guatemala (Chapter 3) and the Cerrejón and Drummond coal mines in Colombia (Chapter 6), bring out other similarities that cross national borders. Luis Solano's description of the Canadian mining company in Guatemala failing to treat "local residents as people peacefully defending their lands" and instead producing a "militarized security strategy [that] seemed designed to face an insurgency" echoes strongly with the experiences documented by Rosalvina Otálora Cortés in the case of Colombia. Court cases, both locally and internationally, have brought important attention and awareness to these cases but have failed to bring meaningful justice for communities.

In addition, there is a powerful connection to be made in bringing together discussions of Colombia's violent extractive industries and changes that may emerge there after the signing of the Peace Accords in 2016, with present-day extraction in Guatemala following the signing of Peace Accords in 1996. This comparison would allow for the development of a greater breadth of understanding of the futures connected to neoliberal peace, with obvious and painful shortcomings. We hope that bringing together chapters on extractive violence in a context of official declarations of peace from Guatemala and Colombia will contribute to an increasingly sophisticated and informed dialogue among activists and academics.

This brings us to Mexico, which is today widely recognized to be experiencing a deep and deadly crisis of forced displacement, executions, and disappearances (Aburto et al. 2016; Correa-Cabrera 2017; International Institute for Strategic Studies 2015). Violence in Mexico has spiked in conjunction with the us-funded war on drugs, with previously peaceful areas transformed into war zones, while foreign direct investment surges (Paley 2014). Although a difficult task to carry out as violence continues to ravage cities and rural areas throughout the country, the chapters on Mexico provide what we consider to be a valuable contribution to the notion of organized violence in a context where violence has been heavily depoliticized and victims themselves extensively criminalized.

The Mexico chapters look at the criminalization and imprisonment of the poor (Chapter 12), corruption and graft by state officials as violence escalates (Chapter 11), and increased violence in resource-rich (Chapters 7, 8, and 9) and logistically strategic (Chapter 10) areas. Each state, and even each region, of Mexico is experiencing different kinds of violence, making Mexico notoriously ripe for the "microhistory" proposed by González y González (2003, 72). In Chapter 9, Antonio Fuentes Díaz delves into the complicated world of self-defence groups in Michoacán, in one of three chapters about this resource-rich coastal state.

As is clear in the chapters on Mexico in this volume, the extreme violence of the drug war is taking place alongside transnationalization and increased extractive projects. Mexico is a key destination for foreign direct investment (FDI) in Latin America. "FDI into Mexico rose 18% in 2015 to reach US$30.285 billion, one of the highest levels for seven years, with the largest investments going to the manufacturing sector, mainly the automotive industry, and telecommunications," according to the Economic Commission on Latin America (ECLAC) 2016 report on FDI in Latin America (ECLAC 2016, 9).

However, the ECLAC report also shows that Mexico was the site of six of Latin America's largest twenty economic mergers and acquisitions in 2016. The manufacturing sector, which is highly connected to global supply chains, continues to be a key driver of the Mexican economy. That brings us to another area for future research suggested through this volume: a focus beyond the extractive industries and logistics infrastructure to understand how organized violence also impacts the lives and conditions of workers in manufacturing sectors in Mexico and elsewhere. As time goes on, we hope these links are made clearer and that the voices of pro-workers' struggles are joined together with those involved in land defence and given the attention they deserve.

ORGANIZED RESISTANCE TO ORGANIZED VIOLENCE

Another area we hope to see taken up further in future research is the range of responses to organized violence taken by affected communities and individuals, including by women organizing against the patriarchy. Organized resistance is most visible in struggles against extractive projects, and especially mining, where spectacular environmental destruction and ongoing repression couple with transnational solidarity activism to bring to the attention of people around the world, at least for brief periods. We are given insight into resistance in non-mining communities in three chapters of this volume—Chapter 5 on Afro-Colombian women defending territory, and in Mexico, Chapters 8 and 9 on armed community defence movements, and Chapter 12 on resistance to prisons—but references to organized responses to violence also run through other chapters. As a final word in our exploration of organized violence, this section of the conclusion considers a range of forms of organized resistance within a broader historical context and highlights the importance of making visible the many existing struggles that are currently carried out under the radar of international attention.

If organized violence has become diffuse in the post-Cold War period—with the "old" or "political" violence of twentieth-century state and guerrilla armies giving way to a range of often overlapping or coordinated armed groups (Koonings 2012; see also our discussion in this volume's Introduction)—organized resistance is even more scattered. As with the shift in categories of armed groups, a period of Left preference for revolutionary capture of state power—an approach that dominated popular organizing from approximately the 1960s through the 1990s—has been supplanted by a dizzying array of social movement forms that, taken together, appear to lack a unified goal, such as the control of state institutions.

The early 2000s saw a number of social movements join political parties that eventually were elected to power as part of a "Pink Tide" of left-leaning governments. In every case, however, the same movements were let down by governments that conformed to the demands of the capitalist state: Rafael Correa in Ecuador and Evo Morales in Bolivia both attempted to address decolonial demands without abandoning extractivist economies, bringing them into confrontation with Indigenous movements; Brazil's Lula da Silva and Argentina's Nestor Kirchner lost the support of local movements by reducing broad-reaching platforms to moderate social welfare programs; other leaders, particularly in Central America, were "Left" in name only and did little to advance popular demands (Dangl 2010; Petras and Veltmeyer 2005; Webber and Carr 2013).

In place of movements involving some combination of armed resistance, class analysis, and a focus on the national scale, movements across Latin America today are characterized either by brief rounds of protest addressing specific grievances, or by a focus on grassroots alternatives to dominant political, economic, or social models. These alternatives include prominent movements such as the Zapatistas in southern Mexico, who have constructed an alternative form of governance based on Indigenous perspectives and anarchist-inspired direct democracy; the Landless Workers' Movement in Brazil, which organizes alternative agriculture and social organization across thousands of occupied plantations; and the "worker-recovered enterprises" or "factories without bosses" in Argentina, a movement of factory occupations that has brought industrial production under the control of worker cooperatives (Stahler-Sholk, Vanden, and Becker 2014; Zibechi 2012). Movements focused on alternative models also include the many examples of devolved political autonomy to recognized Indigenous territories, espe- cially across the eight Amazonian countries. Recognition and influence of Indigenous political organization and world views have also grown significantly outside of autonomous zones (Erazo 2013; Martí i Puig 2010; see also Hale 2011 for a critique of neoliberal approaches to territo- rial autonomy).

While popular organizing and resistance no longer confront the state in the same way as seen through the late twentieth century, and in many cases intentionally reject the temptation to do just that (Escobar 2008; Holloway 2002), a glance at social movements in the region nevertheless reveals a mosaic of organized communities and sectors with deep local, national, and international impact.

How, then, have people resisted the shifting forms of organized vio- lence that so many now face? First, we should recognize that, in terms of numbers, the most common response has been to leave rather than to fight. Behind the tide of Mexican and Central American migrants heading north, and the estimated seven million displaced or exiled Colombians, is the decision to seek safety elsewhere (Martínez 2016). While migration is often seen as an individual action, in reality it con- tains an element of collective resistance in its mass reaction to the vio- lence tied to capital expansion.

Aside from migration, collective responses to organized violence have taken a number of mostly defensive forms, through the insistence of maintaining communities and movements despite violence, through opposition to the economic drivers of violence, or through the direct con- frontation of violent groups themselves. Instances of this last option, direct confrontation, are rare, and mainly concentrated in the Mexican states of Michoacán and Guerrero. There, a series of armed groups have formed since 2011 to defend communities against the violence of nar- co-trafficking. As described in Chapters 8 and 9, these groups have taken two main forms: *policías comunitarias* (community police forces) mobi- lized by Indigenous communities and overseen by traditional assem- blies, and *autodefensas* (self-defence groups) formed by non-Indigenous farmers. These forms of armed community defence have generated mixed results, with some community police forces collapsing under the pressure of state cooptation and organized crime, while the *autodefensas* have been unevenly incorporated into state structures while interrupt- ing and sometimes siding with local armed groups.

Much more common across Latin America are instances of collective resistance to resource extraction projects threatening a community's way of life, such as mines, hydroelectric dams, monoculture plantations, and forestry. These actions, while directed as opposition to the projects themselves, bring communities into contact with armed groups, either by protecting territory from state and non-state violence, or, with tragic frequency, when targeted with violent repression. A review of land and environmental defenders murdered for their work reveals an enormous and growing number of cases worldwide. Latin America stands out as the most affected area, with the six hardest-hit countries of the region—Brazil, Colombia, Honduras, Peru, Mexico, and Guatemala—together accounting for at least 536 murdered activists between 2000 and 2015 (Global Witness 2016). Despite this violence, however, these acts of community resistance do occasionally succeed in blocking harmful development projects. In Guatemala in 2016, for example, the Spanish-owned Hidro Santa Cruz company pulled out of a planned hydroelectric dam in Huehuetenango after years of resistance by surrounding Maya Q'anjob'al communities (De Luca 2017).

A third form of defensive resistance to armed groups overlaps significantly with the second, in the insistence of some communities to maintain their way of life in the face of violence. This does not always involve opposition to economic projects, however, and often entails Indigenous communities protecting traditional territories, whether these are recognized officially by the state or not. There are many such cases in Colombia, where Indigenous and Afro-descendant communities first gained autonomous control over territory following the country's 1991 Constitution but later faced displacement by armed groups fighting for territorial control. A refusal to abandon territory and an insistence on continuing traditional socio-economic practices, even in exile—as Paula Baldunio de Melo observed among Afro-Pacific Colombians and recounts in Chapter 5 of this book—amounts to resistance to organized violence. Similar resistance is seen across Mexico, Honduras, Nicaragua, Ecuador, and elsewhere.

Resistance to organized violence, then, while itself organized, is not always visible to outside observers and certainly lacks the universal structure of past armed movements. But these are not negative aspects of contemporary resistance, just ones that make resistance difficult to identify. By protecting ways of life and creating alternative models, all while resisting violence, today's social movements against violence embody what Ana Cecilia Dinerstein (2015) calls "prefiguration": the fostering of alternatives within the political imagination and the autonomous creation, at a smaller scale, of the nonviolent world they encourage.

By creating functioning experiments of alternative and peaceful societies, while also resisting violence and destruction, social movements offer some of the most effective fronts against organized violence. Their success, however, also requires pressure to be placed upon the state and transnational corporations. An international outcry against the murder of Honduran activist Berta Cáceres, as described by Tyler Shipley in Chapter 2, led to a ripple of divestment from the Agua Zarca dam project. Similarly, Luis Solano discusses in Chapter 3 one of two active court cases in Canada that aim to hold Canadian mining companies responsible for the violence they carry out or instigate in Guatemala and elsewhere.

There is a role to play, then, for outsiders to listen to those resisting violence and support them as requested. Similarly, and despite the autonomous nature of many movements that disregard the state and prefer to create grassroots alternatives, there is an important role for the state in reigning in its own violence and that of non-state actors in order to allow alternatives to flourish.

Recent decades have witnessed a growing wave of organized violence carried out in support of capitalist expansion, a destructive swell that shows no signs of slowing. Across the countries of Mexico and Central and South America—as in the United States, Canada, and many other parts of the world—economic globalization has fuelled a thirst for expansion and accumulation that holds previously not-fully-incorporated peoples, territories, and resources in its sights. As mentioned above, much of this violent expansion is enacted through various extractive industries but is not limited to these. Regardless of the form of economic project, from extraction through assembly, and from tourism through finance and service sectors, armed groups have made themselves available for the suppression of grassroots resistance. A focus on violence as organized in its relationship to capitalism helps to illuminate and theorize the actions of those armed groups. As research into violence keeps pace with its evolution, we hope an expanded focus will shine light on the many complex webs of interaction between capital and violence, on violence carried out in economic sectors thought to be experiencing less repression, and on the struggles of those affected, who insist against all odds that, in the words of Eduardo Galeano (1992), "we say no."

REFERENCES

Aburto, José Manuel, Hiram Beltrán Sánchez, Victor Manuel Garcia Guerrero, and Vladimir Canudas Romo. 2016. "Homicides in Mexico Reversed Life Expectancy Gains for Men and Slowed Them for Women 2000–10." *Health Affairs* 35 (1): 88–95.

Brown, Alleen, Will Parrish, and Alice Speri. 2017. "Leaked Documents Reveal Counterterrorism Tactics Used at Standing Rock to 'Defeat Pipeline Insurgencies.'" *The Intercept*, May 27. https://theintercept.com/2017/05/27/leaked-documents-reveal-security-firms-counterterrorism-tactics-at-standing-rock-to-defeat-pipeline-insurgencies/.

Correa-Cabrera, Guadalupe. 2017. *Los Zetas Inc.: Criminal Corporations, Energy, and Civil War in Mexico*. Austin: University of Texas Press.

Dangl, Benjamin. 2010. *Dancing with Dynamite: Social Movements and States in Latin America*. Oakland, CA: AK Press.

De Luca, Danielle. 2017. "Hidro Santa Cruz Terminates Dam Project in Barrillas, Guatemala." *Cultural Survival Quarterly* 41 (1). https://www.culturalsurvival.org/publications/cultural-survival-quarterly/hidro-santa-cruz-terminates-dam-project-barillas-guatemala.

Dinerstein, Ana Cecilia. 2015. *The Politics of Autonomy in Latin America: The Art of Organizing Hope*. New York: Palgrave Macmillan.

ECLAC (Economic Commission for Latin America and the Caribbean). 2016. "Foreign Direct Investment in Latin America and the Caribbean." Santiago, Chile: United Nations. http://repositorio.cepal.org/bitstream/handle/11362/40214/6/S1600662_en.pdf.

Erazo, Juliet S. 2013. *Governing Indigenous Territories: Enacting Sovereignty in the Ecuadorian Amazon*. Durham, NC: Duke University Press.

Escobar, Arturo. 2008. *Territories of Difference: Place, Movement, Life, Redes*. Durham, NC: Duke University Press.

Galeano, Eduardo. 1992. *We Say No: Chronicles, 1963–1991*. New York: W.W. Norton and Co.

Global Witness. 2016. *On Dangerous Ground. 2015's Deadly Environment: The Killing of Land and Environmental Defenders Worldwide*. https://www.globalwitness.org/documents/18482/On_Dangerous_Ground.pdf.

González y González, Luis. 2003. *Otra invitación a la microhistoria*. Colleción Fondo 2000. Mexico, DF: Fondo de Cultura Económica.

Hale, Charles R. 2011. "Resistencia Para Qué? Territory, Autonomy, and Neoliberal Entanglements in the 'Empty Spaces' of Central America." *Economy and Society* 40 (2): 184–210.

Holloway, John. 2002. *Change the World without Taking Power: The Meaning of Revolution Today*. London: Pluto Press.

International Institute for Strategic Studies. 2015. "Armed Conflict Survey 2015 Press Statement." https://www.iiss.org/en/about%20us/press%20 room/press%20releases/press%20releases/archive/2015-4fe9/may-6219/ armed-conflict-survey-2015-press-statement-a0be.

Koonings, Kees. 2012. "New Violence, Insecurity, and the State: Comparative Reflections on Latin America and Mexico." In *Violence, Coercion, and State-Making in Twentieth-Century Mexico*, edited by Wil G. Pansters, 255–78. Stanford, CA: Stanford University Press.

Martí i Puig, Salvador. 2010. "The Emergence of Indigenous Movements in Latin America and Their Impact on the Latin American Political Scene: Interpretive Tools at the Local and Global Levels." *Latin American Perspectives* 37 (6): 74–92.

Martínez, Óscar. 2016. *A History of Violence: Living and Dying in Central America*. London: Verso.

Paley, Dawn. 2014. *Drug War Capitalism*. Oakland, CA: AK Press.

Petras, James, and Henry Veltmeyer. 2005. *Social Movements and State Power: Argentina, Brazil, Bolivia, Ecuador*. London: Pluto Press.

Stahler-Sholk, Richard, Harry E. Vanden, and Marc Becker, eds. 2014. *Rethinking Latin American Social Movements: Radical Action from Below*. Lanham, MD: Rowman and Littlefield.

Webber, Jeffery, and Barry Carr, eds. 2013. *The New Latin American Left: Cracks in the Empire*. Lanham, MD: Rowman and Littlefield.

Zibechi, Raul. 2012. *Territories of Resistance: A Cartography of Latin American Social Movements*. Translated by Ramor Ryan. Oakland, CA: AK Press.

ACKNOWLEDGEMENTS

We would like to thank the many people who made this book possible. First of all, to the fifteen contributors who wrote chapters for the book: thank you for all of your work and for the many insights delivered through your writing. We thank you for lending your words to help create this book, and we hope this project can become a tool for peace.

A big thanks is due to our editor Karen Clark, who believed in this project from the beginning, and the rest of the team at University of Regina Press. We also thank Weldon Hiebert, the cartographer at the University of Winnipeg who created the two overview maps for the book, as well as Elisa Díaz for her translation work. Thanks are also due to the two anonymous peer reviewers whose comments significantly strengthened the final version of this manuscript.

We also want to thank the countless people who shared their stories and time with us over the course of our academic and journalistic research. Much of our understanding of violence is owed to those who faced it and chose to speak with us about it. We are grateful for the permission and opportunity to share your experiences. Without your bravery, this work would not be possible.

—*Dawn Paley and Simon Granovsky-Larsen*

ABOUT THE CONTRIBUTORS

Patricia Alvarado Portillo has a bachelor's degree in economics and a master's degree in geography. She is currently a doctoral student in social anthropology at the Ibero-American University in Mexico City.

Michelle Arroyo Fonseca holds a master's in environmental studies from York University and a PhD in sociology from the Latin American Faculty of Social Sciences, Mexico branch (FLACSO Mexico).

Paula Balduino de Melo is a Brazilian anthropologist whose doctoral studies were conducted at the Universidad de Brasília. She carried out ethnographic research on the Pacific coast of Colombia and Ecuador in connection with the Universidad Nacional de Colombia.

Guadalupe Correa-Cabrera holds a PhD in political science from the New School for Social Research, and is Associate Professor at the Schar School of Policy and Government, George Mason University, and Global Fellow at the Woodrow Wilson International Center for Scholars. Dr. Correa-Cabrera's most recent book is entitled *Los Zetas Inc.: Criminal Corporations, Energy, and Civil War in Mexico* (University of Texas Press, 2017).

Ana Del Conde is a PhD candidate in anthropology at the University of Massachusetts Amherst. Her work looks at the role of women in novel governance strategies that emerge as a way to resist structures of oppression and resource devastation in contemporary Mexico.

Arturo Ezquerro-Cañete is a PhD candidate in international development studies at Saint Mary's University in Halifax, Nova Scotia, and the Universidad Autónoma de Zacatecas in Mexico, and also Visiting Researcher at the Centro de Estudios Rurales Interdisciplinarios and BASE Investigaciones Sociales in Asunción, Paraguay. He is currently researching the political strategies of new peasant movements in Paraguay resisting the neoliberal transformation of agrarian capitalism.

Mary Finley-Brook is an associate professor of geography, environmental studies, and international studies at the University of Richmond in Virginia. Finley-Brook's research over the past two decades documents social and ecological harm rooted in incongruous development policies, leading to her advocacy for human and cultural rights protections and holistic ecological assessments during energy transitions.

Antonio Fuentes Díaz holds a PhD in sociology, and is a professor and researcher at the Institute of Social Science and Humanities at the Meritorious Autonomous University of Puebla, Mexico. His areas of research include the issue of collective violence in Mexico and Guatemala, analysis of the relationship between security and neoliberal governmentality, and the study of community defence against organized crime.

Simon Granovsky-Larsen is an assistant professor of politics and international studies at the University of Regina and author of *Dealing with Peace: The Guatemalan Campesino Movement and the Post-Conflict Neoliberal State* (University of Toronto Press, 2019). His current research explores connections between non-state armed groups and mega-development projects in Guatemala.

Carlos Daniel Gutiérrez-Mannix was born and raised in the town of El Naranjo, San Luis Potosí, Mexico. He started his post-secondary studies at the law school of the Autonomous University of San Luis Potosi, graduated with a BA in sociology at the University of Texas at Brownsville, and obtained his master's degree in public policy and management at the University of Texas–Rio Grande Valley. He is currently a PhD student in political science at the University of Texas at Dallas.

Elva F. Orozco Mendoza is an assistant professor in the department of political science at Texas Christian University. Her areas of teaching and research interest are interdisciplinary in scope and mostly engage with contemporary political questions that explore the nature and meaning of democracy, justice, gender violence, protest and resistance politics, material ontology, and public life broadly understood.

Rosalvina Otálora Cortés is a professor and researcher at the Universidad Libre de Colombia, and a doctoral candidate in international relations at the Universidad del Salvador, Argentina. She has a master's degree in political studies and international relations and is an economist and a lawyer.

Dawn Paley is the author of *Drug War Capitalism* (AK Press, 2014). She is trained as a journalist and has worked as a freelance reporter for over ten years. She holds a PhD in sociology from the Meritorious Autonomous University of Puebla, Mexico.

Heriberto Paredes Coronel is an independent journalist who has been working for the past six years for the Agencia Autónoma de Comunicación Subversiones, and regularly collaborates with Animal Político y Horizontal. His investigations focus on the processes of autonomy of Indigenous communities, and the effects of violence of the misnamed war on drugs.

Jorge Rebolledo Flores holds a bachelor of arts in international relations from the National Autonomous University of Mexico and a master's of government from Georgetown University, Washington, DC. He has a PhD in international studies and comparative politics from the University of Miami, and is a professor and researcher at the Colegio de Veracruz in Mexico.

Tyler Shipley is a professor of culture, society, and commerce at the Humber College Institute of Technology and Advanced Learning in Toronto. He is Associate Fellow at the Centre for Research on Latin America and the Caribbean, and the author of *Ottawa and Empire: Canada and the Military Coup in Honduras* (Between the Lines, 2017).

Luis Solano is a Guatemalan economist and independent journalist, who began his career in 1987 with Inforpress Centroamericana. He currently lives in Berkeley, California, and is an investigative journalist for the Guatemalan publication, *El Observador*.

INDEX

Note: *Page numbers for figures, tables, maps, and illustrations are listed in italics.*